A
LONG TIME
Coming

A
LONG TIME
Coming

Race, Inheritance and an Extraordinary
Childhood Odyssey in Modern Day Britain

J. W. VIMIKH

authorHOUSE®

AuthorHouse™ UK
1663 Liberty Drive
Bloomington, IN 47403 USA
www.authorhouse.co.uk
Phone: 0800.197.4150

Published by AuthorHouse 11/09/2015

ISBN: 978-1-5049-4308-6 (sc)
ISBN: 978-1-5049-4307-9 (hc)
ISBN: 978-1-5049-4309-3 (e)

Print information available on the last page.

*Dedicated to
my father*

table of contents

Acknowledgements

Had it not been for the unwavering support and Job-like patience of my wife, children and other family members this memoir would not have been possible. Like the best traits of any family, after reading selected chapters, they did not mince their words, whether brutal reprimand or glowing praise. Sincere thanks also go to those colleagues at work who bothered to read various chapters and followed up with constructive feedback. Other beautiful people to whom I am indebted include several lifelong friends. Antipodeans Charlie and Neal, for their constant encouragement over countless years and unrelenting belief that I had a way with the written word and a story worth telling. A final debt of gratitude is owed to brother Rey, known to me since our teenage years, who gave of his priceless time to read the entire manuscript, checking facts and sources, grammar, punctuation, providing an uplifting flow of encouragement and rigorous analysis as the deadline approached for the submission of my first draft.

Prologue

Known as Willson to family, friends, colleagues, and line manager, the full name on the burgundy identification issued to me by the UK passport office in Petty France, just a stroll from London's St James' Park underground station, reads JEAN WILLSON VIMIKH. Between 1982 and 1983, I found myself attending one of London University's pre-eminent art education institutions, studying for a teacher qualification on a one-year postgraduate certificate in education (PGCE) course. The first written assignment was to "produce a piece of work, roughly 2500 words, based on your own personal experience of education". I traced my intense love and acquisition of gramophone discs – seven-inch, nine-inch, and twelve-inch vinyl records – during the harsh learning curve of my youthful years following expulsion from secondary school at age fifteen, after a one sided, bare-fisted assault upon a fellow pupil, perpetrated with gleeful malice. From that fateful day, my informal education included haphazard risk-taking, spiritual conversion, and rebellious teenage escapades, spanning adolescence to early manhood when, at age twenty-one and with much apprehension, I once again embraced formal learning. I had little inkling that what I'd written in that postgraduate essay – professionally typed up for a tidy fee in the days before laptops – would, a quarter of a century later, trigger a more complete autobiographical effort. I attempted to commit to paper a true tale of human struggle against adversity that stretched back to 1950s London. In so doing, I sought cathartic inner peace and a sense of closure to deeply buried, rarely spoken memories of a scarred childhood.

Warping forward to autumn 2008, with much idle time on my hands following severance, I resurrected my storytelling. The two-year build-up to being deemed supernumerate with its resulting consequences, was an emotional roller coaster. Beneath my projected optimism, the strongman exterior, and confident fellow who seemingly coped with being laid off to join the multitudes of British jobless, was an individual traumatised to the core by rejection. Before then I had worked for over a decade with some of the country's most severely damaged and disturbed children, many of whom had committed unimaginably heinous crimes. My job role had been to manage, educate, and assess many of society's most notorious, high-profile, and dangerous adolescent offenders incarcerated in Lederer Manor (named after seventeenth century Appalachian Mountains explorer John Lederer) London's only remaining prison for children under fifteen years of age.

This valuable public protection resource faced privatisation in 2006. Being sold off would conclude years of negotiations between powerful Whitehall mandarins, corporate philanthropists, local politicians, legal teams, and impotent trade unions. The actions of these power brokers, by opting for profit-making, blatantly sounded the death knell of the oft-spouted mantra **good practice**. Privatisation signalled the end of support for Lederer Manor Secure Children's Home, with its inherently large wage bill for the high staffing levels intrinsic to intensive, child-focused social interventions in secure accommodation.

Following the takeover, in fact from the very first day under new ownership, the writing was on the wall as financial austerity decimated the Secure Children's Home's renowned mental health team, which had been headed by one the country's leading child forensic psychologists. Company cuts then slashed vital medical nursing cover. Vehicles used for court escorts and emergency hospital trips were ill-maintained, and no longer legally roadworthy. The programme of staff training and development was ended, admin staff and cleaners vanished overnight, and mealtime portions for the children shrank noticeably, much to their ire. Such events heralded the beginning of Lederer Manor's descent to closure in 2009, when some voices cheered good riddance. The saddest irony however, was, that such a London institution remained an imperative need given chronic levels of youth crime; unprecedented incidents of alleged teenage gang rapes; and worst, the capital's epidemic of brutal teenage gun and knife murders, which escalated to twenty-six in 2007, and then increased again to a total of twenty-nine victims in 2008.

Post redundancy is never a good state for anyone let alone an out-of-work fifty-year-old. It was a time of pervasive gloom and despair, utterly depressing as everywhere in the capital there were scant, ever-shrinking employment opportunities. In desperation, as part of a survival strategy, I reluctantly paid an enrolment fee to join a social care agency and obtained ad hoc work with vulnerable, frail, elderly folk for a salary mere pennies above the national minimum hourly rate. The darkest of moments, anguish, and despondency after repeated failure at job interviews or my bank account being regularly overdrawn, heavily outweighed the brightest, the inspiring educational triumphs of my four beautiful children, or the audacious, tangible optimism proclaimed to the world's citizens by unimaginable results in American ballot boxes, resulting in Barack Obama's presidential inauguration.

The beginnings of a worldwide recession gathered tempo, triggered by Lehman Brothers (the Wall Street investment giant and the fourth largest bank in the United States of America) filing for bankruptcy on 15 September 2008, listing total assets of $639 billion. The largest bankruptcy filing in US history was no mere blip. It signalled a dire warning, a declaration to our world of an unfolding global financial crisis that would just not go away. Unimaginable social, political, and economic upheaval in Western economies set in, like a slow motion avalanche. Yet the wealth gap between rich and poor continued to grow rapidly. In Europe over the next few years, the economies of Ireland, Portugal, Greece, and Spain would respectively be deemed failures, their huge debts forcing European Economic Union leaders to agree to multibillion-euro bailout funds for each in turn.

By spring 2009, British newspaper headlines about unscrupulous, greedy corporate city bankers gave way to unrelenting wave upon wave of daily scoops under lurid captions like "Snouts in the Trough". These seemingly unending stories exposed corrupt, greedy Members of Parliament (MPs), the high and mighty denizens of the Palace of Westminster, allegedly fiddling their expenses – all "within the rules", they said – as the worst economic crisis since the 1930s Great Depression took root. This expenses scandal led to criminal investigations that concluded with several MPs being sent to prison for swindling hard-pressed British taxpayers.

Enforced idleness during this tumultuous period led me one day to browse through the house's dusty bookshelf and stumble across the PGCE assignment. That act spawned fresh attempts at creative writing as, with time on my hands, I became single-minded, doggedly fixated on the task of chronicling my tale in far greater detail. In tandem with writing, I began converting my entire beloved vinyl collection into a digitized library, and by April 2010, fortune had it I was once again settling into regular employment. This was as Eton-educated, Conservative Party leader David Cameron, with elections looming, uttered his rallying call to British voters: "We're all in this together!" and the world's passing events began to blur.

As a married, settled family man and proud father, my initial purpose was for the narrative to be part of my legacy for blood relatives. Unintentionally I had also arrived at that moment of lucidity when one takes an overview to contemplate life's rationale and true purpose.

So I dug deep, scraping together enough precious sterling to purchase a laptop, and continued writing, morbidly composing the data I believed would eventually assist an obituary writer rather than allowing fate to dictate posthumous third party anecdotes and eulogies delivered from a church pulpit or mourners gathered at my wake. Over time the project grew out of all proportion as my spirit became driven, determined to tell its humble story. Upon reaching an unfinished draft of fifty thousand-plus words, I pondered this accomplishment and tentatively approached a publishing house as it dawned on me this was uncharted territory.

What is the difference between a publisher and a literary agent? Would my manuscript be worthy, judged as wheat, not chaff that only close friends or family might find curious? Was I not being naïve, overambitious given my abject failure at secondary school, never even sitting an English literature exam after hours spent studying the drama, poetry, and prose of literary greats like Byron, Shelley, Austen, and Dickens? Why not consider releasing my memoirs via the World Wide Web? After all, Obama's successful 2008 presidential election campaign was the first to recognise and deploy the power of Internet websites to devastating effect in defeating the Republicans, an act the Democrats, led again by Obama, repeated in the 2012 election. In the literary-revolution era of e-readers and tablets like Kindles, iPads, Nooks, Samsung E61s, and Sony Readers, perhaps the answer lay in an e-book and self-publishing.

But a memoir penned by a violent, ignominious high school dropout rousing a sustained desire in the anonymous reader to turn page after page! Come on! Somehow I had unwavering self-belief that my storytelling, like the convincing yarns spun by politicians and bankers, would directly tempt many ordinary professionals working or living under the jurisdiction of the British criminal justice system. Modernist educators, social reformers, and cultural historians might also be lured to its pages.

So might people who are in or are the fruit of interracially mixed relationships. Likewise parents, persons seriously contemplating parenthood, or individuals consumed by genealogy and tracing the perilous journey of their ancestors. And so for several more years I wrote on.

chapter 1

I claim not to have controlled events, but confess plainly that events have controlled me.
—Abraham Lincoln (1809–1865)

Amidst a leafy, hilly district of south London, barely half a mile from the underground station and nearby home of the All England Lawn Tennis Club, was once to be found Southfields Boys High School. This massive, sprawling educational institution was in its era one of the largest comprehensive schools in the whole of England and Wales. Here each day the wide, magnolia-painted corridors and stairwells heaved with some two thousand adolescent boys and young men. The institution was a sweaty, masculine-scented, testosterone-plagued environment, sparsely graced by females – some dinner ladies, a school nurse, the head teacher's secretary, and less than a handful of women teachers.

A regime of strict rules, codes of conduct, and discipline, including corporal punishment – canings were common – helped teaching staff instil and maintain orderly behaviour. Every pupil respectfully stood to instant attention whenever a teacher entered the classroom, and only upon being told to do so resumed sitting. Southfields was the only school in the land to boast its own planetarium for the study of all things celestial. It had an outdoor swimming pool for compulsory lessons in the bitterly cold winter months and boasted an internationally renowned Grammy-winning boys' choir, famed for musical recitals of the then-living English composer Sir Benjamin Britten.

I entered this daunting arena on the first day of term in the early autumn of 1968, alongside more than three hundred other new pupils, all fresh-faced eleven-year-olds, some very bright, some not so, with many in between, who ranged from the apprehensive and timid to the bold and excited. In the lower school playground, our high volume of chattering gradually diminished to a hum as we gathered chaotically to be addressed at 08.30 hours by a towering middle-aged man, balding, stern-faced, and wearing an imposing black cloak draped upon sloping broad shoulders. With dark, sagging bags of loose skin under bulbous, bloodshot eyes, this giant mounted the steps to a temporary plinth and stood behind the lectern, from which he scanned the boyish horde, ushering in complete silence. Introducing himself as Mr Bacchus, the lower school deputy head teacher, he gave a short welcome speech about standards, expectations, and the six school houses our year's intake were to be divided into, followed by instructions to commence lining up in our respective classes.

Sturdily built, I confidently barged and jockeyed a path through the juvenile flock to join two lines of peers standing in front of a school prefect carrying the placard marked "Theta" in large letters. In next to no time, the entire unruly mass had assembled into twelve orderly forms or classes, each form two rows abreast, waiting for Mr Bacchus's command to follow their placard-bearing prefect, who would lead them into the building towards their respective classrooms for morning registration. At 08.55 precisely, high-pitched pips sounded on the system of Tannoy speakers, as if mimicking BBC Radio's hourly Greenwich mean time signal chimes, indicating to all pupils the official start of their first school day.

Early on in that first term I participated in school choir auditions, having enjoyed singing since early childhood. However, before the October half-term break, during choir practice, my voice broke, putting paid to any choral ambitions. I excelled academically, my favourite subject being history. And on the sports field I demonstrated much prowess, particularly in rugby, basketball, and track and field. Each of the twelve forms of my intake year at Southfields Boys High School numbered roughly thirty students, all streamed according to ability. I was placed in One Theta, academically the fourth highest class – every class being named after letters in the Greek alphabet. That academic year witnessed my good progress in all curriculum areas, culminating in excellent end-of-year examination results and my promotion that forthcoming autumn term to the highest class, Two Gamma.

As the end of that maiden secondary school year approached, I became excited when my parents, Mr and Mrs (Billy and Victoria) Vimikh, arranged a visit to a photographer's studio after school. The photos taken were submitted with my application to the UK passport office. Soon, Billy informed me, I was to embark on my first aircraft flight during the long summer recess.

With my stepmother, Victoria, I flew to the United States of America on El Al Airways in August 1969 for a three-week vacation to visit her elderly relatives, Aunt Inez and Uncle Selwyn. Victoria was a puzzling person: a modern, progressive woman who had occasionally taken me to Speaker's Corner in Hyde Park at weekends, where fiery orators on soapboxes ignored hecklers to spout controversial messages. She was a dressmaker, avid admirer of Dr Martin Luther King's message, and a lover of the Christian god, but disinclined to attend church. She always played the records of Sam Cooke, Fats Domino, and Brook Benton on the front room's stacking gramophone. Victoria was unable to bear children of her own and never prone to spare the rod of correction. Decades earlier, before settling in mainland USA and retirement, Victoria's relatives had emigrated to Panama from Jamaica to work on the construction of the canal. Now octogenarians, they lived in the heart of Harlem, an area of New York

City densely populated by African Americans and where, during the twentieth century, ever-increasing numbers of migrants from the Caribbean and Africa would settle. Time spent in the Big Apple as my teenage years loomed would prove to be a genuine cultural and political baptism.

NASA astronauts Neil Armstrong and Edwin "Buzz" Aldrin had arrived safely back on earth from that very first manned moon landing at the end of July 1969 to much national elation, and Victoria took me to their ticker tape parade in central Manhattan's crowded streets. There was, however, a flip side to America's nationalistic moon race euphoria. University campuses across the USA witnessed surge after surge of rebellious student protests; popular and undisputed world heavyweight boxing champion Mohammed Ali (aka Cassius Clay) was still banned from boxing following draft evasion; anti Vietnam War sentiment was rife; and the Civil Rights movement had created a new dawn of optimism for millions of African Americans after many years of struggle and sacrifice to defeat Jim Crow (segregationist) laws and gain the rights of suffrage.

Martin Luther King's assassination in April 1968, which provoked the eruption of civil unrest in over a hundred cities, was followed by the iconic moment of that October's Olympic Games in Mexico when, during the playing of the Star Spangled Banner, black sprinters Tommie Smith and John Carlos, 200-metre gold and bronze medal winners respectively, stood proudly but in silence, black-gloved, fists clenched, heads bowed, and in bare feet, actions etched eternally fresh in the memories of all who dwelt in Harlem. Two framed photographs, one of Dr King and another of Smith and Carlos on the Olympics podium, decorated the walls of Aunt Inez's living room. I learnt from stroke-ridden Uncle Selwyn that the white guy in the Olympics picture, silver medallist Peter Norman of Australia, sympathised with the stance of the black Americans, so wore an identical human rights badge and also stood on his rostrum in bare feet during the protest. Norman was severely reprimanded by the Australian athletics team for his actions—in contrast to the USA team, which immediately expelled the Americans from the games, their competitive careers destroyed.

As I scanned the vista from the window of Aunt Inez and Uncle Selwyn's second floor apartment on Lennox Avenue and 125ᵗʰ Street, or when I ventured forth onto Harlem's bustling streets, its hot, sticky, sultry atmosphere pulsated. The urban noise was tangible, generated by huge American cars traversing the wide roads of multicoloured neon-lit billboards; shop fronts playing vibrant, soulful music; street vendors hawking gum, candy, and fresh watermelon slices; and the loud chatter of the most generously proportioned women shamelessly sporting brightly coloured, tight-fitting hot pants.

Testosterone levels were seriously kicking in at the adolescent age of twelve, and as my awareness of the opposite sex grew, I experienced those private moments. None more so than when alone back in my parents' flat off East Hill in Wandsworth when, time and time again, I would peruse the women's lingerie pages of Victoria's Freemans catalogue with furtive excitement. My parents also took weekly delivery of **Tit-Bits**, a British magazine with thrilling human interest stories, scandalous gossip tales, the odd rude joke, and what needless to say caught my eye the most, pages of bikini-clad, buxom females. In Manhattan, at Aunt Inez's Harlem apartment, I avidly scoured her coffee table's reading material, ignoring newspapers like the **Amsterdam News** and **Jamaican Daily Gleaner** to home in on **Jet**, an A5-sized weekly publication, and **Jet**'s sister magazine, the monthly A4-sized **Ebony**. Both contained articles on black African-American culture; its political figures; creative luminaries, and icons from the sports of American football (gridiron), basketball, baseball, boxing, and track and field athletics. And there were always, in glorious colour, full page photographs of beautiful, curvaceous, dark-skinned women attired solely in swimwear.

That August 1969 experience became a most comforting social reality because after a lifetime of being different, strange, considered an outsider, alien, the other, or in the minority, literally everyone else I gazed upon, despite varying grades of skin tone, was black just like me. I learned about influential African-American photographer and cinematographer Gordon Parks through seeing his autobiographical film **The Learning Tree**, which told about the coming of age tale of Newt Winger in segregated, small-town, 1920s America. Trailblazer Parks went on to direct one of the biggest box office movies of that era: **Shaft** (1971), starring Richard Roundtree as detective John Shaft. That film won composer and musician Isaac Hayes a Grammy award for best score soundtrack album and an Academy Award for best original song for the movie's theme. Parks's son, Gordon Parks Jr, would direct **Superfly** (1972) with Curtis Mayfield's wonderful soundtrack.

Most memorably, I experienced a moment of epiphany when I witnessed the creative genius of Nina Simone singing "Young, Gifted, and Black", her tribute to untimely deceased playwright Lorraine Hansberry, in a free concert at the Harlem end of Manhattan's Central Park. In the sweltering sunshine atmosphere, the majority of the joyous crowd were proudly adorned in colourful dashikis, had glistening Afro hair styles, and gave Black Power salutes. Many other magnificent artists, including the Staples Singers, Sly and the Family Stone, Stevie Wonder, B. B. King, Mahalia Jackson, and Dizzy Gillespie, to name but a few, performed at the Harlem Festival '69. Intriguingly, popular culture has always thrust Woodstock to the fore as the pivotal American musical example of that radical, rebellious era, with its LSD-taking, dishevelled flower power hippies, muddy quagmires, free love, and alternative musical icons.

Early in September 1969 in London, my cultural initiation in that Yankee metropolis was but a distant memory as I joined classmates in Two Gamma, taking my seat at one of the many weathered wooden desks, all with orifices for inkwells used in a bygone era. Next to me sat Mickie O'Connell, the second-youngest child from a large Irish-Italian Catholic family. Over the coming years, Mickie and I became great friends, a camaraderie forged by mutual respect and an ability to excel in team sports. Both of us had represented the school rugby team since the previous year – Mickie was captain. And we soon discovered far more in common as his father and mine worked together on shifts at Fulham Power Station. But as this school journey unfolded over the next few years, both of our lives were destined to follow markedly different academic paths.

During the Whitsun half-term break of May 1970, with the end of another successful year at Southfields Boys High School approaching, I went on a school residential trip. Alongside fellow classmates and teachers, I journeyed by coach to the magnificently named Devil's Punchbowl in Hindhead, Surrey, for a terrific week of outward bound activities. On returning home with my holdall of dirty clothes, some of which were torn or heavily muddied, my stepmother, Victoria, began her harpy-like, non-stop nagging, repetitiously announcing in a shrill, high-pitched Jamaican tone: "Yuh wutless wretch!" Her ranting became frenzied, reaching fever pitch. It forewarned me of the lashing to come. I was having none of this, however, and in a jiffy made off with great haste, running away from home after grabbing a handful of coins from my savings jar on top of the wardrobe. I made my way to Bolingbroke Road on the north side of Wandsworth Common, to a children's home where I knew that an ex-classmate, Thomas, resided. At age thirteen I had finally had enough of Victoria's frequent, harsh discipline, wielding the rod of correction, and incessant nagging. Former classmate Thomas was the son of friends of my parents, close neighbours who resided on the same East Hill street. He, too, had been subject to much heavy-handed Caribbean style corporal punishment before fleeing.

Vowing to never, ever return home, I steadfastly stuck with that decision, much to the annoyance of social workers at Wandsworth Town Hall's social services children's department. The social workers' many persuasive attempts to alter my stubborn mindset failed. I simply would not be reasoned with. Such was their umbrage that they resolved to break my disobedient stance by sending me to Stamford House. This was a detention centre of some notoriety, a large complex built in the Victorian era, housing close to one hundred male adolescent juvenile delinquents, aged eleven to seventeen years, located on Goldhawk Road in Shepherds Bush, West London. I resided there, billeting in one of four dormitories. We were securely locked in each night at 21.00 and were issued a clean change of clothing, including underwear and socks, just twice weekly, and marched in orderly lines two abreast. I held my own against much older, more mature boys, incarcerated for ten weeks as punishment for not complying with social services' requests to return to live with my parents, Billy and Victoria.

During that 1970 summer's detention, I watched on television the legendary Brazilian football team, with dark-skinned maestro Pelé conducting at its heart, win the Jules Rimet trophy by triumphing in the Football World Cup and listened to reggae hits like Nicky Thomas's "Love of the Common People" and Nora Dean's "Barbwire". By mid August social services had a change of heart. Perhaps somebody in the department had realised my imprisonment was unjust. I was transferred to another residential placement, one that did not incarcerate, called Beecholme, just outside London in green belt Surrey. Beecholme was located at idyllically named Fir Tree Lane in the commuter town of Banstead on a picturesque, tree-lined street where many of the houses were children's homes. In each house resided a family who provided short or long term care for orphans like me.

Because I was influenced by being locked up in Stamford House, my descent into petty crime may have been inevitable. While on a seaside holiday to Clacton on Sea with Beecholme during the last week of August, the police arrested me for shoplifting. Alongside three other youths, I made daily excursions into the town centre, shoplifting sprees that saw us wander into various retailers to innocently browse and then secrete knick-knacks and trivial objects like paperweights in our pockets or down our Y-fronts before gleefully retreating back to our seafront holiday house to stash the stolen goods.

By December 1970 I had moved to another children's home called Frogmore, just off Putney Bridge Road near Wandsworth High Street. Then in early 1971, just after my fourteenth birthday, I returned to live with my father at the flat off East Hill. I'd been encouraged to do so by the news that Victoria had departed for the United States with her marriage to Billy on the verge of divorce. When she suddenly reappeared on the scene a few months later, adolescent growth spurts meant I now presented an imposingly pugnacious figure at five feet seven inches tall and a muscular thirteen stones in weight. This terrifyingly feisty teen now confronting Victoria was arrogant, self-confident, and physically mature. The tension was immediate, and sparks flew, yet I sensed in her a cautious apprehension. She dared not contemplate raising her hands to me as in the past, nor would she utter to my face one of her preferred, oft-used derisory phrases like "Yuh tu dam wutless!" Predictably, our often trivial disputes led to greater, intensely festering conflict as a powerless Victoria unsuccessfully attempted to curb my independent thoughts and actions. She could no longer dictate when I went out nor my choice of friends. But she could influence my father.

Soon she issued Billy an ultimatum – either I get out of the family home or she would leave. My arrest with two friends, Bernard and Charles, followed within days for taking a MINI Cooper car without the owner's consent and crashing into another vehicle. On collecting me from custody at the Lavender Hill Police Station, my father advised that by keeping up this petty criminality, borstal beckoned, and this time I would be imprisoned for a much longer period. Billy would definitely not, he sternly chided, bother to visit me as he had previously felt duty-bound to do when I was secured in Stamford House. This vehicle theft incident and irreconcilable differences with Victoria resulted in my swift return to local authority care, the children's orphanage Frogmore.

At Frogmore staff members were addressed as Aunt or Uncle. Uncle Robert, a no-nonsense Scotsman, who coincidentally had been a staff member at Stamford House during my incarceration there, now held down two jobs – one at the children's home and the other in the metropolitan police, based at Garrett Lane police station near Earlsfield. Uncle Robert recognised something of the wild in me and one day counselled "You're a cheeky fellow, far too gallus! You'll come to nothing if you cannot iron a shirt." He proceeded to teach me how to iron my Ben Sherman shirts to an impeccable standard, a life skill that would never desert me. The disruption to my education was minimal because Frogmore was only a short bus journey or within walking distance of Southfields Boys High School. By the year's end, my parents on-off fragile relationship had concluded in permanent separation, and Victoria returned to her American East Coast relatives, where she eventually obtained a green card and US citizenship.

The high-achieving academic image of Southfields Boys High School, with its famed choir and Latin lessons, the Eton Fives, squash courts, fencing tradition, planetarium for students of astronomy, and the ball boys provided every June for the Wimbledon Tennis tournament were all indicators of its heyday as a grammar school. By the early 1970s, this reputation was beginning to free-fall, blamed by some on its comprehensive status and the Inner London Education Authority (ILEA) liberals at Westminster's County Hall. Whatever the reasons, its glorious past was long gone, steadily in decline. During my days as a pupil, an opposite view, a reputation for toughness, grit, and brutality common to many inner city schools gained ground.

A number of belligerent youths attended the school, some of whom were proudly allied to Chelsea Football Club, Shed End supporters from the nearby Argyle and Ashburton housing estates. The majority of pupils were just rough and ready plebeians, the offspring of hard-working families of mainly English descent, with a scattering of Irish, Mediterranean, and African Caribbean types, all of whom would always stand their ground in physical disputes. Indian subcontinent pupils (Asians) were scarce, known for their meekness, academic prowess, and considered easy pickings by some warlike, white skinhead lads. These moronic youths loved etching the letters NF onto wooden desktops, a permanent declaration of their loose links to an openly fascist organisation called the National Front. It was an era notorious for Paki bashing weekends or the alternative, stalking Nancy boys for a spot of queer bashing in and around the Brompton Road area of Earls Court.

Fights were commonplace and for the most part fair – one-to-one bare-knuckle bouts. They would routinely take place during break time in the playgrounds and, on occasion, in neighbouring roads outside the school. Opponents would square up, first making sure to remove their expensive maroon school blazers, embroidered on the chest pocket with the We Serve badge, to be held by best mates. The combatants would be encircled by a swiftly gathering tide of one hundred plus adolescent boys, every one of them baying "Fight! Fight! Fight! Fight!" and all keen to see the protagonists quell their anger in a flurry of violent punches or kicks. Being engulfed in these unruly scrums bought time for aggression to take its natural course. A crowd would act as a temporary barrier to intervening teachers unluckily burdened with playground duty. By the time an authority figure arrived, the victor or vanquished would be known and his status among peers would be enhanced or diminished.

One clash in particular gained tragic notoriety in 1971. In an innocuous mid-morning break time game of football that cold autumn day, a heated dispute arose over a penalty kick. Roy Peters, aged fourteen, was stabbed once, a sudden, violent thrust to his chest with a penknife, wielded by the clenched hand of one of the Johnson brothers. He collapsed instantly into a motionless heap upon the damp tarmac. I was present, though not a witness, and I helped carry limp Roy from the playground to the school medical room while his mouth oozed bright maroon froth, his grey shirt became increasingly bloodstained, and his bellows laboured, as he gurgled audibly. Back in class, when lessons resumed I would tell fellow pupils of my fervent belief that Roy would not survive such a mortal blow to his pierced lung. Later that day he died in Queen Mary's Hospital, Roehampton. On the day of the funeral, I stood alongside two thousand other pupils plus teaching staff, respectfully assembled outside the school as Roy's funeral cortège drove slowly past en route to his final resting place.

At age fourteen, my ego's burgeoning sense of omnipotence was jolted by the spectre of death, which seemed ever close at hand. A good school friend called Rudolph "Legs" Smith lived near my family home in East Hill area of Wansworth and was in the year above me at Southfields Boys High School. One Friday night at a reggae dance held above the Clapham Hotel pub in South London, he was cut up across his face, chest, and forearms by an older jealous rival for a girl's affections, action that was intended to warn him off. As befits his nickname, Legs had a lanky yet muscular physique, was tall as a tree (six feet five inches), and was a great all-round athlete with a basketball jump shot that I coveted. He had fallen for sixteen-year-old Dorette, a voluptuous, Afro-haired Jamaican girl with a passion for short skirts and platform shoes. She attended

West Hill Girls School near Wimbledon Common, roughly one mile away from Southfields Boys High School.

This equally large girls school was a daily haunt where alongside schoolmates I viewed the eye candy disembarking at the No. 37 bus stop. Outside West Hill's school gates I encountered and began my pursuit of Dorette's equally beguiling, slimmer, yet vivacious younger sister, Yvette. Sadly, Legs would die within the year, not the result of a further knife attack from his Battersea adversary, but smitten by invasive cancer of the liver. His formerly athletic physique had become a ghastly, haggard corpse, displayed for mourners in a casket in his bereaved parents' living room while country and western songs of Jim Reeves played sombrely in the background.

Beautiful Yvette became a passion, my first serious girlfriend, though our romance, like many adolescent trysts, was short-lived. This relationship gave me my first real taste of going to reggae dances. I remember being on a dimly lit, crowded dance floor, entwined in Yvette's loving embrace as her warm, tasty lips murmured "Mmm" into my ear above the loud musical sounds of John Holt's "Stick by Me". This love also brought to bear corporal punishment (legally deployed in British schools until banned by an Act of Parliament in 1987) that I routinely received from various senior teachers for sneaking out of school. Bunking off (truanting) was punishable with an expertly wielded cane. I would bunk off regularly to meet groovy Yvette during lunchtimes. So strong was my craving for her company, fragrant smell, and gentle caress that I was oblivious of the consequences. If truth be told, I simply did not give a damn. Thus after being discovered bunking off on a sixth consecutive occasion, I stood once again outside the office of the dreaded Mr "Killer" Heath-Miller's office awaiting my punishment.

When summoned by the school secretary's call: "Vimikh, you may go in now!" I entered, closed the door with care, and stood respectfully to attention. Ritualistically, Heath-Miller arose from his brown leather seat behind the highly polished desk and approached a metal umbrella stand from which he deftly selected a thin cane roughly three feet in length from among several others of varying thickness. Killer barked an instruction: "Hand out!" I obeyed, accepting without flinching six of the best across the palm of my extended left hand while observing this deputy head's facial expression contort and grimace with each noisy, downward swoosh of the cane. Heath-Miller seemed pitiful, I mused, and not deserving of such a fear-provoking alias.

Despite the ongoing upheavals in my domestic life at Southfields Boys High School, there was always a constant: physical education. PE teacher Gwyn Evans, originally from a mining village in Camarthenshire, South Wales, always selected me for the various under-fifteen school sports teams due to my precocity, ignoring my deteriorating school behaviour and truancy record. In track and field athletics, I won the **victor *ludorum*** – Latin for "winner of the games" – a tradition practiced in quite a few public and grammar school sports days, where a trophy is awarded to the most victorious athlete, the competitor who accumulates the greatest number of points for the team. I excelled in basketball, demonstrating sound leadership skills as team captain and representing London schools at under-fifteen level.

I also loved rugby union, representing Surrey Schools at under-fifteen level. Every Saturday afternoon, after school rugby matches, I would accompany Mickie O'Connell to Mr Chen's fish and chips shop on Garrett Lane where Mickie's elder brother Seamus, a prefect at our school, had a Saturday job. We would always receive a free meal of pie 'n' chips. Even more special would be the times when I was invited to Mickie's family home where his mother was always welcoming. She would generously give me a delicious meal of pasta and spicy meatballs accompanied by fresh, home-baked ciabatta bread. His father, close to retirement, would recite tales of how he'd stood up for my father at the Fulham Power Station when bullying Anglo-Saxon English workmates sought to make trouble.

At this time my academic work began to free-fall dramatically. The potential and diligence of earlier years was replaced by erratic performances in all subjects except physical education. This was no surprise in view of my recent social care history and the influential criminal peers I had encountered, lived with, and come to admire during my time in Stamford House. In searching chaotically for identity, life's meaning, and where I fitted in to the grand scheme of things, I explored sexual, racial, religious, and moral issues: Who am I? What are my beliefs? Do I believe in a just and fair God, or in evolution, as depicted in Darwin's fascinating **Origin of Species** that I'd liberated from the school library? How far should I go if three of my friends want to have sexual intercourse with one girl? Will I join in? Everyone I knew gambled with coitus interruptus, but what about cunnilingus? Will I embrace the widely held belief of misogyny? Where am I actually headed? Who – what friends – will I go with?" These were among the many unresolved questions racing through my youthful mind.

I was now overwhelmingly attracted to wayward behaviour, which included swearing in a manner that would make Satan proud. Kissing my teeth – some would say sucking my teeth – disrespectfully was too juvenile, so I learned how and when to deploy a repertoire of the foulest profanities, becoming skilled at jive talking or cursing, not simply spouting with a Cockney twang "Effing w*****!", "Effing b******!" or "Effing c***!" but far more venomous Caribbean slurs such as "Go suck your mother's c***!" I practiced and perfected my gait to emulate elder youths, strutting with self-assured arrogance and a cocky swagger that I understood signalled to the opposite sex my virility, that I had the wood to light their fire, and forewarned other males that here was a tough guy, a Killer Joe, cock of the roost, or rude boy not to be messed with.

This youthful time was my transition, graduation, progression from bouts of simple French kissing, passionate groping, and fumbling to the wildness and reckless abandonment of full, unprotected sexual intercourse. (Nobody I knew ever bothered with billy bags or Durex.) Mine was indeed a promiscuous adolescence, but on reflection it was a sexualised teenage culture verging on innocence when compared with the porn-obsessed, texting, sexting youths of today's cyber age.

My impetuous character often adopted a stroppy sneer when I scornfully, insubordinately questioned adult authority figures who showed signs of weakness. One exception was when in the presence of the religious education teacher, the Reverend Hubert Montgomery, whom all of the African Caribbean boys at Southfields Boys High School respected and warmed to. Mr Montgomery was a rarity: a bearded, black, African Caribbean teacher with a noticeably strong accent who often displayed a youthful fun side but was fiercely able to control a class full of the most disruptive pupils. Driven by wanting his students to gain a love of learning, this teacher somehow commanded deference and respect, just as actor Sidney Poitier had done in the 1967 movie **To Sir With Love**. Perhaps it was that Mr Montgomery mirrored our fathers and therefore ourselves, namely the ever-swelling ranks year after year of first generation black pupils. We were promising youths, just beginning to formulate clear attitudes, identities, and beliefs as we embarked on our adolescent journeys to manhood and positions in British society.

Try as he might, Mr Montgomery's mentoring could not save me from those malicious demons within, that aspect of my personality increasingly attracted to expressions of hostility and enmity. My school days were numbered. Always at my aggressive, belligerent best on the rugby pitch, I had become equally combative in the dingy school corridors, routinely displaying poor self-control by shoulder barging or violently lashing out at other boys who, it was rumoured, had the temerity to suggest they were my physical equal or dared to screw (eye) me up the wrong way. This was my habitat, my territory, where I felt omnipotent and feared no one, like Roman ruler Julius Caesar uttering "Veni, vidi, vici!" However, my declaration was muted. I was never prone to stand and brag to any foe: "Oi! Who are you f****** looking at?" More like a sniper, my unhinged ego's strategy was passive stealth and silent circumspection that neither forewarned nor broadcasted malevolent intent.

Little did I realise that by exhibiting such Neanderthal conduct I was unwittingly living up to the stereotypical, machismo character that some held to be present in all black males: animalistic, bellicose, quick-tempered, impulsive, and with chips on both shoulders. One of my numerous violent outbursts in the hallways came to the attention of the school authorities after I unleashed a flurry of fists upon one fellow student for no justifiable reason. The ramifications were instantaneous as first thing the next morning, my battered victim's furious but liberal parents stormed into the school demanding a meeting with the headmaster. They stipulated that there would be instant police involvement unless the perpetrator, the boy responsible for their beloved son's injuries, was asked to leave the school immediately.

Fortunately there was an element of forgiveness in their demands which, only after many years had elapsed, I recognised had probably saved me from certain confinement in a youth detention facility. Without further ceremony, the headmaster sanctioned my expulsion. I was swiftly escorted through the school gates before the lunchtime recess that day in October 1972, carrying only a leaving certificate hastily drawn up by the head of year, Mr Watson, who gave me a final parting look of exasperation. I strode nonchalantly down Augustus Road, past the nicely maintained semi-detached houses, towards Southfields underground station. I'd departed school in disgrace, with neither formal examinations nor qualifications, and yet at that precise moment, my braggadocio – my swagger – indicated no rueful sensations, not a second thought as to my future. I had no opportunity to bid farewell to fond friends like Mickie O'Connell, who would deservedly advance over the coming years to head boy status, university, teaching, and a successful career in Perth, Western Australia.

That coming weekend I embraced recidivism, the inevitable relapse towards criminal behaviour, by means of a further brush with London's forces of law and order that resulted in my arrest for shoplifting in bustling Brick Lane Market, Liverpool Street. Four months short of my sixteenth birthday, hell-bent on ignoring sound advice, I was increasingly making the wrong life choices and spiralling out of control. Gravitating towards petty criminality almost as frequently as night becomes day meant that my imminent prospects held little promise, and ahead lay only a gloomy destiny.

chapter II

That ends this strange eventful history,
Is second childishness and mere oblivion,
Sans teeth, sans eyes, sans taste, sans everything.
—William Shakespeare (1564–1616)

Within one month of my expulsion from secondary school, England's grim winter of 1972 had set in. Though merely fifteen years old, I'd outgrown Frogmore Children's Home and now resided in a bed and breakfast (B & B) hotel accommodation paid for by Social Services. Located a ten-minute stroll from the major transport hub of Clapham Junction Station, this B & B was a seedy establishment whose obese, balding pederast proprietor, Cyril, began making unwelcome sexual advances towards me. Just then I recollected events that occurred two years earlier when, on becoming a newspaper boy, another similar predator had accosted me early each morning in the nearby East Hill Housing Estate during my deliveries. The locally known sex offender ceased these actions only after I informed my father Billy, who swiftly went to confront the pervert, brandishing his cut-throat razor, a tool used for his hairdressing work at Ivan's Barber Shop in Clapham High Street.

Cyril's unsolicited approaches halted abruptly when he was threatened by the glinting blade from my lock-knife. Shortly afterwards I transferred to another B & B closer to Clapham Common, again supported by my social worker, who deemed me mature beyond my years and more than capable of coping with independent living. Soon, by a stroke of good fortune, an opportunity to redeem myself and alter my life's trajectory arose when I found regular employment as a salesman at Rueben's menswear store near the recently built Wandsworth Arndale Centre. Serendipity, it seemed, was my guardian angel.

Portly and full-bearded, the yarmulke-wearing shop owner, Philip Rueben, was a jovial, fatherly character who little by little bestowed upon me much faith and responsibility in return for a decent salary plus commission as from day one my work ethic and manner with his customers impressed. I'd secured the job following a preliminary half-day trial in which Mr Rueben deployed an integrity examination. He had deliberately secreted cash about the changing rooms, seemingly spilled from an unwary customer's pocket, to elicit either a trustworthy or unscrupulous response. Passing this test, I was taken on and soon, with extra money in my pocket, was at last able to visit Ronald Perry's Fulham Road tailor shop, recommended by older peers as the place to get measured up for the much coveted three-piece mohair tonic or Glen check – aka Prince of Wales check – suit. In next to no time, I assisted with banking the weekly takings, and was soon entrusted with a set of keys to unbolt the shutters, unlock, and lock up the shop each day. The wondrously uplifting sensation of ecstasy, gratification, and pride that overcame me that day Mr Rueben first handed over to me his shop's keys would not be forgotten.

This proprietor, a married father of two, learned before long of my family problems, that I lived in bedsit land and had a history as a tearaway, and yet he was prepared to gamble and give me a chance. Mr Rueben told me harsh tales, facts of life that he himself had undergone and survived during the past years developing his small business. His faith helped nurture in me a growing sense of self-belief. Appearing at Marylebone Magistrates Court in December 1972 for the theft offence that past October could have seen me sentenced to custody in a

Borstal or Detention Centre but for the presentation of Mr Rueben's written character reference, which depicted a much trusted, hard-working, praiseworthy young man. The court outcome was a fine, a conditional discharge, and the sternest of warnings from the magistrate that any further offence would definitely result in a custodial sentence.

The Jewish shop owner's reference was intrinsic to my good fortune that day at court. So was another event, as I believed. By this time I was renting a small second-floor room in a large Victorian terraced house on Stephendale Road in Fulham. The chain-smoking landlord, a sinewy, dark-skinned man called Israel with a wispy goatee from the island of Dominica, claimed to be religious, though exactly what faith he practised was rather a mystery. Israel persuaded me that for no significant cost he could prepare some vague, unspecified talisman that would be beneficial and work in my favour at court. The landlord actually thought himself to be a necromancer, a bit of a medicine man. What he required was the purchase of a brand new, unused fountain pen, an unopened bottle of ink, and some new writing paper of the very best quality. A few days later, when presented with these items, Israel proceeded to scribble some illegible text onto the pristine paper, stating the scrawl was simply a line or two from the Old Testament, while muttering some vague incantations. To conclude, we both drank a small measure of overproof Caribbean rum after he first drizzled a small quantity onto the linoleum-covered floor – a libation to divine spirits and ancestors. Israel advised that I carry the piece of paper on my person at court, and its magical charm would do the rest. A little Caribbean obeah, or so I believed, in tandem with my Jewish employer's reference had saved me from certain incarceration.

Each Friday evening, upon receiving my Rueben's wage packet, I would seek out some trusted source to purchase a quarter of an ounce. Smoking marijuana, collie, weed, tampi, or ganga had become a regular pastime for me and many of my companions. I had begun smoking regularly before leaving Southfields Boys High School, yet for some unknown reason wisely chose never to pull on a spliff either before or during employment at the clothes shop. Away from work it was a different matter. One Saturday afternoon in February 1973, with a pre-rolled joint inside my box of Benson & Hedges cigarettes, I headed for Chelsea Football Club's home fixture against Sheffield United with a good friend, ardent Blues fan James "Guinness" McLean, his Jamaican alias on account of his dark hue. Attending football matches in this era was an extremely hazardous pastime. Intolerance, ugliness, and bigotry blighted the English sport. Pitch invasions were the norm; hundreds of moronic hooligans would often prearrange fist fights, brawls, or mini riots inside and outside football grounds; and bananas were thrown onto pitches at the few black players gracing the game. People, including the authorities, shrugged such conduct off with "It's just football, innit?"

That afternoon, walking down Fulham Road towards Stamford Bridge, Guinness and I shared the spliff and once through the turnstiles joined thousands of other supporters in the terraces of the Shed End, the designated territory of ardent home fans. With the referee's whistle barely blown, the Shed's mighty chorus rang out loudly from song to song and then worryingly turned. "Sieg Heil, Sieg Heil, Sieg Heil!" cried many Chelsea supporters in unison. Looking about in every direction, we witnessed a sea of fascist salutes given in tandem with the intimidating chants which, interestingly, were directed at the opposition fans. Within minutes, avid fan Guinness and I skulked out of Stamford Bridge, our apprehension, sense of persecution, and paranoia exacerbated for having had the earlier smoke. It would be another twenty years before I attended another professional football match.

Sweet smelling and with a distinct aroma, ganga was, alongside reggae music, an integral element of our youth subculture. Loveable reggae had evolved considerably in stature since the sexually explicit hits of the late 1960s, when artists like Max Romeo sang "Wet Dream", and Prince Buster produced an album which included such tracks as "Wreck a Pum-Pum" and its opposite "Wreck a Buddy". Reggae had developed into a far more sophisticated genre by 1973, and youngsters like myself who gravitated towards the music were unconsciously making choices that entailed distinctly different social, political, and cultural pathways. The clubs and musical venues where we let our hair down, the companions whom we trusted, and the girls we sought out were almost exclusively black. Many of our male contemporaries who favoured soul (rhythm and blues) music were attracted to more racially integrated dance venues like Waterloo Birds Nest or Hammersmith Palais where, significantly, they pursued and dated white girls, and black girls dated white boys. Dressed in our glad rags, my closest friends and I raved at reggae clubs every Friday, Saturday, and Sunday night. Before hitting the town I'd don an immaculate, tailor-made mohair suit, always dry cleaned to provide razor sharp trouser creases, and polished black brogues, after which I'd splash on Brut aftershave, sprinkling some onto the cotton flannel stuffed in my back pocket to be used to mop the sweat from my brow.

With my gang of friends, sometimes up to a dozen in number, I travelled the length and breadth of London for the pleasure of listening to sound systems such as Fatman, Coxone, Duke Reid, Count Shelley, and the Mighty Sufferer. And it mattered not that we hailed from South West London. We never encountered any of the notoriously territorial postcode rivalries that decades later, in 2009, began to plague many of London's poorer neighbourhoods. At these musical venues, my peers and I competed with each other to see who could get the most dances with the opposite sex. The manner of our dancing was very different from the uncoordinated, chaotic way many white people danced, especially those fans of British heavy metal rock bands like Deep Purple or Led Zeppelin.

We skanked and swayed in controlled time to the offbeat rhythm, and if lucky, with the right female partner dancing oh so close, the extremely erotic, slowly gyrating pelvic motions guaranteed to elicit a stirring in one's loins. At the night's end, when the lights were turned on and the DJ signed off with his last record, one just might get lucky and secure a girl's phone number. On a London Transport underground train, Red Routemaster bus, or when walking home afterwards, our banter jibed, ridiculed, and teased: Who had danced with the fittest, most attractive girls? Or who was the recipient of rejection, refused a dance and therefore publicly shamed?

By the spring of 1973, having just turned sixteen, I had moved to a rented £10 per week first-floor room in a shared terraced house off Fulham Palace Road. Several old school friends lived nearby, and in their company I partied every weekend. We raved at clubs like the Metro in Westbourne Park on Fridays. Sometimes on Saturdays we were at Four Aces in Dalston Junction, Phoebe's on Amhurst Road, Mr Bee's in Peckham, or All Nations off Hackney's Kingsland Road. And always a Sunday night favourite: the Red Lion in Leytonstone.

Another preferred weekend haunt, near the end of the Piccadilly Line, was Bluesville in Wood Green, North London. One Sunday evening I took a girlfriend named Carol along. She had given birth to a baby (not mine) some months earlier, was merely fourteen, and always ensured my fridge was stockpiled with quality foodstuffs like rump steak and fresh fruit acquired from local supermarkets. As a young, low-ranking member from a group of streetwise South London women, Carol excelled in deception, sleight of hand, and hustling, and at that moment in time being a ponce or bludger did not affect my moral compass one little bit.

Arriving at Bluesville's first-floor dance hall and licensed bar, located above a High Street public house, we positioned ourselves next to a wall alongside many large, stacked, pounding speaker boxes. Being very egotistical at the time, and out to impress Carol, I visited the bar and purchased our drinks of choice, a rum and black on the rocks for her and Stingo barley wine for me. During that first hour, I rolled a spliff, downed my beverage, and danced up close with my girlfriend. Soon the dance floor was full, jam-packed with revellers, and the heat suffocating. Halfway through another spliff, I left Carol's side, easing among the packed, sweaty partygoers to seek out a couple of pals in the less crowded centre of the hall. Passing on the still-lit spliff, I spoke over the loud music into one friend's ear, stating my intention to go out for some fresh air, took two steps in the direction of the exit, and collapsed flat on my back from the combined effects of stifling temperature, alcohol, and too much weed. My companions picked me up and hauled me outside to revive in the cool, clean air. Humiliation quickly kicked in, and so as not to appear weak-hearted, I promptly rolled another spliff and entered the dance hall with it placed in my mouth. Travelling home on London underground, my friends ribbed me about my Christ-like posture while horizontal on the floor, mouth agape and eyes glazed. Carol, who had no clue I had collapsed, joined in the ridicule as I vowed never again to mix Barley Wine with weed.

One former school friend from my Fulham neighbourhood, Amos Hanson, had two influential elder siblings: Alexander, who was in the Royal Air Force and always purchased the latest reggae tunes when on home leave; and Adam, who had recently completed a maths degree at university. The latter was a conscious brother who convened meetings with my companions and me on Sunday afternoons in nearby Bishop's Park to explore the development of our latent talent. We talked politics and the importance of family, of the desperate need for black youth to organise, pool resources, form community support groups, and most important of all, become educated. Adam's oratory was fiery, a call to arms. He declared at each gathering "Young brothers: Education is the key!" persistently referring to the brandished, yet caressed, reading material held aloft in his hands, books like **Invisible Man**, **No Easy Walk to Freedom**, or **Seize the Time**.

"There is nothing you cannot accomplish!" Adam asserted as he stood tall before us, looking stylishly militant, Fulham's mirror image of Huey P. Newton, Eldridge Cleaver, or Bobby Seale – donned in his black beret, black polo-necked top, and bottle green trench coat, belted around the waist. Moreover, the initiatives he preached about made good sense, and shortly our small group formed a savings scheme with individual subscriptions of fifty pence paid in each week. The idea lasted about seven months, after which interest waned as our individual paths moved off in teenage life's diverse voyages. However, with minds like sponges, the seeds sown by radical Adam meant that intellectually, spiritually, and morally we were more certain, assured, and explicitly headed in the right direction.

Other friends in my peer group, sixteen-year-old Henry Gyan and his younger brother Stephen, declared to everybody that their family was originally from Guyana, South America. Then one day after visiting Henry's family for dinner and conversing with his ever-so-hospitable mother, whose accent was recognisably not Caribbean, I persistently queried my friend's stated origins, especially their ownership of the surname Gyan. Eventually Henry confided that his mother and father were from West Africa, from Sierra Leone, and Ghana respectively. If truth be told, I too had lied to my peer group ever since attending Southfields Boys High School by declaring my birth mother to be a light-skinned coolie woman from Antigua, my father's birthplace.

By claiming he had Guyanese origins, Henry was signalling "I want to be in the in crowd!" merely seeking grace and favour among a predominantly West Indian or rather African Caribbean peer group, some of whom, it has to be said, ignorantly engaged in a type of cultural snobbery that ridiculed Africans. I had no false sense of cultural superiority and advised Henry to drop the pretence and proudly state his African roots. Why I was so perceptive, so insightful as to Henry's identity plight can perhaps be linked to the other tenants living in the property off Fulham Palace Road. Phillip Obi was a short, stocky, quiet Nigerian man, a student of mathematics, who rented the room next door to me while a young family, Mavis and Derek John and their one-year-old baby, rented the ground floor rooms and, interestingly, were from Sierra Leone and Guyana respectively.

Henry, an aspiring drummer and sixth form pupil at a respected Hammersmith school, introduced some of us to his drama teacher, Theophilus Bridgeman, who rented a flat on a neighbouring Fulham street and hailed from the Caribbean island of Barbados, also known as Little England. Soon we gathered regularly at our gregarious thespian mentor's flat, a venue that provided a forum for us to listen critically to music, mingle with girlfriends, and engage in intense, lengthy conversations from twilight into the early morning hours. These rap sessions were an alternative education because, teaching drama aside, Theo was equally enthusiastic about music and politics. Our dialogues increasingly focused on issues like Theo's experiences in the teaching profession; the problems impacting on London's black community such as the unexplained deaths of African Caribbean men in police custody; the hated stop and search (SUS) laws; and more broadly international events in the wider so-called Third World.

What we gleaned from these late-night gatherings was far removed from what formal British education had instilled in us. Our secondary schools had never taught us about ancient African civilisations like Nubia, Ile Ife, or the Kush city of Meroe; that most of Egyptian history is the history of black African or Negroid peoples; that the English language is rooted in the ancient Indian language of Sanskrit; or that many European or Caucasian scientists and intellectuals had contrived a sophisticated structure of ideas – social Darwinism and scientific racism – to assert the African's supposed inferiority. A spark combusted in my mind, and suddenly my thirst for answers led me back to the effortless, most satisfying act of reading, something I'd abandoned following being expelled from school the previous October.

These nocturnal debate sessions inspired me to enrol at the local public library and at weekends to habitually visit Grassroots Bookstore in Goldborne Road, Ladbroke Grove. One Saturday at this bookshop I browsed through reading material with subjects ranging from Karl Marx's writings on economics and philosophy to the biography of Dr Kwame Nkrumah, who had steered Ghana (formerly the Gold Coast) to independence from Britain in 1957. I came across books on the eighteenth-century Jamaican Maroon Wars and George Jackson's **Soledad Brother**, its poignant, angry letters detailing Jackson's intellectual response to incarceration and a sentence of one year to life for stealing less than $100 when he was a teenager. I purchased this paperback and a hardback entitled **Africa's Gift to America** by J. A. Rogers, the distinguished African-American historian.

The following Saturday a friend took me to a bookshop located in the front room of a house in Ealing whose owner, Jessica Huntley, had recently published Walter Rodney's **How Europe Underdeveloped Africa**, which I, of course, purchased. Totally absorbed and engrossed by the sheer magnitude and diversity of history before, during, and after the Atlantic slave trade, our Maafa or African holocaust. I read avidly any book, newspaper article, or magazine connected to the umbrella term **African studies**.

Running concurrent to my resurrected enthusiasm for literature and learning was an ever-increasing melomania, an unquenchable passion for reggae, a music form in its adolescence that was verging on becoming an international genre and shortly to evolve into the greatest cultural movement to come out of the island of Jamaica. In the decades ahead, reggae would heavily influence the growth of elements of American rhythm and blues along its path towards rap music. It would attract adherents from white British working-class backgrounds. Due to the good money I earned as a salesman in Mr Rueben's shop, I could now afford to regularly send £10.00 per month to Derrick Harriot's record store in Half Way Tree, Kingston, Jamaica for pre-released records – seven- or twelve-inch vinyl, fresh off the press and not in general release in UK record stores. Coincidentally, Half Way Tree was where my stepmother Victoria had lived and attended elementary school as a child when growing up in Jamaica.

Following the arrival of my airmail packages, I'd play each new disc over and over at high volume through the large speakers of my Leak stereo system, with the bass always switched to maximum. By mid 1973 I became increasingly aware of and influenced by Rastafarian ideology, the faith that permeated this wonderful music from Jamaica, with its infectious embrace of concepts like the legalisation of cannabis, peace and love, and support for the liberation struggles of oppressed Africans throughout the world. A number of my friends were equally attracted to and swept along by the influential tide of ideas in reggae music.

Seeking out elder Rastafarians at every opportunity, I enquired and reasoned with them, listened carefully, and heard talk of a black king who ruled modern-day Ethiopia. Ethiopia was much lauded in Jamaica as the only African nation to have remained independent and unconquered by Europe throughout the decades of tumultuous exploitation when under colonial rule. Ethiopia's ruler, King Haile Selassie I, was believed to be a direct descendant of the Queen of Sheba and King Solomon. Like Solomon of the Old Testament, Haile Selassie was considered to be a great and wise King, a true prophet who was accorded God- or Christ-like status. Selassie was the King of all black people scattered worldwide as a result of slavery and the iniquities of the Western World, Babylon. Under his divine leadership, and the name of Ras Tafari (Rastafari), Africans scattered in the diaspora would eventually arise and repatriate back to the lands of their forefathers to reclaim their birthright. Rastafarian ideology immediately struck a chord, appealing to my lapsed Christian background and evolving racial awareness. It became plausible as, approaching the age of seventeen, I sought culture, identity, enlightenment, and truth in my voyage to adulthood.

Regretfully, along this spiritual journey a not-so-subtle shift in attitude towards my peers took place. Trusted acquaintances like Guinness and Amos, whom I had known since the age of eleven, became lost to me as my evaluation of, fascination with, and the eventual adoption of this new ideology took root. Other young men like the Gyan brothers, Henry and Stephen, would also choose the Rastafarian path. My chosen estrangement left friends bewildered, even embittered, as I espoused my belief that they were crazy baldheads, unbelievers, disciples of Babylon. I overtly rejected their company over the days, weeks, and months that went by. My hair became unkempt and natural as I ceased to groom it by daily combing or trips to the barber shop. Growing one's locks was considered an essential act of faith for a Rastafarian. Proof of its godly relevance was to be found in the Bible's Old Testament, to which I was referred by one elder Rasta brother who counselled me on knowledge of my new faith. The book of Numbers, chapter 6, verse 5 reads concerning the vow of a Nazirite: "All the days of his vow of separation no razor shall come upon his head. He shall be holy and let the locks of hair on his head grow long." To my impressionable mind, this passage was a further revelation and served to reinforce my new-found belief system.

Instructions written in the book of Numbers detailed the type of foods believers, the "chosen few", could eat or what was deemed unclean, unfit for a devout man's consumption, including pork (swine) and strong drink (alcohol). When I became an avid Bible student, lots of things began to make sense. After all, black people in the Western world were the modern-day children of Israel, and history, as then known, had merely been distorted by European people. Four hundred years of African enslavement by Europeans was historically significant and mirrored the period of slavery meted out to the Hebrews in ancient Egypt.

Within the book of Revelation there seemed sufficient proof of claims by Rastafarians that Haile Selassie was the returned Christ, the living God. Revelation chapter 5, verse 5 reads, "Weep not, lo the Lion of the Tribe of Judah, the root of David, has conquered". This, alongside other excerpts from such a revered religious source, supported by Haile Selassie's claim to be a direct descendant of King David, helped confirm in my mind's eye the undeniable truth that lay within Rastafarian ideology. However, I did not immediately accept its entire message. During the coming months, my initial scepticism was overcome by hours of reasoning with Rastas at every opportunity, reading and daily evaluation of Biblical texts, and other relevant literature, all underpinned by sweet, sweet, sweet reggae music and the blessed herb. By the age of seventeen, no longer reticent, I fully embraced Rastafari, convinced my salvation and that of all shackled black people scattered throughout the Western world had arrived.

With self-imposed estrangement from past friends, the void was gradually filled by brethren. I declared to former trusted peers in the starkest terms that they were now divided from me, my stance physically evident by my dishevelled, natty dread and beard. As unbelievers they were unrighteous, impure, and blind to the truth. Their only deliverance, my doomsday scenario preached, was to accept what I now fervently acknowledged: that Haile Selassie was the Messiah, Jesus Christ reincarnated, that Ethiopia in Africa was the rightful homeland of black people, and finally that repatriation to the motherland was the means by which people of the African diaspora could be saved from the impending destruction of Babylon. They, of course, refused to be indoctrinated by my fealty sermons, rants expressing allegiance to some far-off king, and thus our friendships were severed. These old companions must have felt a confused bitterness following such scornful rejection when their place in my social network was replaced by Rasta brethren.

Each passing day my beliefs hardened as the conviction in the genuine truth of Rastafarianism took root, bolstered by my dramatically increasing daily consumption of ganja. By December 1973 I was spending an average of £10 to £15 per week on the holy herb. As Rastafarians we incorporated the smoking of ganja into our cosmogony, the herb being deemed sacred and sanctified by God himself. Weed was judged as most earthly, natural, and organic, a tenet that influenced my decision in later years to shun any temptation to dabble in progressively popular drugs like cocaine. As an **earth man** I would never, ever pop the nervous system stimulant speed (amphetamines) or experience the psychedelic effects of LSD. However, the high produced by hash oil, a thin streak of which was applied to Rizla papers before rolling up with ordinary cigarette tobacco and smoking, was another matter.

Impromptu gatherings regularly occurred at the homes of various Rastafarian brethren. These were times to reason and explore Biblical philosophy, quote holy scriptures, and smoke weed as thumping away through speakers in the background would be the bass line of music like "Door Peep" (Burning Spear) or the Nyabingi drums of "Hundred Years" (Count Ossie and the Mystic Revelation). We would smoke either spliffs or the pipe (chillum). Smoking spliffs was an informal sharing affair, as my brethren or I would expertly roll a joint, rarely ital – pure cannabis, unadulterated by mixing with cigarette tobacco – due to the cost. We would light up, take several pulls, and then pass it on. Failure to share was poor etiquette.

Pipe smoking was totally different and always linked to Rastafarian festivals like the celebration of Haile Selassie's birthday (23 July), Ethiopian New Year (11 September), the anniversary of the coronation of Haile Selassie I (2 November) or Ethiopian Christmas (7 January). Chillum smoking also occurred at other special events like a brother's birthday, the birth of a child, or the reunion of old friends, where the atmosphere would be reverent, solemn, and almost churchlike. The pipe was made of several sections, including a receptacle with water therein to cool the hot smoke, an outlet to which was attached a pliable rubber tube, and a conical device made of fired clay into which the ganga, in its ital form only, was carefully packed. Once prepared, a chosen brother would bless the pipe by reciting a verse from the Bible, and it was then lit, each person in turn puffing a deeply inhaled lungful before passing it on.

Physically and psychologically the effects of pipe smoking were traumatic. A brother might choke, become oblivious to his surroundings by entering a trance-like hypnotic state, faint momentarily, or even become unconscious. Years would pass by before I openly acknowledged that the intoxicating effects of the chemical THC (tetrahydrocannabinol) in this "sweet, blessed herb" sent some brothers into a permanent mind-altered state akin to schizophrenia from which they would never, ever recover. Brethren like Melvin, a bright youth who a couple of years prior had left school having passed ten GCE O level exams; or Desmond, a talented footballer and apprentice plasterer, respectively, became bedraggled, psychotic street wanderers or one day just disappeared, never to be seen again by friends nor family.

Dazed and red-eyed after chillum smoking, I would become withdrawn, my lungs feeling as if stretched to their utmost, but my mindset remained fixated. I would not, **could** not succumb and thus demonstrate weakness to those present. Several hours after one such pipe session I belched, expelling from deep down inside my innards an immense cloud of smoke, much to the amazement of myself and others present. On reflection, I became aware of the absence of women's participation in pipe smoking, whereas they would often share a spliff. In fact, sisters, referred to as **queens**, were peripheral background figures, domestics who prepared food, cleared away afterwards, looked after children, and presented a submissive character.

Events in my life moved rapidly. I proclaimed to all who would listen that I was now and for eternity a convert to the Rastafarian message, that Babylon was Europe, and that Europeans were in essence evil. Reality, however, meant compromising, given that I worked alongside white people, a fact that often brought issues of conflict to the fore. By this period I had long since stopped working for Mr Rueben, whose Arndale Centre shop had closed, relocating to Caledonian Road. Following this, I had found temporary employment in various dead-end jobs: hod carrying, assembly line work in an electronics factory, and a brief spell in the kitchen of a major High Street restaurant chain. Then in June 1974, aged seventeen, I took up permanent employment as a handyman, following recommendation by my social worker, in a local authority run residential home for the elderly called Green Lands, set amidst five acres of gardens near Wimbledon Common. Initially I enjoyed the job, being responsible for building maintenance, general repairs, changing light bulbs, and other light tasks, but after a while its daily routine became mundane. My soul yearned for more challenging work.

Almost immediately I found myself directly involved with the senior citizens themselves, often listening to or chit-chatting away with them, a trait soon recognised by management. Significant numbers of these folks were physically frail and demented but interesting characters nonetheless. Fewer were lucid, sharp-witted and mobile, and many had a remarkable story to tell. One ninety-something-year-old Cockney man, Mr King, often recounted sad anecdotes of the eerie sound played by pipers during combat, of the bravest teenage Tommys, his fallen comrades at the Somme – the "meat grinder" he called it. Mr King recalled this bloodiest battle in British military history, the effects of shrapnel, and the loathed chateau generals, months in muddy trenches, then the extreme cold of winter, the onset of gangrene, the bully beef, biscuits, and rations of cigarette and matches. The old ladies, many spinsters or widowed by that Great War, gave vivid accounts of living with neither wedlock nor children, and their subsequent lifelong service in the palatial households of the wealthy.

At Green Lands a job vacancy shortly arose for the position of Geriatric Care Assistant, and I applied with instant success. My wages increased and also my responsibilities, which entailed caring for the needs of six elderly men: daily shaving, weekly baths, clipping nails, laundry, and so on. One day on arriving for work, I was informed by the matron that Mr Judd had died early that morning. As Mr Judd preferred to sleep butt naked, I was instructed to give him some dignity by assisting with putting some pyjama bottoms on him. I refused to touch him! This was a step too far and clashed with my religious principles. I declared emphatically, "Is it not written in the Holy Bible 'let the dead bury the dead'?" The middle aged matron, a thick-set and far from dour Scottish woman called Mrs Kirkbride, insisted I complete this unpleasant task, but I remained resolute. Mrs Kirkbride then phoned a senior manager responsible for the council's old people's homes who also spoke to me, yet I still refused. Both eventually conceded that my non-compliance was a lost cause but ensured it was documented on my employment record.

Afterwards, the matron warned me sternly that if my ultra-religious philosophy was rooted in such ideas, I should exercise the greatest of care as old, vulnerable white people might become scapegoats and face maltreatment given my attitude that European people and their values were inherently flawed. "You might," she stated, "harm an old person one day, and we cannot have that happen!" This set me pondering deeply, as did Mrs Kirkbride's later comments in which she divulged to me facts of her own teenage years, when she was a zealous convert, a religious disciple in the sect known as the Plymouth Brethren.

Influential reggae artist Burning Spear released in Jamaica his 1975 album entitled **Marcus Garvey**. This album arrived along with other records in one of the regular packages sent over from Derrick Harriot's Halfway Tree record shop. Burning Spear's songs were rhythmically hypnotic, with lyrics that referred to the struggles of Garvey, the slavery era, and Africa. At the time I knew little about Marcus Mosiah Garvey except that he was a Jamaican national hero. Then Larry, one of my brethren, enlightened me further by handing me a book to read entitled **The Philosophy and Opinions of Marcus Garvey**. This book, compiled by Garvey's wife Amy, set out the details of his life from his boyhood days in Jamaica at the turn of the twentieth century to the growth of his Universal Negro Improvement Association (UNIA) organisation to three million members in the USA, to his last five years living in West Kensington, London and death in 1940.

Garvey, a pudgy, dark-skinned man, stood out as a great historical figure who took immense pride in his African ancestry and believed in the Holy Bible. Garveyism made popular the idea that black people in the western hemisphere should return home to Africa and were destined to play a major role in the future of world economics and politics. Rastafarians believe him to be a prophet, sent by Almighty God to show black people the way forward. Garvey was said to have prophesised the crowning of a great black King – Haile Selassie I – who would eventually free black people from the iniquities of Babylon. As a result of this prophecy, Rastafarian ideology was born in Garvey's island of birth in the 1930s. I reasoned that these jigsaw pieces made a whole narrative: Haile Selassie was the living God; he ruled a nation never conquered by Europeans; he was a descendant of King David; and he was black. Was not Ethiopia mentioned in the book of Genesis, chapter 2, verse 13? And was not Babylon – Europe – guilty of numerous historical acts of barbarism?

Brother Larry soon introduced me to the Ethiopian Orthodox Church in Ladbroke Grove, and for a short while

I'd proudly travel there on the 295 bus, Bible in hand, to attend Sunday worship. While there I was particularly taken by the aroma of frankincense, the sweet-smelling incense obtained from the gum or resin of the Bosiwellia papyifera tree that grows in Ethiopia's rocky habitat and which was burnt in tandem with the priest's chants and prayers.

Working at Green Lands had many perks, including the five-acre garden to relax in during breaks while reading the **Guardian** broadsheet. The **Sun** tabloid newspaper, much loved by me when I sat at the back of class in Southfields Boys High School, I now deemed too juvenile a read. There I enjoyed free hot meals prepared by Grace, the wonderful Trinidadian cook, and the resident's lounge, with its sizeable colour TV always tuned in to BBC television. There on the screen in the summer of 1975 I watched elegant, Afro-haired African-American Arthur Ashe inflict a four-set defeat on the previous year's champion and favourite, Jimmy Connors, to win Wimbledon, considered by many to be the world's most prestigious tennis tournament.

That August I saw a brief BBC news bulletin: Haile Selassie had died of a prostate ailment after being overthrown following a military coup. The broadcast reported that Ethiopia had been gripped by the ravages of unprecedented famine since 1972. Selassie's army, in particular junior ranking officers influenced by Marxist ideology, could no longer countenance the many royal idiosyncrasies – like the pets he kept, including a beloved poodle, maintained in extravagant luxury – while his emaciated people endured starvation. Old black and white film footage depicted Selassie's life, his triumphant return to Ethiopia from exile following the Italian invasion of the 1930s, and his role in the Organisation of African Unity (OAU).

Trauma and confusion set in that day, and after work I sped home to seek the counsel of other brethren. "Lies! Damn, blasted liars!" they uttered emphatically. Babylonian society simply wanted to throw Rasta into confusion.

Brother Larry, however, rationalised the probability of some truth in these tidings, stating: "Every mickle mek eh muckle."

Shortly after the military takeover, further news reports surfaced: Haile Selassie had actually died in prison. Again most brethren refused to accept this as factual. "CIA sponsored Babylonian propaganda!" they countered. In my heart of hearts I did not know what to believe anymore. Larry once again was among the few who dared speculate, at least in private, that only those in Ethiopia could know for sure that Selassie was dead.

One year later, summer was a scorcher, one of the hottest since English meteorological records began. With average daily temperatures of 30 ºC during June and July across South and South East England, the 1976 heat wave saw virtually no rainfall, only daily news reports of drought-induced forest fires. At summer's end the Notting Hill Carnival would erupt into violent skirmishes between black youths and the police. That season three black sisters, including the cousin of a well-respected brother, came down to London from Leicester. All were natural in appearance, deceptively demure, wearing no make-up, just simple, modest attire with minimal jewellery. Two had their hair covered with brightly coloured head ties, while the third sported an almost perfect, medium-sized Afro. Following introductions I sat upon a floor cushion in the living room alongside other Rasta brethren as we began reasoning with the sisters. I formed an immediate impression. Good looks aside, they were intellectual, articulate, yet far too opinionated.

These were modern day furies, liberated young black women posing queries that neither my brethren nor I could adequately answer, points of view that felt antagonistic to the sanctimonious values we held to be true. Why was there a famine in Ethiopia during Haile Selassie's time in power? Why did he live in lavish luxury, flaunting his wealth and pampering a beloved pet poodle while his people withered from famine and starvation? Was this behaviour not simply the way of all royalty the world over? How do you repatriate to a country where you do not speak the native language of Amharic? Why do Rasta queens act subservient and submissive to their men? Had we no understanding of the American Civil Rights struggle, a battle not just for racial equality but for women's rights? And had we not heard of the revolutionary, iconic radical, Afro-haired Angela Davis, number one on the United States of America's most wanted list? Was not the Holy Bible, lying open before us on the nearby coffee table, written and translated for King James I, a European ruler? What did the Bible have to do with Africa and African people, who had their own indigenous religions prior to the white man's arrival? Were not Rasta, the Holy Bible, and Haile Selassie's divinity one big lie? **How f*****g dare they?** I thought.

To say we were bewildered by such brazen hyperbole would be an understatement. The meeting left me feeling uneasy, nauseous, and emasculated. These Leicester women were formidable debaters, clearly educated and well read. They fired off question after question, statement after statement, each one ever more probing and analytical. As we jousted verbally, my brethren and I replied with ideas, explanations, and biblical rhetoric about the Rastafarian perspective on worldly matters, ripostes that were fundamentally weaker and lacking in substance.

When they left the house, boy oh boy did we curse! They were nasty Jezebels, in need of a good slap, harlots, decadent lesbians, Babylonian spies who fornicated with European men. They spoke only wickedness and would face a painful death worse than that inflicted on the inhabitants of Sodom and Gomorrah.

Later on, and for weeks thereafter, my thoughts ran amok. If truth be told, I had no answers to the daring questions these terrifyingly haughty sisters posed. Other brethren seemed equally feeble, unable to offer explanations other than outright condemnation based on

Rastafarian oratory or the Holy Scriptures. All except Larry, that is, who in private again wisely counselled, "Every mickle mek ah muckle. They could be right!"

Larry Anglin was a couple of years older than me and originally someone whose parents and siblings I knew from the East Hill area of Wandsworth where my father Billy used to cut Larry's hair in his pre-Rasta days. Not an extrovert like me, but quietly self-assured and rational, Larry often provided me with measure and clarity when I was confused. After the clash of ideas and principles upon debating with the three Leicester sisters, I began to visit him more often at the flat in Balham where he lived with the mother of his two young children. There, after his day's work as an electrician, Larry would practice playing his electric bass guitar, eventually progressing to the double bass, and we'd broaden our intellectual and musical horizons by listening to jazz greats Charlie Mingus, Bird, John Coltrane, and Miles Davis, or Gil Scott Heron and a trio of American rappers called the Last Poets. Here, more often than not, Larry and I would simply investigate themes that were outlawed, taboo when among our brethren.

All rebellious young men break rules and question the status quo and wisdom of their elders. Our breach commenced with becoming Rastafarians in the first place, much to the ire of our parents, and now here we sat querying Jehovah's instructions to mankind. How, for example, could we go forth and multiply without having the economic means to provide for our offspring? The Bible stated that women should remove themselves from men and refrain from cooking and certain other activities while menstruating. How on earth could such ancient legislation make sense in the latter twentieth century? We explored the hot political issues of the day and the incredible wealth of industrialised northern hemisphere countries compared to their poorer southern hemisphere counterparts, an economic divide so crystal clear. Did not European nations reign over the entire planet and have the means to ensure their continued dominance: the guns, the bombs, the gas, the money, the transportation infrastructure, and so forth? Were not the majority of our brothers and sisters in the African diaspora mentally enslaved by Eurocentric thought processes, unwittingly still guided by our slave masters? Maybe black people had been fed too much religion, we dared postulate, as after all, didn't most of us adhere to the Bible in ways that caused Europeans to express quiet disdain and scornful amusement?

Slowly my attitude transformed, my world view broadened. I sensed myself becoming dissimilar to other more steadfast brethren and eventually accepted that Haile Selassie was dead. Deep down I pondered how on earth I could have ever publicly declared such blind loyalty to a feudal ruler. My concentration focussed on the book **Blood In My Eye**, written by George Jackson, the imprisoned African-American radical, just before his shotgun death at the hands of prison guards in San Quentin maximum security prison. George wrote that when compared to the likes of Ho Chi Minh, Kwame Nkrumah, or Che Guevara, His Royal Highness Haile Selassie I, Jah Rastafari – my god – was merely a punk.

I was developing an awareness of a school of thought that the white man had a God complex and the Holy Bible was a key tool among his arsenal of weapons. South of the Sahara, where my ancestors would have been shipped from, indigenous African religions prior to the arrival of Europeans were definitely not Judeo-Christian in origin. My intellectual shift was moving at a pace. As I consumed newly found literature, my ideas changed rapidly, and I found myself occasionally daring to openly disagree with other Rastafarians. Deep down it was only a matter of time before things came to a head. Sometimes I discussed transformation with Larry, the possibility of a day arriving when I might summon up the courage to trim off my dreadlocks. That far off time, just a sinful notion then, would be a kind of judgement day, when brethren and my entire social circle would indeed know I was not a true believer.

Late in July 1976, I moved out of the rented Fulham bedsit, having been invited back to the flat in East Hill, Wandsworth, where my father lived. Billy had been made redundant from his main employment at Fulham Power Station and was finalising preparations to leave England for the shores of his native Antigua. At age nineteen I jumped at this golden opportunity. I had been paying £10.00 per week for the first floor bedsit so would have been extremely foolhardy to turn down the chance of a ground floor two-bedroom flat with its small garden in Wandsworth for even less weekly rent. That month my transfer application from Green Lands in Wimbledon to another council-run geriatric home located near Clapham Common was approved.

My experiences working alongside many wonderful carers, predominantly mature African-Caribbean women, looking after the elderly taught me a valuable lesson about the human condition and the seventh age of man. Providing personal care for previously independent, physically healthy pensioners was most sobering. Watching these men and women wither, drool, and waste away, seemingly overnight, left an unforgettable memory as many developed permanent putrid bedsores so loathsome to smell. The unpleasant, foul-tasting odour literally clung to my clothing. Some of these poor souls succumbed to senile dementia, whether they were formerly bus drivers or mathematicians, assembly line workers or middle managers. Once intelligent minds became babbling, half-conscious zombies, decaying cabbage-like without dignity or memory, no longer able to recognise their own visiting beloved sons, daughters and grandchildren. A few of these old folk also had what was described as double incontinence – enuresis and faecal leakage – and the presence of both physical ailments, combined with dementia, made their existence far more woeful.

This second childhood is that most cruel of fates for which there is absolutely no cure. I resolved that when I'm old like them, with cracking knees and miles of wrinkles, with a body and senses that can no longer differentiate between flatulence or the passing of faeces, when my muscles waste and breathing becomes progressively more difficult, when I'm able to consume only foods macerated to a gooey pulp and am terminally ill, I will have control; I will be in charge of my life and not burden loved ones or society. Decades later this mindset would evolve, given the high probability that the autumn of my life in the twenty-first century might well become undignified or unbearably painful, with worsening physical frailty and incurable dementia. Should this become my fate, and having worked hard every day from the age of fifteen, I can neither comprehend nor contemplate reaching my earthly journey's end to then spend all of my accumulated, modest wealth on expensive nursing home care. To hell with the sanctity of life. I plan, therefore, to end it all by embracing euthanasia, to quietly commit suicide in the comfort of my own bed with medication and a glass or two of the finest, perfectly matured, single barrel Caribbean rum.

The lengthy hot summer of 1976 proved to be one of great turbulence as vast tracts of England's green and pleasant land turned a parched, grubby, dull yellow ochre hue from months of record high temperatures and low precipitation. The drought brought to areas of forest and heath raging fires. Food prices soared as £500 million pounds worth of crops failed or were destroyed, and reservoirs and rivers were at seriously low levels. Such relentless heat and sparse rainfall led to the passing of a Drought Act by Parliament, water rationing, and a hosepipe ban, even at cricket grounds.

Speaking of the gentleman's game, the long heat wave and rising clamours against social injustice in English inner cities coincided with the arrival of the touring West Indies cricket team for what would become a historic series of Test matches. Until this iconic series, I had never been a cricket fan, despite playing the odd game during school days. I held the belief that only nerdy, bourgeois snobs, pompous lovers of Latin, and rich public school types who struggled with repetitions of ten press-ups played such a boring sport. Cricket was about class – elitism – and epitomised that which was most English. My imagination was stirred, and I took note as England's captain, a blond-haired, white South African called Tony Grieg, in an explosive television interview, made a most arrogant statement that became emblazoned on the sports page of every national daily newspaper. Grieg confidently predicted an English victory. The West Indies, he declared, would be made to grovel. Such comments served only to motivate the talented Caribbean visitors, resurrecting in some the bitter memories of slavery, empire, and colonial rule. Had the captaincy of the West Indies cricket team not always been about the ruling class and race? That leadership role had always been the preserve of affluent white men until unstoppable independence struggles ushered in a new mindset, and with it the first black West Indies cricket captain, Frank Worrall, back in 1960.

The first two Test matches in 1976 between England, the former colonial ruler, and her subjects from Caribbean countries like Antigua, Barbados, Guyana, and Jamaica both ended as draws. However, a West Indian victory by 425 runs in the third Test at Manchester's Old Trafford would set the tone for the remainder of the series. The fourth Test, played at Headingley, a suburb of Leeds, ended with another Windies victory by 55 runs. England's eleven would have one last opportunity to deliver for Grieg and salvage some home pride as the Test series concluded in South London.

Kennington Oval Cricket Ground overflowed that sultry August week with colourful, raucous West Indian supporters who gathered like pilgrims from cities all over England. To their cricketing heroes, the atmosphere in the ground simulated home crowd support, as if playing before crowds at Queen's Park Oval in Port of Spain, Trinidad, or

Sabina Park in Kingston, Jamaica. This fifth and final test witnessed England's demise. They were overwhelmed by 231 runs. The West Indies side, captained by the majestic Clive Lloyd, contained prolific batsmen Vivian Richards and Gordon Greenidge and a quartet of supreme fast bowlers including Michael Holding and Andy Roberts. These players, and all other members of the team, became legends, cricketing giants, as they went on an unbeaten Test match run that would last for more than a decade. England lost the Test series 3–0, a drubbing – a **blackwash** we in the African-Caribbean community called it – and their captain Grieg had been humiliated, made to eat a huge slice of humble pie. The game of cricket would never be the same again. The Windies team had played above and beyond the boundary, like immortal Nubian gods, and the record books were rewritten forever. Two weeks later revelry at Notting Hill Carnival would commence.

August Bank Holiday Monday celebrations in 1976 witnessed more than three hundred police officers injured, thirty-five police vehicles damaged, numerous shops looted, and at least sixty people arrested as black British youths rioted on London's streets during the Notting Hill Carnival, fighting pitched battles with the racist Babylon – Metropolitan Police and officers from other regions drafted in to control the event. These youths sardonically decried being hindered when walking while black, driving while black, shopping while black, or simply waiting at a bus stop while black. Many, having fallen victim to police brutality when stopped and searched under oppressive Stop and Search under Suspicion (SUS) laws, sought payback as sound systems pumped out Junior Murvin's "Police and Thieves", resulting in one national daily newspaper headline: "Ulster in Portobello Road". This definitely was not cricket.

Ushering in the change was my uncharacteristic purchase of a soul album, Stevie Wonder's breathtaking, pioneering **Songs in the Key of Life**, and after twenty-two years residence, my father's exodus from England. Before

Billy's homeward journey, he proffered some final sage, paternal guidance: "I cannot insist you gain a qualification, stop you smoking weed, or change your friends, but give serious thought as to where you will be in ten years time." The council flat, he declared, was now mine, pointing to my name on the tenancy agreement, along with all of the furniture therein. This was my inheritance. All I had to do, Billy advised, was keep the place in good order, and pay the weekly rent (£7.76) and quarterly utility bills on time. His softly spoken guidance upon departing echoed the many conversations between Larry and myself on the vices and virtues of our ganja-inspired world, merely serving to strengthen the gathering winds of change within.

It was mid September 1976, and aged nineteen, I was truly isolated, rudderless like a refugee unaccompanied by any loving kith or kinfolk. Exactly how this situation arose – the total absence of known blood relatives and no family's comforting succour – will shortly be unveiled. My return to living in the neighbourhood of SW18 coincided with ever more scepticism vis-à-vis my role in the Rastafarian movement. Alongside that nagging disenchantment was one other ever-present, concrete fact. Having now entered the adult world, I was untrained, unskilled, and unqualified, had neither a trade nor profession, no plans nor aspirations and, dead end jobs aside, no resources to pursue a meaningful career. At least Billy was a qualified, highly skilled hairdresser who always made good money cutting hair at Ivan's Barber Shop near Clapham North Station, or from those friends and neighbours who visited the East Hill flat for a trim.

The previous year I had begun drawing on an A3 sketch pad in my leisure time and often ogled the graphics on posters displayed on billboards around London, thinking the artistic content was weak. Convinced I could do better, I drew images from either memory or photographs, honing my skills with plain lead pencils. Art as a livelihood seemed an appealing option.

Ever since 1972 I had enthusiastically associated with individuals who not only smoked but peddled weed – Jamaican sinsemilla, Durban poison and Thai sticks – in clubs or from their homes. Becoming a Rastafarian took this association to another level. Early on, several brethren pooled money and purchased a couple of imperial pounds in weight of ganja, which was subdivided into £5 or £10 draws (wraps) made with expertly folded pieces of magazine pages. Yielding a steady profit by the end of 1976, several thousand pounds was invested in this enterprise. The idealistic motive behind our business was accumulating enough capital to repatriate back to Africa. It was decreed that Rastafarians had to leave England by the seventh day of the seventh month of 1977, a time drawing imminently closer that would witness terrible events, divinely inspired natural disasters, and an apocalypse throughout Babylon. To some brethren this was merely a ruse. They lacked sincerity, flaunting the profits on materialistic, worldly possessions: gold rings and neck chains, travelling everywhere by minicab, entertaining friends extravagantly, and generally having a good time enjoying Babylon's forbidden luxuries. Whispers here and there alluded to frequent quaffing of the king of wines – champagne – and even the snorting of cocaine by respected brethren. Compelled by a brooding sense of betrayal, my ganja consumption began to decrease.

After transferring employment to the Clapham geriatric home, little by little I severed my links with this group and its enterprise. My mindset was undergoing much alteration, and to those Rastas who noted the change, I was suspected of heresy, was a **Canis lupus**, and wolves were not to be trusted. Inwardly I'd begun trekking on a steeply downward descent towards anti-Rastafarianism, though to all external appearances I was still a dread. To bring about a sea change and make my break concrete, a significant trigger was required.

Tuesday, 7 June 1977 was a UK public holiday, with all banks closed for the Silver Jubilee celebrations of hereditary monarch, Queen Elizabeth II. Festivities were in full swing throughout London. Many streets were festooned with red, white, and blue bunting and Union Jacks. There was an abundance of national pride as blue-blooded, true Brits loudly sang "God Save the Queen" or "Rule Britannia" at every opportunity. Evolving in my mind was a knowledge that whenever the chorus rang out "Britons never, never, never shall be slaves", it excluded me and mine.

Let's get this discourse on track. Life in the UK is wonderful and exceedingly civil. People have universal rights; free education, including public libraries; employment opportunities; the National Health Service, free at the point of delivery; and hot and cold water. However, anti-royalist seeds were sown as it dawned on me that I would never again sing the dourest of national anthems, much beloved by British military patriots and empire builders, which I'd innocently sung with gusto as a child. And yet I felt such rousing passion for the Welsh anthem "Land of My Fathers" and equally the republican "La Marseillais", sung as the French triumphed unbeaten in that year's Five Nations rugby competition.

Amidst the Silver Jubilee revelry, the minds of us Rastafarians when gathered together smoking, stoned on some good sinsemilla, were focused on that day one month ahead. Thursday, 7 July 1977, would be an alternative celebration, a date to usher in a divine apocalypse, when the Two Sevens Clash, supposedly based on a Marcus Garvey prediction and popularised in a 1976 song by Culture, a Jamaican roots reggae group. According to Culture's prophetic lyrics, all past injustices would be atoned for on the seventh day of the seventh month of the seventy-seventh year. The date passed without incident.

My smoking habits decreased further with the realisation that when stoned, I could not focus on reading. My capacity for sustained concentration was severely compromised whenever I was in a brain-numbing, ganja-induced stupor.

The job in the geriatric home had stimulated in my mind the notion of finding some kind of career path, of gaining access to training, and I flirted momentarily with the prospect of becoming a registered mental nurse. This idea soon dissipated when it dawned upon me that working for the rest of my life with the unpredictable mentally ill or with frail, demented elderly folks, whose physical condition only deteriorated as their final days approached, was not my vocation. But how on God's earth could I overcome having left school a violent miscreant, a total academic failure, with not one single examination passed? Turning my attention towards art, I speculated that it just had to provide more interesting career opportunities than the daily grind of the old people's home. Creativity could become an alternative to cleaning faeces, emptying bedpans, to incinerating incontinence pads or compassionately nursing bedridden pensioners towards a semidignified death while putrefying bedsores ate away at their flesh.

In September 1977 I enrolled for evening classes in life drawing, the study of the human form, at the Camden Arts Centre near Finchley Road. On my first evening I nervously joined others in a spacious art room for introductions to the class tutor, Margaret Fannington. Then, following other students, I selected an easel and clipped my A2 sheet of cartridge paper carefully to my drawing board, made ready my rubber and sharpened pencils, and awaited the arrival of the life model. At precisely 19.00 a middle-aged white lady with a flowing brunette mane entered the studio wearing only flip flops and a loose, brightly coloured, floral-patterned silk robe. The woman cheerfully greeted the art tutor and then, after the briefest of conversations about what particular pose she should assume, nonchalantly disrobed to reveal a physique far grander than a Rubens Venus, in fact a shape akin to a Palaeolithic Hottentot Venus fertility figurine or bloated Henry Moore female bronze.

The unflappable model positioned herself on a cloth-draped chair, and when comfortable, froze facing my direction, no more than ten feet away, gazing unfocused into the distance. Far from being the sexual innocent, I was temporarily awestruck by her blatant lack of inhibition as there she reclined, naked as the day she was born, with large melon breasts, pronounced nipples, the broadest of hips and pudenda covered by a thick nest of reddish brown pubic hair. Exposed basket of fruit aside, her image conveyed a primeval motherliness, with voluminous milk-giving mammary glands and ample hips conveying the warmth of motherhood. Her feminine shape was far removed from the oft-portrayed modern, slender-hipped, hermaphrodite-looking females of chic fashion magazines.

My peers in that first life drawing class, all mature men and women, began sketching away feverishly, with an eye for detail and confident hand strokes born of experience. Attempting to follow their lead, my hand just would not steady, but shook and trembled with embarrassed, nervous anxiety. It took until the second half of the lesson, following a short interval during which I immediately reached for the nicotine fix in my box of Benson & Hedges, for my composure to regain itself and my first nude drawing to emerge. That sketch was not a great effort. But Fannington, the tutor, praised the attempt. Over the coming weeks and months, consistently attending this class honed my observational drawing skills. Before long my portfolio of drawings in pencil, charcoal, or Conté crayon grew, and I explored my options: possible graphic design, illustration, or fine art on part-time or full-time courses at a further education college.

With the new year of 1978 approaching, I was ever more outspoken, confidently opposing ill-conceived ideas when in the company of my Rastafarian brethren. Many brothers were blindly full of praise for the actions of Idi Amin, the dictatorial ruler of Uganda, who in 1972 had expelled thousands of Asians from the landlocked central African country after confiscating their financial assets.

My wide reading had led me to alternative knowledge, so I countered their views, stating that this despot was a creation of the British army. Amin had in fact fought as a sergeant in the King's African Rifles regiment, who were allegedly responsible for many brutal acts, including torture, rapes, amputations, and castrations against ordinary Kenyans and the Mau Mau freedom fighters during the struggle for Kenyan independence. By digesting books on diverse historical, philosophical, and religious teachings about Buddha, Hinduism, Marxism, Chairman Mao, and the thoughts of Black Power advocates in the United States of America, I had come to understand that there were ground-breaking struggles for the minds of men far more concrete and rebellious than Rastafarianism. Dreadlocked, weed-smoking Rastas, despite the songs of freedom, were about escapism and pusillanimous by comparison.

While I was in Grassroots Bookstore days before my twenty-first birthday in mid February 1978, I stumbled across and purchased a significant classic piece of American literature that told the true tale of an orphaned African American boy called Malcolm Little. This boy grew up to be Detroit Red, a handsome, charismatic, Lindy Hopping, reefer-smoking adult character. Named after the American motor city and his light-skinned appearance, Red became a hustler in the thriving criminal circles of post-World War II Detroit and New York City. That paperback, **The Autobiography of Malcolm X**, was the result of collaboration between Malcolm X and Alex Haley, author of the best-selling **Roots**, which told the tale of Haley's search for his African heritage.

During the next seventy-two hours, while avidly examining the 460 pages of Malcolm's story, I temporarily shelved smoking the holy herb. Here was the most engrossing book I'd ever come across, a publication that became my "road to Damascus" moment, radically altering my life's course, as within its pages I discovered much that mirrored my own tale and shadowed my history and search for the truth. Malcolm's schooling had ended prematurely after some years in the care system. He'd gravitated towards a pleasure-seeking career of criminality and socially unproductive behaviour until he was caught, convicted, and incarcerated for years in the harsh US penal system. During imprisonment, Malcolm read, educated himself, found religion (Islam), and transformed into an articulate, fiery orator, an outspoken advocate of black people's resistance against oppression and racism in segregated America.

By the time of his release from custody, Malcolm was an adherent of the Black Muslim faith led by Elijah Mohammed. Malcolm's organisational and motivational leadership skills helped the movement grow more than tenfold. Years later Malcolm split acrimoniously with Elijah Mohammed to form his own organisation. He made the pilgrimage to Mecca, and was invited to speak at Oxford University's debating society before falling victim to an American establishment assassination plot that exploited the internecine rivalries within the Black Muslims. On 25 February 1965, Malcolm, aka El-Hajj Malik El-Shabazz, was brutally gunned down while making a public speech at Harlem's Audubon Ballroom. He was thirty-nine years of age and on the verge of becoming the greatest spokesman for the African diaspora since Marcus Garvey.

I admired Malcolm's deeply felt convictions, how he'd found the strength of mind to change from hedonistic rogue, pimp, and dope dealer to a morally upright, powerful religious and political leader. On the verge of even greater change, with ideas beginning to embrace all forms of injustice worldwide, issues beyond mere religion and race, he was murdered. Come the second decade of the twenty-first century, Malcolm's light remained eternally bright, vividly undiminished, forever alive, and unforgettably iconic. Just like many of history's proven, most effective leaders, he told a simple story that was easily grasped by adherents around the world, from Johannesburg to Rio de Janeiro, Chicago to Dar es Salaam, or St George's, Grenada to Hong Kong.

I read the autobiography a second time, and then thrice. Transform oneself! Self-directed change! These were the significant vibes screaming out, the underlying messages I gleaned from its many pages, and I reflected in my dreams over the coming nights on eulogist Whitman's 1865 poem "O Captain! My Captain!" 'Steady keel, grim and daring vessel, bleeding drops of scarlet and my fallen Captain, cold and dead. O Brother! My beloved Brother!'

I needed to deconstruct then reconstruct, controlling change for the good of myself, others, and ultimately society. At this juncture my metamorphosis was nigh on complete. Malcolm's large hand had gently yet firmly grasped my shoulder reassuringly, his oratory rearranging my brain's development forever. By evolving into a Malcolmite, conversion to another monotheistic, conservative faith beckoned. My uncut, thick beard projected religious purity, and some indicated that the growth would have made the transition easier, yet I doggedly resisted. I would not be inveigled, beguiled by the call of Islam, a world faith that a few otherwise intelligent souls naïvely believed practiced no racism. My compulsion to alter became overpowering, but ultimately conversion to Islam, Malcolm's faith, could not enter the frame. Islam was after all a belief system just like Christianity, with hereditary royalty, tainted historical links to African slavery, and an unspoken hierarchy based on race, contrary to what some academics and leaders would have people believe. No longer my opium, religion had become for me an anathema.

Buoyed by having touched the hem of Malcolm's garment, the physical act of trimming my dreadlocks was to become the catalyst for my own revolution in May 1978. One evening in my bathroom, I washed my thickly matted, shoulder-length dreadlocks for what would be the last time before sinking into a relaxing, steaming hot bath. On pulling out the plug, my contemplation was over. Cleansed, purified, and refreshed, I stepped onto the bath mat, standing for some minutes before the mirror that was clouded by condensation, inhaling and then exhaling deeply but otherwise motionless. Smearing the glass partially clear with a couple of hand strokes, I examined my reflection, and then, with a pair of Billy's old scissors, cautiously cut half an inch from my scalp, removing one lock at a time. Gathering the shorn locks together, I placed them in a plastic bag and secured them away in Billy's old brown suitcase, where they remain to this day, housed on the top of my wardrobe.

Five years of disciplined, grogless sobriety as a London Rastafarian, though roughly one quarter of my existence, was in reality merely an ephemeral segment of my entire life's journey. Though I was cursed and shunned by many brethren, it had taken this ultimate physical act to proclaim my renunciation of their core beliefs. Brothers Larry, Henry, and Stephen, who would eventually teach me valuable carpentry skills, remained close. However, out of earshot other brethren condemned my treachery, saying that all along I had been a heretic, a Babylonian spy, a wolf in sheep's clothing. Some even alluded to the percentage of European blood pumping through my veins. "Dat mulatto, red skin ras!" To them I was not only an apostate but a Judas, an agent of Satan and pseudo black man, hence my weak-hearted betrayal. However, divine retribution, godly wrath, and brimstone and fire did not rain down upon me. Rather my actions propelled me forward, onwards to my life's most fruitful phase.

chapter III

I will go back to the great sweet mother.
—Algernon Charles Swinburne (1837–1909)

During 1978 I made contacts with several individuals involved in an organisation called the Pan African Exchange Scheme (PAES) as a direct result of my frequent trips to Grassroots Bookstore. This group, funded in part by the United Nations Educational Scientific and Cultural Organisation (UNESCO), had affiliations with other English inner city black community organisations, namely George Jackson House from Manchester's Moss Side, and Harambee based in Handsworth, Birmingham. PAES was coordinated by a slim, soft-spoken, baseball cap-wearing Senegalese man called Omar Diarra, who invited me to join the ranks of other young British African Caribbean women and men from these three cities' fundraising. The rationale behind our charitable efforts was to finance the journey "home" to one of several West African countries, and once there to experience the life and culture while working as volunteers in remote rural villages on building projects like schools or pharmacies. However, fund raisers were given no guarantee of automatic selection to travel to Africa. Eventually three mixed-gender groups of equal number were chosen as volunteers for journeys to Ghana, Nigeria, and Togo. As providence would have it, I was selected. I joined a quartet that included Patrick; another Londoner, Mavis from Birmingham and; Audrey from Manchester, all bound for Togo that July and August.

Togo? My ignorance about Togo was complete; I knew absolutely nothing so did some hasty research. Togo, I discovered, was geographically 360 miles long and merely 100 miles wide at its broadest point. It was bordered by Ghana to the west, Benin to the east, Burkina Faso to the north, and the cold, choppy waters of the Gulf of Guinea on its sandy southern shores. In the late nineteenth century, it was the German colony of Togoland. After British and French military forces invaded in 1914, Togoland fell and following World War One was divided up by the League of Nations for shared administration between Britain and France. In 1957, the population of British Togoland united with the Gold Coast to become part of Kwame Nkrumah's newly independent nation of Ghana. French Togoland became Togo in 1960, achieving independence from France under the leadership of President Sylvanus Olympio. Togo's population of several million people was composed of more than twenty ethnic groups, of whom the Ewe in the South and the Kabye in the North are major groups. Most people in the south speak the closely related Ewe or Mina languages alongside the official language of government, French.

Togo was a member of the West African Economic and Monetary Union (UEMOA), which fiscally grouped together eight West African countries: Guinea-Bissau, Mali, Niger, Senegal, Togo, Benin, Burkina Faso, and Cote d'Ivoire – all of whom used the CFA franc currency. Subsistence agriculture was one of Togo's main economic activities, which the majority of the population depend upon. Cocoa and coffee are the traditional major cash crops for export. Other crops grown for food include sorghum, millet, groundnuts (peanuts), corn, cassava, and yams. Research aside I began preparations for travel to the tropics by purchasing a large rucksack, lightweight sleeping bag, torch and batteries, and a supply of mosquito coils. I organised my tetanus, cholera, and yellow fever inoculations alongside sufficient malaria tablets for the four-week experience. It dawned on me that socially, economically, and culturally I was in for an almighty shock.

With my United Kingdom passport and inoculation certificates in hand, I arrived at Heathrow Airport, where those volunteers destined for Togo rendezvoused excitedly alongside those headed for Ghana. It was late July 1978, and at last I was to make the pilgrimage, my hajj back to West Africa, becoming the first known member of my blood family to return to the lands of our forefathers. Omar, the coordinator, was also travelling and handed to us the tickets for the flight. Our schedule was to fly out with Ghana Airways to Kotoka International Airport in Accra, the Ghanaian capital, where one quartet would remain in Ghana and my quartet would proceed onwards by road to Togo. Upon arriving at Terminal 3 with our baggage, a scene of utter confusion and disorganised chaos welcomed us at the Ghana Airways check-in desk. Our flight had been heavily overbooked.

After optimistically queuing for hours alongside swarms of other passengers, some of whom were extremely patient, impassive, and seemingly used to such inconvenience, the flight departed without many, including us volunteers. A few passengers sighed and quietly commented that this was "the Ghanaian way", just standard practise. Our group, some of whom had travelled down from Manchester and Birmingham, made the decision to remain overnight in the terminal's passenger lounge, crashing out on the floor and catching the next available flight the following day at sunrise.

The flight was otherwise uneventful until we touched down on the runway in Accra when an impromptu chorus of happy voices and loud applause rang out as all aboard cheered and clapped in unison, offering thanks for a safe landing. Disembarking through the aircraft's door was akin to stepping into a sun-kissed sauna. Suddenly we were enveloped by the invisible mist of searing humidity and 35 ºC tropical heat. Across the shimmering tarmac,

I surveyed the scene of Africa's ancient, rich terracotta-hued earth beneath palm trees swaying in the light zephyr.

After going through immigration control and collecting our luggage, my group were met by two smiling, welcoming Ghanaian volunteers who, following introductions, escorted us through the melee of chattering small boys, all vociferously touting trade for the nearby parked taxis, towards an awaiting minibus. This moment was to be the first of countless occasions when I heard the adjective "***Obruni, obruni, obruni***" being called out in my direction. With baggage and visitors aboard, our vehicle made the short northwards journey to Madina, a suburb of Accra, where we lodged overnight in a sparsely furnished high school dormitory. That night I was horror-struck when I was informed that **obruni** means "white foreigner", a generic term of reference, applied not only to European people but also to those of African-American and African-Caribbean descent regardless of their skin colour.

Early the next morning, dawn's warm rays had barely arrived when we were roused by the blaring horn from a brightly coloured Peugeot with the writing ***Gye Nyame*** (except for God) emblazoned in large letters across its bonnet and doors. This was my quartet's taxi ride, accompanied by Omar Diarra, for the onwards journey to the Ghanaian–Togolese border, about one hundred miles away. Patrick, Mavis, Audrey, and I bade farewell to our other UK companions who were themselves preparing to head off shortly into Ghana's interior. Our drive to the border was uncomfortably hot and sticky, even with all of the vehicle's windows down and intermittent stops en route for roadside refreshments. On one occasion our Peugeot slowed to a stuttering snail's pace, joining a small queue of traffic delayed by an army checkpoint on the road up ahead where stern-faced, AK-47-toting Ghanaian soldiers waved our car on its way, but only after receiving a payment, a customary bribe from our driver.

A much larger military presence was at the coastal Ghana–Togo border crossing where, weighed down by rucksacks on sweaty backs, we said farewell to our driver. It helped that French-speaking Omar was present as questions were asked and our travel documents thoroughly scrutinised, before finally being stamped by French-speaking Togolese military border officials. Without further ado we crossed into Lomé, the bustling capital city of Togo. The intense heat and scorching sunshine made everyone extremely thirsty, so we paused for refreshments at one of many market stalls fronted by sturdy, confident, chattering women clad in traditional dress and headties made from brightly coloured batik or Dutch type printed cloth. Omar then interpreted, negotiating a fair price on our behalf for the juiciest, most succulent pieces of freshly cut pineapple chunks. I had only ever eaten such tasty fruit from a tin and found there was absolutely no comparison.

Travelling onwards, the two-hour journey headed inland, some sixty miles north of Lomé, to the large town of Palimé. Transport was a seriously overcrowded minibus in which both English foreigners and Togolese sat tightly squashed in seats, hip to hip, with virtually no leg room. Some passengers even sat on small wooden aisle stools. Along winding, potholed roads hemmed in by lush tropical rain forest, there appeared every so often standing roadside a solitary person or two, motionless, eyeing the passing vehicle while balancing seemingly monumental loads upon their heads. Arriving in Palimé, we stayed overnight at the house of wonderfully named Bacary Babacar Souleymane, the Togolese volunteer coordinator. Omar, his task concluded, shook hands and waved au revoir! This was our final night of reasonable comfort: a bed with a mattress, electricity, a tap with running cold water, and a somewhat modern toilet, albeit located in a telephone box-sized shed with a huge bucket beneath a hole in a wooden plank seat. It was slopped out daily at dawn by sewage collectors.

Our quartet was divided up the following morning: Patrick paired with Mavis and Audrey with myself. After introductions to local Togolese volunteers, all higher education students on summer vacation, we commenced the final leg of our journey through more forested hills, valleys, and small hamlets. Once again driving through the densely forested interior, we would pass statuesque pedestrians, mainly women and children, pausing at the road's edge, gazing as Bacary Babacar Souleymane's car sped by, all burdened with unbelievably huge loads balanced precariously, yet ever so gracefully, on top of their heads.

Our destination, residence, and place of work for the next few weeks was the remote village of Ahlon Sansanou – not found on any map – set amidst huge hardwood trees and tropical vegetation. Warmly received by the villagers, we were shown to our quarters, a one-storey compound encompassing an inner courtyard. The large room was devoid of furniture except for several floor mats made from a woven, dried leaf frond material, laid out on the cool ground. When we unfurled our sleeping bags to bed down for the night, a symphony of croaking frogs and chirping crickets resonated as darkness descended outside. Inside, a dull, yellowish glow from the single kerosene lamp illuminated our faces.

At dawn, tropical heat aside, I was awoken by the shrill, incessant crowing of a cockerel and the sound of music playing nearby on a neighbour's battery-powered transistor radio. This annoying rooster's call, day after day, was as repetitious as one particular Highlife tune with infectious guitar riffs and a catchy chorus that played out over the wireless: "Sweet Mother", one of the most popular songs ever to come out of Africa and sung in Nigerian pidgin English, was a celebration of all things maternal.

Ahlon Sansanou lacked the conveniences of every day modern life. We had neither gas nor electricity, and no cooker, television, or fridge, which meant that after dusk we relied totally on kerosene lamps, a torch, or the soft moonlight. In addition, there were no indoor taps or street standpipes with fresh running water. Our H_2O, which had to be boiled before drinking, was sourced from a nearby small river reached via a short trek, bucket in hand, along a centuries-old earthenware-coloured path that snaked through the humid equatorial rain forest whose luxuriant viridian canopy provided partial shade from the relentless sunshine.

Having arrived "home", all our romantic notions faded within twenty-four hours, and I made essential mindset adjustments in order to cope with such Spartan conditions. That first morning in the village provided for me the most abrupt of lessons on human existence as my group of volunteers happily strolled some one hundred yards from our courtyard, each holding a metal pail, to the swift running stream to gather water with which to wash. This was the daily routine: fetch a bucket full of Adam's ale and return to the compound without accidentally stepping on the many observed lines of marching soldier ants, with hands aching from the load. Unlike the villagers of all ages and Togolese volunteers, who walked elegantly and effortlessly with the water goods balanced upon their heads, my attempt to carry water this way was clumsy in the extreme. I then washed and brushed my teeth in a small, mud-bricked, doorless cubicle as the sun's rays pleasantly heated my back, carefully saving just enough of the bucket's precious liquid to then hand wash my soiled, sweat-ridden underwear.

There was no option but to adjust to the slow pace and tranquillity of rural village life, collective mealtime preparations and cooking, and eating meals communally. I tasted new foods like fufu (pounded cassava – which I struggled with), fish stew, and a savoury dish containing a popular delicacy, a type of bushmeat known colloquially in Ghana as "grasscutter", or cane rat. This large rodent's habitat was in reed beds, riverbanks, and plantation farms where, feeding on agricultural crops such as maze, sugar cane, and cassava, it was said to grow to a length of more than half a metre (two feet) and weigh in excess of six kilograms (fifteen pounds). I observed heterosexual men who, like their womenfolk, were touchy-feely and publicly tactile, at times hold hands while strolling to and fro, acts that back in London would attract howls of homophobic derision or worse. Adult males, friends from birth, would innocently clasp hands while on their way to the pit toilet. Or if strolling under the brightest of moonlit, starry nights, when all villagers became nocturnal, youths courted, and children played, clapping, dancing, and singing games.

Despite life's austere hardships, the Togolese appeared to be robust, happy survivors. We volunteers made adjustments to varying degrees and managed to focus on the arduous weekday tasks of carrying building materials for the new village school extension, which would turn one classroom into two. Saturdays meant shopping for the next week's provisions, and Sundays attending the village church, which was for me abhorrent. I struggled to maintain a respectful demeanour while enduring the two-hour church service, my thoughts racing amok as the villagers sang hymns with gusto and loudly declared "Amen" in French. I tried reconciling the weird contradiction before me – such unwavering religious fervour from the darkest-skinned, most forgiving of humankind, all demonstrating sincere reverence to an alien deity with yellow hair, blue eyes, and pale dermis. I mulled: Had the painted icon before the assembled congregation been of a black Christ, my annoyance and sense of irritation would have been far less.

Relief arrived that evening when I joined a night-time gathering of villagers dancing to drums; attended shrine; met a dreadlocked, middle-aged, female fetish priestess with several youthful, orange-clad, clay-smeared initiates in attendance; and learnt about animism. Indigenous, traditional African religion, also known as juju or voodoo, was alive, integral to daily life, and said to be practiced by one third of the population.

When the end of our time as volunteers drew nigh, the village chief presented us with some gifts: a goat, a crate of Castel beer, and a large receptacle of jam-packed, huge, phallus-like yams for a celebratory thank you feast.

I excitedly offered to slaughter the goat, and had my photograph taken gleefully cutting the bleating beast's throat while others held it still for the blood to drain into an aluminium pot. My nerve, however, deserted me when soon afterwards someone offered some of the seasoned, cooked, and congealed blood to eat.

Throughout my stay in Ahlon Sansanou, I had sketched away, and the village chief, having witnessed this, requested that I draw his portrait. I gifted the chief the completed pen and ink image, and in return he bestowed upon me, after noting my date of birth, an Ewe name: Kofi (male child born on a Friday) Amegbo (to return). Now with an African name, a portion of my quest for cultural identity, self-knowledge and self-image had been fulfilled. The moniker Kofi Amegbo would, from that day onwards, be my aka, the signature on all of my future artwork.

On leaving Ahlon Sansanou, Audrey and I returned to Bacary Babacar Souleymane's house in Palimé, enjoyed some R & R and modern creature comforts, and reunited with Patrick and Mavis. Patrick, who was born in Clarendon, Jamaica, revealed excitedly that he, too, had received an Akan name, Kodzo, as he was born on a Monday. He was overwhelmed with pride as this moniker is also that of a Jamaican national hero.

Patrick, a history undergraduate, was highly animated as he explained further.

"Kodzo is also spelt Cujo, Cudjo, Cudjoe or Kojo in other regions of West Africa. In the early eighteenth century on the island of Jamaica, enslaved Africans, originally from the Akan-speaking region of modern Ghana, bravely resisted captivity, fleeing into the hinterland to evade the harsh brutality of European-owned plantations. The escapees sought and found refuge in the nigh on impenetrable Clarendon Hills, where they were mercilessly pursued. These freedom fighters were known as **Maroons**, and from the hills they waged a successful guerrilla war over many decades against the military might of the English redcoats or mercenary militia with their bloodhound hunting dogs hired by the plantation owners."

Patrick, or rather Kodzo, stared momentarily into the eyes of Audrey, Mavis, and finally myself as his retrospective declaration concluded.

"History will one day compare the Jamaican Maroons' resistance to another more famous campaign for freedom in the Americas, that of Cochise and Geronimo over one century later during the Apache Wars of the late 1880s in mainland North America. Captain Cudjoe was one of the Jamaican renegades' most famous leaders – a man of squat muscular stature, warrior virtues, and physical courage, fearless, skilled with weapons, and able to survive in the harshest Jamaican terrain."

A few days later, we made the awkward return journey to Accra via Lomé, this time without assistance from Omar or any locals. Back in the Ghanaian capital, my group changed our remaining English pounds for Ghanaian cedis on the black market, acquiring a vastly superior exchange rate, over 500 per cent higher than what official banks offered. Then we travelled north to the city of Kumasi, home of the Golden Stool, in Ashanti region, for several days sightseeing. During this trip the women, Audrey and Mavis, having left some clothing hung out on a line overnight, including washed brassieres and knickers, were angry to find the line bare the next morning, much to the hilarity of Patrick and myself. While in the Ashanti capital, we haggled with street traders over the price of carvings and other such souvenirs. Then on returning to Accra, we rejoined the other English quartet, those who served as volunteers in Ghana, for the homeward flight to England.

In West London the day after landing at Heathrow, I jumped aboard a No. 37 Red Routemaster bus and, sitting comfortably with no overcrowding, went shopping for provisions at my local Sainsbury's supermarket in Clapham High Street. I was overwhelmed by the quality, quantity, and diverse range of both fresh produce and tinned goods, and the contradiction posed by one whole aisle of shelves stacked entirely with provisions for pets, with merely half the space again devoted to baby food.

Inspired by events from my pilgrimage, where I'd witnessed poor people survive and achieve so much with so little, I embarked in determined fashion upon a period of higher education, becoming a full-time student in September on a one-year Arts Foundation course at an art college in trendy Notting Hill Gate. This was the era of punk rock. McLaren's Sex Pistols had released "God Save the Queen", which some viewed as an assault on the monarchy, and Blondie, flying high in the pop charts, would soon cover "The Tide is High", originally by John Holt and the Paragons. By the end of that academic year, I had assembled a promising portfolio of artwork and successfully passed a fine art degree course interview at one of London University's pre-eminent, avant-garde art education institutions. Despite no formal academic qualifications, a window of opportunity had opened, and I would receive a full government student grant for basic living expenses upon starting in September 1979.

Having caught the travel bug, I spent the long summer recess of 1979 in my father's birthplace, the stunning tropical island of Antigua in the Caribbean. "Discovered" by Christopher Columbus in 1493, Antigua was named after a church in Seville, Spain called Santa Maria de la Antigua. **Antigua**, meaning "ancient" in Spanish, was also known affectionately to the islanders as Wadadli, a native Amerindian word. I stayed with Aunt Esme, my father Billy's half-sister, at her single-storey dwelling on Bishopsgate Street, in the capital St John's, where she lived with her youngest son, seventeen-year-old Vivian.

I met for the first time my paternal grandmother, Susie Aitken, then aged sixty-eight, who resided on the outskirts of the small village of Parham, located to the north of the island in the Parish of Saint Peter. Susie was diminutive, less than five feet tall, and had smooth, soft, burnt umber toned dark skin. With the rising sun, she travelled by bus into St John's every Saturday to visit the local farmer's market and shops for weekly provisions, and I noted how she gracefully balanced her purchases in a bag upon her head, exactly as I'd witnessed people doing in Ghana and Togo the previous summer. Before Susie's homeward journey, she would visit her daughter Esme's to cook and share food, then catch the bus back to Parham before the fall of darkness.

Throughout my Antiguan vacation, I made a particular effort each Saturday to walk my grandmother to her bus stop and carry her bag of shopping. On a few occasions, I also made the hot, sweaty, and uncomfortably crowded bus journey (again like Ghana and Togo) to her village, Parham, and the building she called home. En route I observed, scattered among picturesque tropical foliage, derelict granite, conical sugar mills, structures from the bygone era of slavery. Susie's small, sparsely furnished abode was just a wooden shack with a single planed, sloped corrugated iron roof, originally grey but now weathered intermittently with an orangey brown patina of corroded patches. Her one musty room, in which my father Billy had been born some four and a half decades earlier, was no more than twelve feet by ten and lit by a beam of light from a tiny window draped by an aged, frayed, yellowing cloth for a curtain. Susie's sleeping area was divided from the remaining space by a wooden partition, and nearby stood an old kerosene hurricane lamp. There was no electricity, gas, nor running water. A communal street pipe stood about fifty yards away.

Immersing myself in the joie de vivre of island culture leading up to Antigua's annual Carnival, I hung out each sunshine day with cousin Vivian and his pals. We spent many hours **liming**, a word originating from **limey**, the adjective for scurvy-ridden nineteenth-century British seafarers and local terminology for vagrancy, idly hanging out, or killing time – pure cloud nine.

Vivian also played tenor pan – a steel drum – in a steel band, and I accompanied him to the pan yard where I gazed attentively at the method of pan creation as a vast, discarded forty-five gallon oil drum evolved into a shiny, perfectly tuned steel pan at the hands of a Trinidadian craftsman named Rafael. Twilight arrived each day in the Pan yard, serenaded by the chorus from nocturnal creatures in nearby bushes and treetops, as Vivian joined his steel band troupe practicing their harmonies over and over into the early morning hours.

Trailing Vivian's band at Antigua's Carnival with the Technicolor hordes of dancing, gyrating revellers moving in time, "chicken" style, through the streets of St John's was liberating. My understanding and appreciation of this powerful cultural phenomenon, which had evolved from the previous century's abolition of slavery celebrations, its radiant high spirits, celebration of sweet liberty, and the joy of living, meant that back in London at the Notting Carnival in the years ahead I could never again bond with the idle, static sound system crowd. Rather, year after year, I turned into a partygoer who would jump up with the insatiable crowds behind mobile floats carrying steel bands or lorries that blasted out infectious calypso or soca. The unique social commentary of these music genres, often times humorous yet equally serious, year after year covered everything from cricket, Black Power, obeah, hair, and salty sweet cunnilingus, to US-inspired military coups, economic austerity, lustful seamen, and sexual infidelity.

In Antigua, when I wasn't lazily strolling here and there, the feting or partying felt endless, especially as romance had blossomed with a tantalizing local girl called Octavia. Many weeks of build-up to Carnival eventually climaxed on the streets of St John's. The atmosphere of revelry that had become fever pitch for the final days of the first Monday and Tuesday in August was followed by an eerie aftermath, a tranquil silence, with both locals and transient visitors to the island exhausted. The climax of Carnival was as if it was a signal to the supernatural. Suddenly hurricane season had arrived. During the next week and beyond, the skies darkened for days on end, squalls became lengthy storms, and the heavens opened. Rarely did the sun's rays pierce the grey clouds as Hurricane David grew, becoming ever more forceful, gathering unbelievable power to eventually wreak havoc across the island and wider Caribbean region.

I alighted back in London that September with a weighty suitcase laden with sodden, unwashed clothes – laundry was the least of priorities that last fortnight in Antigua – and several bottles of the island's finest distilled Cavalier rum, soon to embark on a bachelor of arts degree course in fine arts at London University's Camberwell Campus. After that carnival summer, my paintings in acrylics, drawings in charcoal, etchings, silk screen prints, linocuts, and photography explored with greater zest my past history and my quest for cultural and racial identity. As a student I explored my capital, becoming intimate with the citadels of art and culture, from the ICA, Courtauld, Hayward, the Photographers' Gallery, and the National Portrait Gallery to the Museum of Mankind, Tate, Royal Academy, Chelsea Physic Garden, and Horniman Museum. Bacchanalian memories of Antigua remained bright in that fresher's year as I deliberated over a topic for my first art history assignment.

Holding deeply ingrained convictions that much of known history was based on the concept that Europe was the world's epicentre and any history other than European history was none too significant, I pondered exactly where to begin. Intense as my beliefs were, among predominantly white art students and the teaching intelligentsia I was cautious, extremely reticent about verbalising my opinions let alone writing them down. Damn! It was one thing to have a gut feeling that historical facts were distorted, wrong, or prejudiced but another to actually articulate or write about that feeling with confidence and coherence and to quote sources of evidence in the intellectual forums of the college.

Artistic creativity aside, London University undergraduates were expected to successfully complete two 2,500-word essays in their first academic year, three essays of the same word count in year two, followed by a 10,000-word dissertation in the third and final year. I quickly realized that the majority of my fine art peers were not poor, working class, or undereducated as when witnessing one exceedingly scruffy, bedraggled student (the vogue was to dress down), an abrasively eloquent debater in seminars, saunter out of the campus gates, hop into his black Porsche, and drive off at speed. Some such individuals chose to write about their favourite Botticelli painting, modern sculpture artist Henry Moore, the meaning of Carl Andre's **Bricks**, Duchamp's urinal, minimalism, the Mexican muralist movement, religious iconography, Andy Warhol, or great Spanish painters like Goya or Dali. However, what was pertinent for them was not so for me.

Having spent the summer with blood relatives in Antigua, I embarked upon a historical study of this most beautiful tropical island. As I researched material on Antigua and the wider Caribbean, tentatively embarking on my first essay since expulsion from Southfields Boys High School, what gradually emerged was a picture of this region, post Columbus but prior to the twentieth century, whose annals were littered with cruelty and oppression. My first rough draft initially lacked the structural sophistication, depth of argument, and clarity expected – clearly the legacy of an unfulfilled, failed secondary education. But I was a fast, determined learner.

Of all the subjects taught at school, my favourite was always history. **Why history?** I pondered. Because it teaches where mankind has been, which in turn influences and informs where mankind is going. I was fascinated by this subject's various characters and the great events that in one way or another shaped the past, present, and future. Books on Egyptians, Persians, Greeks, and Romans were full of vivid accounts that engaged my young imagination, with Hannibal and Alexander the Great among my preferred historical figures. Christopher Columbus was another icon who caught my attention. It was Columbus who, against all the odds, "discovered" the Americas, and all historical accounts presented him as a brave sailor, navigator of unknown seas, and one who disproved the rigid sceptics of the day who believed the earth to be flat. Columbus was deeply religious, a pious and devout Christian, and to my youthful mind's eye a truly heroic figure whose adventures were in some way analogous to the epic travels of Odysseus returning from the Trojan War.

Years later, my intellect having expanded, that history learnt in classroom texts appeared biased, contradictory, and full of voids. Every noteworthy historical hero, indeed heroine, from Aristotle to Isaac Newton, Boadicea to Emmeline Pankhurst was of European origin. It appeared that no people other than Europeans were credited with making significant contributions to humanity's story. For example, Egyptian history had always seemed to be divorced from African history. I recollected that Egypt's separateness from the rest of Africa was reinforced by pictures in text books which presented these ancient people as white or pale-skinned. Genghis Khan was portrayed as the barbaric, primitive, bloodthirsty leader of vast tribal hordes who pillaged and tyrannised the Caucuses, China, and the East. Why, I asked myself, was Genghis Khan a barbarian, a leader of brutal tribal peoples while Julius Caesar or Queen Elizabeth I were rulers of cultured, sophisticated civilised nations? Cultured, sophisticated, civilised nations.

Why? How? When? Who? Why, how, when, and who? These simple questions now preceded my thoughts about the true purpose of history as taught to me at school. I dared to think, freely, what I not been taught: that many aspects of mankind's story, humanity's journey, appeared tainted with deliberate untruths, beliefs that favoured what was European or white. George Washington, the father of American independence, owned a large plantation and many African slaves, facts barely emphasised in the school history books I had read. I could never reconcile the fact that fervent worshippers in Togolese, Ghanaian, and Antiguan churches bore witness to solely blond-haired, blue-eyed, white-only Christian icons. Furthermore, in all of the great historical paintings depicting such iconography – Mexican muralist movement aside – from the Renaissance to the modern era, Jesus Christ and his disciples were always portrayed as Caucasians with greenish blue eyes, and never, ever swarthy or dreadlocked.

Any understanding of Caribbean history that I had was post Columbian. The arrival of gallant fifteenth-century seafarers, funded by the Spanish royal family, ushered in the Atlantic slave trade and plantation system, hence the African blood pumping through my veins. The fact that other peoples had inhabited the Caribbean region before the advent of Europeans had always seemed insignificant. Even during my Rasta years, when in 1977 the popular reggae group Culture sang about "Pirate Days" when "the Arawaks was here first", I had never given a second thought to the two native American (Taino and Arawak) Indians, the indigenous male and female figures, prominent on the Jamaican national coat of arms with its motto "Out of many, one people".

My tentative research for that first composition at London University revealed far greater detail: Prior to the arrival of the Europeans and African and slave labour, there was a very large indigenous Caribbean population which, according to an authoritative estimate (G. R. Crone, 1969), numbered some two million. On his first voyage, Columbus, the brave navigator and hero of history, arrived at San Salvador – now called Watling Island – in the Bahamas on 12 October 1492. By February 1494, on the second voyage, four ships were preparing to return to Europe from the much larger island of Hispaniola, estimated to have had a population of one million. Columbus, agent of God and the Catholic nation of Spain, hurriedly organised a mass slave raid in which fifteen hundred Arawaks were herded up, and five hundred of the best "specimens" selected and shipped to Spain. Only three hundred of these arrived in Spain alive, where they were put up for sale in Seville. By the year 1518, Hispaniola's population was said to have shrunk to eleven thousand. In the next few years, a smallpox epidemic would kill off the survivors.

At the hands of the Spanish, this native population in the beautiful Caribbean endured mass exploitation and suffering, which led ultimately to their genocide. This saddest of narratives became the subject of my first essay. Four years later, after more lengthy and comprehensive research, I revisited this topic in the treatise I submitted to conclude my 1982–83 PGCE year, an account of times long ago that was, and remains to this day, a true story that warrants being retold to future generations.

To clearly state that written history was not just a Eurocentric way of interpreting the past had become extremely important. Yet I was often dumbstruck, terrified to voice any opinion amidst academics or my fellow students, most of whom were from affluent backgrounds and so incredibly articulate, having arrived on the degree course with an array of qualifications following successful schooling. Hence, I read vigorously the works of C. A. Diop, Frantz Fanon, C. L. R. James, Kwame Nkrumah, and Dr Walter Rodney. Such authors were most definitely not on any recommended reading list given to students in my first year at art college. They were, however, relevant to my intellectual development, and as such became the guidelines, the foundations by which I began to re-evaluate the past from a non-Eurocentric stance.

This re-examination of history was necessary in my case for several reasons. Despite having a white birth mother and black father, a mixture of both European and African genetic material, I remained proudly black. But why was this so? Why not remain neutral, sit on the fence, buy into the irrelevance of race and be neither black nor white? Was not the notion of racial insignificance a seed sown by the white side of a mixed-race child in response to the realisation that their child can never, ever be defined as white but will always be defined as black?

My artwork increasingly explored this quandary and the centrality of race in my life's journey. I believed positioning along racial lines by the offspring of interracial relationships was rarely explored either frankly or with any intellectual depth. Many modern, racially mixed British couples of African (black) and European (white) origin naïvely avoid having this candid discourse either beforehand, when lustfully exchanging bodily fluids, or afterwards, once their fused DNA arrives in the world of mankind. Such parents do their young a disservice, as many grow up racially and culturally abandoned, in a no man's land, left to plot their own confused course. "Who am I?" they ask on their adolescent journey, not having been taught the truth, ending up struggling with essential human concepts of identity and the self. And should family breakdown occur, they will, as a matter of course, be disproportionately represented in both the British care and prison systems.

Defined by the world I lived in, my paternal genes and cultural background was of African–Caribbean origin, the end product of the slave labour and plantation system that dominated the Caribbean experience for several centuries. Under this historical process, my African heritage underwent extreme forms of aggressive cultural devastation in which the African personality was ruthlessly suppressed, almost totally destroyed. A confused mentality emerged that embraced the essence of European culture with its clearly defined notions of racial hierarchy. But this proved unsuccessful as that culture had barely begun acknowledging, re-evaluating, and shedding its past imperial doctrine. Post World War II witnessed independence struggles in the Caribbean and many other colonies around the world. The important ingredient in those liberation struggles was identification with the "self" as opposed to the "other". Recovery from centuries of cultural disinheritance and impoverishment meant reconstructing a new identity and consciousness. This reconstruction has taken many forms, ranging from the concept of Negritude, as espoused by Aimé Césaire, to Rastafarianism, to the musical genius of Blue Note artists like saxophonist John Coltrane to the Black Panther movement.

Planning my travel back to Ghana for the summer months of 1981, I shopped around for the cheapest air fares to Accra, eventually booking with Aeroflot, Russian Airlines. The flight proved a mini adventure in itself, departing from London's Heathrow for overnight transit to Moscow's Sheremetyevo International Airport. Terminal F, with its pristine marbled floors, was built to handle the influx of passengers attending the 1980 Summer Olympics, the games boycotted by the United States of America in protest of the 1979 Soviet invasion of Afghanistan. I travelled onwards the next day via Budapest, Hungary, and then a final transit landing in Bamako, the capital of Mali. Standing on the hot tarmac, stretching my legs in the equatorial heat, one fellow passenger informed me that we were standing geographically in the heart of what was the eleventh-century empire of Ghana and that a few hundred miles northeast was the legendary city of Timbuktu.

On arriving in modern-day Ghana for another period of volunteering, I made time for a special sightseeing visit to Elmina Castle, whose walls had witnessed half a millennium of West African history. This coastal monument, constructed from stone hewn in Europe and shipped to Ghanaian shores five hundred years earlier by Portuguese seafarers, would one day become a UNESCO World Heritage Site. With my Olympus OM-2 SLR camera in hand, I snapped away feverishly. The scene of Elmina through the viewfinder was picture postcard perfect. Set against the choppy, iridescent, azure blue waters of the Gulf of Guinea, ultramarine skies, and white sandy beaches, intense sunshine, palm trees, and more distant viridian tropical foliage, the beautiful vista held a unique yet hauntingly tragic history. The granite innards of Elmina Castle retained a vast dank, cool dungeon – one of several – which imparted a pervasive, visceral ambience, a stillness that overwhelmed. A humbling sense of déjà vu embraced my spirit. Within this musty chamber, a grey haired curator pointed out, the solid, stone-like sediment that encased the cold rock floor included residue from centuries of excrement, urine, vomit, and blood.

That excavation, in some sections to a depth of fifty centimetres, was evidence and testimony that here was a sepulchre from hell, a mausoleum which once housed many thousands of living human souls. Renowned Oxford-educated historian A. W. Lawrence, an authority on the history of such fortifications (and the younger brother of T. E. Lawrence, aka "Lawrence of Arabia"), wrote (A. W. Lawrence, 21):

> [I]n all history there is nothing comparable with the effects produced by the forts of West Africa; nowhere have a small and transitory community of traders so changed the life of the alien peoples who surrounded them, and indirectly of a vast region beyond.

With industrialised efficiency, prime young women and men, fortunate or perhaps simply strong enough to survive in this Hades, were shackled, inspected, probed, and categorised like cattle at market for sound mouths, teeth, skin, and anatomical physique prior to transatlantic shipment to almost certain death or, for only the fittest of the fittest like my paternal ancestors, lifelong slavery for generations in the Americas. On an industrialised, continental scale, Mother Africa, the birthplace of mankind, had, not without sacrifice and struggle, surrendered her fruits unto the pale northern horseman.

In a bygone age preceding twentieth-century killing fields in Cambodia, before Hiroshima and Nagasaki, earlier than German death camps like Dachau or Buchenwald, prior to lethal automatic weapons and mustard gas used in World War I, West Africa endured one of humanity's lengthiest and most significant holocausts – that witnessed by Elmina Castle and the system of stone-built fortresses littered along its beautiful coastline. This traumatic event resonates with many as **maafa**, a Kiswahili word meaning "a disastrous, terrible occurrence" or "great tragedy". Tears gathered momentarily as I recollected and came to fully appreciate the haunting melancholic lamentations from Louis Armstrong's recital of "Black and Blue", Coltrane's saxophone, Stéphane Grappelli's violin, Aretha Franklin's vocals, Charlie Mingus's bass, and the Melodians' rendition of "Rivers of Babylon". Five hundred years since its construction, the horrors that Elmina's unnamed and anonymous victims endured were spread-eagle before me. I vowed soberly: "These forebears shall never be forgotten, not in ten years, one hundred years, or four hundred years", knowing I would play my part invigilating, ensuring the fortresses' after-image would last beyond my short lifetime.

On completing this second volunteer stint in Ghana, I flew back to London with a potential wealth of photographs, albeit only precious undeveloped rolls of exposed black and white film, and unforgettable experiences, which were to become pivotal resources in my final year's study. Ahead lay many, many hours of intensive, skilled labour inside the darkrooms at the Camberwell campus, commencing with developing the films into negatives.

In traditional black and white photographic printing processes, a negative image is projected onto light sensitive photographic paper. This exposed photographic paper's latent image is hidden to the naked eye, becoming a positive image – a photograph – only when developed by immersion in three separate baths or trays of chemical solutions – developer, stop, and finally fix. I loved the pungent, vinegar-like smell of the darkrooms, an aroma produced by the acetic acid solution of the stop bath. In order to produce black-and-white prints, a safelight is commonly used to illuminate the work area. I learnt that since the majority of black-and-white papers are sensitive to only blue or green light, a red or amber coloured light can be safely used without exposing the paper. As I beavered away in the darkrooms, the images from Ghana magically emerged in their liquid baths, and the seeds of a final year dissertation were sown. Half a millennium after the fortress of Elmina Castle was built with granite sculpted by Portuguese stonemasons in 1482, I would research the written evidence to present an account of its history.

Having inherited my father's lifelong work ethic, I was habitually the first student to arrive each day at the darkrooms. Being there at 09.00 sharp was the only guarantee of a bay with the best Durst enlarger. The warm, magenta-lit rooms became my habitat for days on end as I studied the development of black and white negative films, making contact sheets, choosing individual frames for enlarging, focusing, exposing, immersing, agitating, washing, drying, cropping, and then critically selecting for exhibition only the most excellent printed images. Through learning this craft I grew acutely mindful of the role of photography since its proliferation following the pioneering work of Louis Daguerre and Henry Fox Talbot in the 1830s. Doing this cultivated in me an awareness that the vast majority of humankind often take for granted or rarely consider the powerful significance of the photographs enmeshed within the unique fabric of their daily lives.

Some 170 years later, our modern, technology-driven cyber era thoroughly embraces the photograph. This imagery is omnipresent, with billions of people owning the means of production: mobile phones with built-in digital cameras. From ordinary school children to university graduates, Academy Awards Oscar winners to presidents and prime ministers attending the funeral of a globally revered world leader, all indulge in the spontaneous selfie. Such everyday snapshots are intrinsic to humankind's knowledge of society and self, as alongside the love and nurturing given by family members and wider society, these photographs provide context, informing us about who we are and where we come from.

Studying this visual medium revealed to me a most sobering realisation: No photographic record existed of my childhood decade from birth in 1957 to 1967, not one single faded, tattered, monochromatic image weathered by loving tender touch or the passage of time. At that precise moment I knew that when my turn at fatherhood arrived, my progeny would have such family heirlooms. For the reader to appreciate the nonexistence, the most unusual absence of significant childhood photographs, this narrative must travel back six decades to 1950s England.

chapter iv

Can a woman's tender care
Cease towards the child she bear?
Yes, she may forgetful be,
Yet will I remember thee.
—William Cowper (1731–1800)

Molly Elizabeth Sherman was a World War II baby and a tad free-spirited, having just turned sixteen in 1956. Always clean, elegantly dressed, and a picture of health, this ample-hipped working class English rose had attractive features, auburn hair, and eyes that glowed, and she was not, so it was rumoured, unused to the ways of the world. Each day before venturing forth, Molly would check her appearance in front of the mirror, carefully making use of elder sister Isabel's lipstick and perfume – her favourite bouquet being Tabu the "forbidden" by Dana. That Saturday night at Hammersmith Odeon, she and several other teens, boys and girls, sat riveted during a screening of **Blackboard Jungle,** a powerful film with a soundtrack featuring Bill Haley and the Comets' hit "Rock Around the Clock", in which novice teacher, actor Glen Ford, struggles to cope in an inner city school against rebellious students led by the ever-so-handsome Sidney Poitier.

Victorian census records indicate Molly's family originated from Chelsea Kensal in London, where her great-grandfather Charles Edward Sherman was employed in the footwear industry, working as an expert machine boot closer. His powerful hands bore the cuts, scars, and two missing digits from a lifetime in this dangerous craft trimming leather for shoes. Charles fathered nine children with his spouse Sylvia, including Molly's grandfather Charles "Clarence" Sherman (born circa 1889). Grandfather Clarence served in the Merchant Navy and, following the Great War of 1914–18, headed westward to the city's Middlesex edge, where his own children, including Molly's father Clifford, would grow up.

Feltham, the rough, nondescript blue-collar suburb of outer West London, was Molly's birthplace and where she lived with her married parents, Clifford Jean Sherman, a skilled plasterer, and his wife Gillian. Clifford owned a Triumph motorcycle, his pride and joy, and Gillian loved warm weather weekends when her husband would tolerate her riding pillion behind him. Both of Molly's parents were at one point Salvationists, evangelizing foot soldiers in William Booth's Salvation Army, with whom Clifford played the cornet, trumpet, and piano. He was also a longstanding member of the Staines Temperance Brass Band.

Gillian had suffered for many years with a disability in her leg, having been struck by a speeding car as a child, and she later contracted tuberculosis (TB) and suffered from chronic asthma. Due mainly to her mother's persistent ill health, Molly's early life had been most unhappy. Despite attending the West Middlesex Hospital for both conditions, Gillian obtained little relief, and consequently had developed a cantankerous and temperamental personality. In more recent years she had grown addicted to alcohol in an effort to drown her depression. Clifford and Gillian's married life had not been a happy one due to Gillian's poor physical well-being and inebriation, which reflected upon Molly and her two elder sisters, Rita and Isabel. Oldest sister Rita, followed by Isabel, would leave the family home on turning sixteen to marry young, thus escaping the household's discordant atmosphere.

Molly had done rather well at school, passing her eleven plus exams and gaining a scholarship to attend the Mary Boon Technical School in Hammersmith. Here she showed some talent for French and as a fashion artist, and intended to become a seamstress. Nevertheless things went awry from several causes, one being the inability of her parents to provide an adequate school uniform and another being that Molly struggled to make friends with the other better-off girls. Over time her attendance at Mary Boon diminished as she increasingly cared for her ailing mother, eventually leaving school at fifteen. Molly's first job as a shop assistant selling confectionary lasted six months, after which she worked on an assembly line in a nearby factory engaged in the making of wire sprung mattresses and bird cages.

As far back as she could remember, Molly had been quite friendly with a local youth, Adrian Gardener, and they courted for a while after she stopped attending Mary Boon. Their relationship, however, was the cause of never-ending friction between Molly and her parents, both of whom disapproved most strongly of Adrian, under whose influence Molly became disobedient and wayward. This young man was a greaser, or in more common parlance, a Teddy boy. Adrian was notorious to local Feltham folk for possession of a most caustic tongue and hasty temper, yet somehow he had shown sufficient diligence to complete his eighteen months of national service. He was industrious, too, holding down regular work, albeit as a lowly refuse collector for the local council. Then one sunny day, a serious adversary for Molly's charms entered the stage, a rival she encountered while toiling at the factory in early May 1956. During a mid-morning break, Molly bumped into new assembly hand Garnett Willson Vimikh, known affectionately to friends as Billy. A short chap, just five feet three inches tall, he was soft-spoken, of stocky, muscular build, youthful, handsome, and in possession of the most irresistibly bright smile, which yielded unblemished, perfectly aligned, sparkling, ivory white teeth.

Not quite a decade before this first acquaintance of Molly and Billy, a passenger ship called the ***Windrush*** had arrived at Tilbury docks in the Thames estuary on 22 June 1948. This date is considered a significant historical milestone as those pilgrims who disembarked were among the first wave of Caribbean immigrants invited to English shores by the post World War II Labour government of Clement Attlee. These English-speaking, dark-skinned travellers from islands like Jamaica and Barbados arrived in the motherland to aid Britain's post-war economic recovery, providing desperately needed labour for numerous factories and government industries such as British Rail, London Transport, and the National Health Service. UK census records from 1951 reveal there were 15,301 people who were born in the Caribbean living in the United Kingdom. By the 1961 census, this figure had increased more than tenfold to 171,800.

Billy was one of these pioneering migrants, barely twenty-one years of age when he arrived at bustling Southampton Docks via the Azores and Canary Islands one bitterly cold, windswept grey December day in 1955, a passenger on board the **SS Ascania**. That morning, standing aboard the docking liner's crowded promenade deck, Billy could hear and feel his heart pulsating. He thrilled at the piercing shrieks and squawks from the many huge herring gulls circling overhead, and watched in amazement as his exhaled breath magically became a cloud of steam before evaporating into the chilly atmosphere. After seemingly an eternity at sea, he had arrived at the shores of his dreams.

Fourteen days earlier, beneath fierce rays from the tropical sun, he had embarked happily from St John's, capital of the British Caribbean colony Antigua in the Leeward Islands, bound for the Jamaican port of Falmouth and then onwards to England. Billy's lifelong home on this island was the simple wooden shack that he had shared with his mother Susie in a small village called Parham in St Peters Parish. His odd surname, Vimikh, was said to be traced to a great-grandfather called Roy Vimikh, who was of Indian origin and who settled in Antigua after serving in Queen Victoria's merchant fleet, where he fathered several children with local women. Esme, Billy's only and elder sibling, but by a different father, had some years prior left home to get married and now had two young children. In Parham he attended the village primary school, advanced to a Seventh Day Adventist senior school until, at the age of sixteen, Billy started helping Susie, who toiled daily on an estate picking cotton. Over the next few years, he obtained ad hoc, short-term jobs like preparing the sugar cane fields with stakes for planting or helping out at Antigua's Recreation Ground cricket venue. Opportunities on the island for employment, personal advancement, and a route out of poverty were scarce. Susie, recognising her son was weary of such futile drudgery in the stifling heat, borrowed the money to fund Billy's passage to England. He promised to repay every penny once he had secured employment in the mother country.

Upon disembarking the **SS Ascania** in Southampton with his small, burnt sienna coloured suitcase in hand, Billy was met by Antiguan friends, including his sister Esme's brother-in-law. Together they made haste for London where he registered with the Department of Social Security and Labour. Within days he found regular work and commenced sending postal orders fortnightly back to Susie, fulfilling his promise. By January 1956 Billy took up employment at a mattress factory in Colnbrook, near Hounslow, where he would work for one year and shortly encounter the alluring Molly.

Billy, this handsome, dark stranger, was the very first black person Molly had ever spoken to, and in his presence her eyes flashed and her heart fluttered. Dare she contemplate crossing the racial divide for that very first tempting, sweetly succulent kiss or perhaps take matters a step further? Powerful, exciting thoughts of sexual intimacy that scorned the staid and ordinary, that broke with cultural conditioning, raced through her mind. Could she ditch the familiar for the shockingly new and find the courage to lie with an outsider, the forbidden, erotic, unusual fruit that many of her kind viewed with utter repugnance? Was it preordained destiny that she would succumb, as had curious Eve in Paradise, and fall for a Moor and, as in the Shakespearian tale, calamity befall both parties? Billy, too, found Molly to be a strikingly exotic temptation.

Indeed Molly was irreversibly smitten by Billy's soft-spoken, mysterious charm, his clean and sharp dress sense, bright smile, and dusky good looks. With humanity being what it is, there was an inevitability to future events. Their romance blossomed at a pace, lust took its course, and in an era before Family Planning clinics and the widespread use of condoms, Molly fell pregnant. Billy, upon hearing this news, was exceedingly pleased and gallantly proposed marriage. He was, after all, a chivalrous fellow of unwavering commitment and great integrity, a man who had been raised correctly, one who would always take his responsibilities seriously. Could this fellow possibly rewrite the script, prove with the passage of time that by simple, understated deeds, his was a worthy character, one equal to that of any man? Molly, for reasons this tale will in due course reveal, declined his proposition. That September of 1956, the film **Rock Around the Clock** – dubbed the story of Rock 'n' Roll, about Bill Haley's Comets, and featuring the unique voice syncopation of the Platters – was shown in picture houses across England. Rioting at many venues ensued, most notably at the Trocadero in central London.

It would not be an untruth to say that this was a period in time when the English found such racial mixing or miscegenation scandalous and unpalatable. However, such liaisons were not unheard of in the history of the British Isles. Before the 1950s, stretching back two millennia, there were many recorded examples of black people – Africans – integrating successfully in all classes of English society, having lifelong intimate relationships with white people. In 80 AD, the Roman orator, public official and historian Tacitus refers to dark-complexioned, unusually curly-haired black Celts believed to have originally migrated to these northern isles from the Iberian peninsula – modern-day

Spain. In tenth-century Saxon Britain, the King of Alban, Niger Val Dubh, also known as King Kenneth of the Picts, was one of the Moors of Scotland, dominant and reigning over black divisions who disappeared in subsequent generations by mating only with native British women, according to archaeologist and folklorist David McRitchie (1851–1925), though to some scholars today his findings are erroneous fantasy. There are parish records, letters, and paintings that evidence the presence of Africans – not enslaved – in Tudor times, and in the seventeenth and eighteenth centuries, many Africans shipped through the thriving slave ports of Liverpool and Bristol did not arrive in the Americas but remained in England. Questions rage as to the genealogy of Queen Charlotte (1744–1818), patron of Kew Gardens and consort of King George III.

In 1789 one former slave wrote and published his autobiography in London: ***The Interesting Narrative of the Life of Olaudah Equiano, or Gustavus Vassa, the African***, about being enslaved as a child, his eventual release, arrival in England, and involvement in the Quaker-inspired abolitionist movement. Equiano married Susan Cullen, a local English girl, in 1792, in Soham, Cambridgeshire, with whom he had two daughters. Walter Tull, born to a Barbadian father and English mother in 1888, was raised in an orphanage and went on to be signed by Tottenham Hotspur Football Club in 1909. Tull fought on the Western Front in 1916 and eventually rose through the British Army ranks to second lieutenant. He died in action, leading his men from the front, on the blood-soaked war fields of Somme during spring 1918. Some English people were known, in the 1950s, for wanting to touch a black person's skin or hair as this, they perceived, would bring them good fortune. "Black for luck, white for pluck" went the saying.

Shortly before Molly's due date, Billy left the Colnbrook mattress factory for better-paid employment as a packer in the stationary department of Harrods in Knightsbridge. She was admitted to West Middlesex Hospital, Isleworth, in the Ealing sub-district of Syon Park where her baby would be delivered. I – Jean (pronounced the French way) Willson Sherman – was born on 17 February 1957. Barely seventeen years of age, Molly still resided in Feltham at her parents' address where, upon discharge from hospital, she returned with me in her arms. On 11 March 1957, while en route to Ealing Town Hall Registry Office to officially have her infant's given name recorded in the births register, mother and child endured stares, nasty comments, thrown stones, and thick, sticky phlegm. This experience was not new. That day Molly gave instructions to the registrar that the spaces on the birth certificate for my father's name, Garnett Willson Vimikh, and his occupation should remain blank. My only link to Billy was my middle name.

Notwithstanding having returned home to Feltham, Molly's relationship with her parents remained fraught. By 7 April, when I was baptised at St Stephen's Church in West Ealing, Molly had departed from the family home to reside in Amhurst Lodge, a home for unmarried mothers and their babies at 47 Amhurst Road in Ealing. My father, then twenty-three years of age, was already making regular weekly payments towards my keep by means of an affiliation order set by the courts. Billy paid regular visits to Molly and me at Amhurst Lodge, and furthermore wrote a letter to her reiterating his proposal of marriage, passionate ardour, and unwavering intentions to renew courtship.

Molly was in absolute turmoil, her heart leaning heavily towards my father's offer of wedlock but her head overwhelmed by a mass of social cues that deflated her spirit. Still brooding over her options a few weeks later when visiting her parents' Feltham home, she bumped into former flame, twenty-two-year-old Adrian Gardener, and informed him of her renewed friendship with Billy, including the possibility of marriage. He exclaimed, "Good Lord, no!" and there erupted bitterly harsh words between them. Adrian, like many of his compatriots, believed in the nationalist mantra "Keep Britain White" to avoid becoming a nation of coffee-coloured half-breeds. He then countered with his own desire to marry Molly, but with one caveat: that she surrender her man-child to the authorities. The dustman's precise, razor-sharp words to her were, "I'll marry you if you get rid of your mongrel coloured bastard."

Perhaps equally influential on her final, heart-wrenching decision was one superintendent Beresford, head welfare official at Amhurst Lodge. Formerly an army officer, zealot missionary, and civil administrator for the colonial office in what was then British East Africa, namely Kenya, Uganda, and Zanzibar and Tanganyika (now Tanzania), Beresford was exceedingly proud of his service record for king and country, controlling the natives while introducing civilisation and the word of Jesus Christ. The superintendent silently opined to himself

> This poor, wretched girl Molly Sherman was brought up knowing the truth, the light, and our Good Lord's beneficence, and yet has yielded to base, incontinent, animalistic desires. As a result of such sinful conduct, she has now become an outcast, one of society's black sheep, a pariah, and even more so the infant.

Beresford then put pen to paper and wrote: "I think we should remove the baby boy, who is another obstacle, so as to facilitate this potential marriage with Adrian, and to improve Molly's life prospects."

Over the coming childhood years I would be targeted with familiar, overtly pejorative adjectives, the socially acceptable racial slurs of the day, combined with subtle metamessages intended to destroy any sense of self-worth that I might possess. People then, and indeed even now in the twenty-first century, mistakenly assume that a young child cannot perceive constant derogatory deprecation communicated by parents, carers, responsible adults, and society at large, messages that signal "You are okay, but your blackness is unforgiveable."

Had these tragic circumstances occurred in any southern state in the United States of America, Billy might well have become "strange fruit hanging from the poplar tree", yet here in England this migrant had the audacity to propose marriage. Liberal Britain, though not inclined to lynch, certainly had its own tried and trusted methods of managing the resulting "stain" from mixed race relationships.

Life for people in those countries victorious in World War II, despite a decade of peace, remained brutally harsh. The era witnessed ever-increasing social tensions as frequent racial violence erupted on the streets of cities like Nottingham and London, and notorious slum landlords seeking new tenants unashamedly displayed signs that read "No Blacks, Irish, or Dogs". Prior to the war of 1939–1945, native Englishmen resented hard-working Irish or Jewish migrants, whom they respectively labelled **finnian** or **Yiddish scum**. Now in the post-war years, such detestation and loathing was directed at the "bloody wogs and darkies"; those equally industrious yet strangely attired Asians, who kept to themselves and spoke their own language; or the ebullient West Indians, strange English speakers, whose lustful men were brazenly developing a taste for white women.

Rationing was still a reality for the majority of British people during the early 1950s. The nation was mired in economic austerity, and order in society was held together by the fabric of long-held conservative values and attitudes. But winds of radical change were on the horizon. The decade witnessed the spread of black and white television, which initially had just the one channel for viewers to watch. By comparison with twenty-first-century technology, the screens were miniscule, but to the average UK citizen, televisions were must-have consumer items. Despite being expensive, many households purchased their first TV sets in 1953 so as to watch the coronation of Queen Elizabeth II. By the mid 50s, British industries had revived and were beginning to outstrip those of many other

European countries, leading to improved wage packets for the average worker. The new era of affluence was summed up in the declaration of Prime Minister Harold Macmillan: "Some of our people have never had it so good".

Increased prosperity gave employed British youths far greater spending power than previous generations had ever experienced, and they explored the latest fashions from across the Atlantic. At the same time, there was a spike, an escalation in delinquency and juvenile crime. By 1953 an urban youth cult had surfaced known as the Edwardian Brigade whose dress style was said to have evolved from that worn by flamboyant Edwardian aristocrats attired by London's Saville Row tailors. These youths had a fondness for sombre-coloured draped coats – some called them coffin coats – with black velvet collars, matching waistcoats, high-waisted drainpipe trousers with turn-ups that exposed the socks, and brogues or crepe-soled suede shoes. Soon identified as Teddy boys by the British press, they quickly gained a reputation for acts of violence, mischief, and non-conformity. Teds were heavily influenced by the novelty and glamour of all things Yankee such as Hollywood heart-throb Tony Curtis's haircut, and dancing, bopping, or jiving to the popular, infectious, syncopated musical genre scorned by their elders known as rock 'n' roll.

Teddy boys, these endearingly labelled working class English delinquents, were allegedly behind many of the recorded violent attacks on black people and any "treacherous" whites who dared to fraternise with them. Slogans daubed on walls appeared: "Down with n******" and "We'll kill the blacks". Such events culminated in the Notting Hill riots of 1958 and, in that same neighbourhood in 1959, the brutal stabbing to death of Kelso Cochrane, a carpenter from Antigua, by a gang of white youths who would never be brought to justice. Notting Hill in the 1950s was destitute of riches, a dilapidated, rat-infested, run-down area of London, crime-ridden and a far cry from the gentrified neighbourhood, home to famous thespians, artists, film moguls, politicians, and hedge fund executives that it would evolve into five decades later. About one mile away as the crow flies was Hammersmith, where Billy resided in a small, shared rented room, which was another violent haunt where Teddy boys would meet regularly to engage in racially motivated affray.

Within this social context, the outcast – Molly – whose son was indeed a bastard, had laboured emotionally, conducting her soul-searching. She loved her swarthy-skinned, curly-haired baby as much as any mother would. However, he was the stone that the builder refused, the stain on the kitchen sink that Ajax, Vim scouring powder, and bleach could not remove. Molly elected to follow the same route as thousands of her contemporaries in English towns and cities, other ill-fated, unmarried young women of that generation who had "lapsed". Her aberration, however, was further aggravated, her name "blackened", her reputation the more sullied by the end result: a half-caste, mulatto baby, the product of her willingness to be intimate with a coloured man. Self examination finally over, Molly made the desperately painful decision that would haunt her to her dying day to surrender me into the care of the authorities.

Her action to be rid of the stigma, her badge of shame, reveals a tragic and most uncomfortable truth about twentieth-century British society: Maternal rejection was normal for countless Annes, Barbaras, Dorises, Elizebeths, Janes, and Susans whose "undesirable" children were shipped overseas to countries like Canada, New Zealand, and Australia. Molly's deed was socially and morally acceptable, in keeping with the times, and a good solution. Ultimately her course of action was a mix of simple, wretched teenage naïvety, influenced by deep-rooted imperialist prejudice and bigotry, an overpowering belief system, oft-denied, that permeated all social classes in England at that time.

Post World War II had witnessed major reforms in how orphaned children were looked after in the UK. The wartime evacuation of many children, and some notorious cases of child neglect and abuse, had led to a 1945 public enquiry and the Monckton Report. In January 1945, as Allied troops advanced through war-ravaged European countries, one infamous UK case stands out, that of a twelve-year-old boy murdered while in foster care. Dennis O'Neill's death at the hands of his foster father led to the enquiry and ultimately the 1948 Children's Act. This legislation officially recognised the role of voluntary agencies, some small and others exceedingly large, in the provision of childcare. Among these larger authorities were the Catholic Child Welfare Council, the Church of England Children's Society and the Jewish Board of Guardians.

Some would say that Dr Barnardo's Homes, founded by Dublin-born Irishman Thomas John Barnardo (1845–1905), is the most renowned of such charitable institutions, and altogether they were then the equivalent of a nationwide social services children's department. In 1862 seventeen-year-old Barnardo converted from Catholicism to the evangelical Christian sect known as the Plymouth Brethren. His missionary zeal led him to Victorian London, where he crusaded to rescue deprived, destitute children from the squalor of its Dickensian streets, and in 1870 he established his first home in Stepney, East London. It was said Barnardo promised to "let the crushed go free" and "shatter the joints of the yoke" that oppressed outcasts and the friendless poor. He would "break his bread to the hungry" and "bring home the wandering poor". By the time of his death, the charity had mushroomed into a national network of ninety-six residential units.

In 1950s England one smaller agency that mirrored the philanthropic work of Dr Barnardo's Homes was St Mary's Children's Charity, who were prepared to undertake my care on condition that steps were taken to ensure my "putative" father's financial responsibility was formally in place. Despite Molly's parents' persuasive arguments expressing their willingness to have both mother and her newborn return to the Feltham family home, Molly stuck steadfastly with her regrettable decision.

Thus on 7 May 1957, Molly's father Clifford Sherman, then in his mid fifties, reluctantly and with a heavy heart signed the agreement form, authorising and consenting to his nine-week-old grandson being brought up in the care of St Mary's Children's Charity. Clifford's signature had been sought by welfare officials as Molly was under eighteen and not legally an adult. On 30 May I was admitted to the branch of St Mary's known as Tiny Tots Palace, an orphanage in the picturesque but somewhat remote village of Madehurst, in West Sussex. Here I was considered an unfit candidate for permanent adoption, something that would have ensured growing up and developing within a stable family environment. A welfare official wrote, "Willson's colour debars him, but recommendations were made for him to be boarded out (fostered) in the west of England".

Tiny Tots Palace, opened by St Mary's in 1896, became the charity's largest home for orphaned babies and young children in southern England. During the 1950s many of the children resident there arrived from London, the undesirable fruit from the growing trend of frowned upon, mixed-race relationships. In May 1959 a local townswomen's guild expressed "considerable surprise" at the large number of "coloured infants" at Tiny Tots Palace. Unless they could be assured – guaranteed – that no white child was being refused admission as a consequence, the townswomen warned their support for St Mary's Children's Charity would cease. They were reassured and the matter blew over. The home closed in 1965 before being used as a geriatric nursing facility, renamed Madehurst Castle. Today the building lies derelict.

As summer turned cooler, the foliage on trees became golden amber, signalling autumn's arrival. Come October 1957, as cultural icon Elvis Presley performed his international R & B hit "Love Me Tender" on the Ed Sullivan Show and the Everley Brothers hit number one with "Wake

Up Little Susie", Molly made no further contact. Then one Sunday in the middle of the month, my father Billy visited the orphanage, bringing me the gift of a teddy bear, and he told a Miss Catherine A. Howarth that Clifford and Gillian Sherman wanted their grandson returned to the family home. Miss Howarth, who trained at one of London's great hospitals, was neatly dressed in her pale blue starched and ironed nurse's uniform, white apron, and cap. As she wrote afterwards of the visit:

> Willson's father, Garnett Willson Vimikh, who was accompanied by his Jamaican cousin, visited Willson on Sunday 13 October for the first time since the child's admission.
>
> As explained in my letter to Mr Sherman, the father wrote to me to ask whether he might visit Willson, and I replied saying that I would be very pleased, but I thought I was writing to the mother, using her new married name. Miss Cook brought a prospective foster mother to visit Willson at the end of September, but as I told her I was hoping the mother would visit Willson, we left it that I would have a talk to her when she came.
>
> Instead of the mother in response to my reply to "Vimikh" the father came, and I told him what intentions we had for Willson's future. At this point he flinched, grimaced and seemed genuinely perturbed about these plans, as he told me that Willson's grandparents wanted him home with them. So I asked him to get the Sherman grandparents to write to me, and then I could possibly do something about it. The young men left me to go to the grandparents straight away on their motorcycle, hence the early letter to me from Mr Sherman.
>
> The father does seem genuinely fond of baby Willson, he took him out in his pram, brought him back and gave him his tea, and Willson himself

seemed to take very well to both young men. Each took a turn in pushing the pram and feeding Willson, which they explained to me is done in Antigua and Jamaica. They were friendly and well turned out young men, and the father seems to be on good terms with Mr and Mrs Sherman.

A few days later, on 16 October, Miss Howarth received a letter from Mr Sherman requesting that his grandson be returned immediately to abide in the Sherman family home. My grandfather's favourable attitude to events, given the social context, can probably be explained by the fact that his mother, Leandra "Ann" Sherman, was affectionately called "our black granny" by Molly and her two elder sisters. It was said that Ann originated from Argentina, South America, and was probably of native American descent. She had sailed to England before World War I with Clifford Sherman's father, merchant seaman Clarence Sherman, to get married.

Miss Howarth replied in writing to Mr Sherman that a welfare officer from St Mary's head office would be in touch and that plans to place me in a foster home would be kept in abeyance. Her report to Mr Sherman added more news.

> A delightful baby – Willson is incredibly affectionate and jolly. He is so even tempered and pleasant, always smiling and happy. He has grown a great deal and is very big for his age, but then he is such a good eater and enjoys his food so much it is not to be wondered at that he grows so quickly. He sends his love to you and his Granny, and he loves the teddy bear his father brought to him on Sunday.

Over the passing months since my admission to Tiny Tots Palace, my mother was now titled Mrs Molly Gardener, having married Teddy boy Adrian. They were domiciled in a two-room rented bungalow, but their union would be calamitous. Molly was contacted by a welfare officer, Mr P. Bannerman, about my restoration to the Sherman household, and he reported his findings to the authorities.

> Mother is most definitely not in favour of restoration to the maternal grandparents, even though the grandfather may be earning good wages, and she would like to resist it. Nor will she agree to boarding out as she would like him to grow up in community life.

Legally Molly was not yet an adult, and given that her father, Clifford Sherman, had signed the original agreement, Mr Bannerman visited the home of Mr and Mrs Sherman as part of St Mary's Children's Charity's investigations. He wrote of this contact:

> The maternal grandparents are still deeply insistent that Willson shall be handed over to them, but, as recently as two weeks ago the mother, Molly Sherman (now Gardener) told them she did not want them to have him. It is alleged her recent marriage already shows signs of splitting but when I saw her and Mr Gardener, no mention was made of it, nor did it seem likely. Mr and Mrs Sherman realise that even though the mother is under 21 years – she has since turned 18 – her wishes ought to take precedence.
> The putative father is most welcome in the grandparents' residence but they deeply loathe the step father. Should the marriage fail, and the mother wanted to make her home with the grandparents again, it would open up the way for Willson to be restored to her, leaving the grandmother to care for him while his mother worked. In some respects I gather they would

95

prefer to see this to happen but it seems a hard bargain to drive.

Although we talked it over at great length, nothing definitive emerged, principally on account of the mother's firm and continued rejection of the plan. I did not tell Mr and Mrs Sherman I had previously interviewed the mother and her husband.

The Sherman's working class home, includes, surprisingly enough, a grand piano (full size) but otherwise it is sparsely furnished with little else of any great value. Mr Sherman is a concrete maker's maintenance hand earning about £12 per week. Rent is 27 shillings per week. He is 54 and his wife Gloria 49. Mrs Sherman's indifferent health (asthma) is not sufficient to make her an invalid, and she was adamant that she can still do all for Willson that any mother could. They have a pram, a cot, a few soft toys and play-pen. There are two bedrooms unoccupied. Both "like their pint" but Mr Sherman said proudly that they were both formerly Salvationists and he at one time played an instrument in the Staines Temperance Band. There are now no children at home and they would dearly like to have Willson.

If I were asked for an opinion as to the advisability of pursuing the application for Willson to be placed in the care of his grandparents, I would feel disposed to oppose it, not that I think they would not do their best by him and love him, but I fail to see how his mother's wishes can be ignored, even though she has not yet reached woman's estate. She is not a simpleton however, is much older in outlook than her years might suggest and I was told she visited Willson at Tiny Tots Palace just two weeks ago. I also gather she is very fond of the child and there must be sound reasons for her not wanting him to be reared by the grandparents.

The decision was rubber-stamped in early December 1957. Restoration to Mr and Mrs Sherman was not recommended. I remained at Tiny Tots Palace while plans for me to be boarded out or fostered were resurrected. The restoration statement recorded an interesting note from the chief executive officer. It read:

> The putative father visits Willson and has said that his mother in Antigua will have the baby. Things may work out that way, however, in the meantime I do not recommend restoration as the mother opposes it.

At Tiny Tots Palace on 5 June 1958, Miss Howarth logged:

> Mrs Gardener, Willson's mother, came to visit him on Sunday, bringing his father (not her husband) Billy Vimikh too.
> Mrs Gardener explained to me that she and her husband have parted for good, that she is now living with her parents, has a part time job and would like to have Willson home with her.
> The father (a West Indian) did have ideas of having Willson flown to Jamaica ...

One can only assume Miss Howarth's geographical knowledge of British Caribbean territories was quite limited, thus she mixed up Antigua with Jamaica.

> ... for him to live with Willson's grandmother (Billy's mother) but now that the infant's own mother wants him back he has cancelled these plans. I will say that Willson's mother has always seemed fond of the child, but her personal

relationships with her husband and Willson's father seems to me to be rather a tangle.

However she asked me to try and arrange that Willson should return to her.

A week later, regarding an application for my restoration to Mrs Gardener, Miss Howarth noted:

Willson is a rather plump, pleasant looking little boy. He used to be awfully shy of strangers, especially his father, and would scream and hide but he is over this stage now, and is very cheerful and friendly towards adults.

He can run exceptionally well, says a few words, loves other little children and joins in their games, and is very affectionate and responsive to affection.

He eats simply splendidly, sleeps well, is dry by day but not at night and is an especially nice and happy little person in every way.

Mr Bannerman, the welfare officer, wrote to the restoration department of St Mary's Children's Charity, under the heading "Urgent":

I have seen the maternal grandparents and mother of the above named, separately, regarding this application for restoration. Both grandparents are thrilled at the way matters have worked out and, to use their own words, will not only be delighted but pleased beyond measure if Willson can come to them now that the mother's husband has deserted her and she is living with them again. Attention is respectfully drawn to reports dated 11/11/57 and 27/11/57 as bearing on the present situation.

Regarding both maternal grandparents I have shown that they "like their pint". Materially, little exception can be taken to the home, it being one that is "lived in" and not kept for show. There are three bedrooms, one used by the grandparents, one by the mother, and a spare for when Willson is older. His cot, pram and play-pen have all been retained. The grandmother's health has improved and whatever may be her physical disabilities they should not prevent her giving all the attention the child needs while the mother is at work. Grandfather is working as a painter earning around £10 to £12 per week. During the winter months he changes to plastering and allied work. They are Salvationists in spite of not being abstainers. The thought that Willson may be restored has put new life into the grandmother and grandfather, and their joy seems profound.

I saw the mother at the maternal aunt's (Mrs Isabel Cotterill) caravan in Chertsey where she was spending the day. We know that the grandparents have always disapproved of her husband Mr Gardener because he was a teddy boy, however, they strangely accepted the putative father. Mother, now pregnant with her husband's child, said that their marriage severance is irrevocable and she would die before ever returning to him. There would be no point of applying for a separation and maintenance order as Mr Gardener would never pay owing to his lazy ways.

Mother is now in receipt of reduced unemployment benefit of 38 shillings and 6 pence per week plus 12 shillings and 6 pence National Assistance Grant. As a skilled buttonhole maker and with some experience of tailoring she should be able to earn quite good wages, but has ideas of finding a nursery post, and in the event of Restoration, the putative father's payments of 25 shillings per week would revert to her. Towards board and lodging, the grandparents will only look for a nominal sum, say £1 per week or nothing if the occasion demands. Their rent is 28 shillings and 6 pence per week. They have no debts or Hire Purchase commitments.

There is thus an almost complete reversal of mother's former attitude in that she is now quite willing for the grandmother to care for Willson during the day, and Molly assured me her mother is completely able to do this. All of the family hope to go to Tiny Tots Palace on our Open Day 28/6/58 and to save expense it is hoped approval for restoration will then have been given so that they can collect Willson. Both mother and grandparents are certain matters will from now on work out right, and in all the circumstances I do not feel able to report adversely thus respectfully recommend approval be given.

So it was that on 28 June 1958, aged sixteen months, I was restored back into my mother's care. However, by December 1958 she had written to St Mary's because restoration was not working out very well. Molly's letter also implied a request for financial help in getting me to my paternal grandparents in the West Indies. St Mary's Children's Charity arranged a visit as soon as possible by another welfare officer, a Mr Walsh. His January 1959 report for the Admission's Department read:

On 11/12/58 I wrote to the mother asking when and where I could meet with her – addressing the letter c/o 21 Alma Road, Wandsworth, SW18, the putative father's address – and on 15/12/58 Molly contacted me by telephone at headquarters saying she was "fed up" with things at home, and that Willson was ever so boisterous, getting out of hand and being spoiled by his grandfather. Whenever our Homes were mentioned with the possibility of Willson being re-admitted, grandmother would threaten to turn her out. Molly was unable to go out to work on account of the young baby. She is still on friendly but definitely not on intimate terms with the putative father of Willson, who visits the boy every week and he is on good terms with both grandparents, who dislike intensely the mother's husband. There is a possibility of reconciliation with Mr Gardener, however, he categorically will not accept Willson.

The mother had been considering the possibility of sending Willson to the putative father's people in Antigua, British West Indies, but has no prospects of getting the fare. I told the mother I would be making a post restoration visit to her home at 42 Percival Road, Feltham and provisionally arranged to see her afterwards at the maternal aunt's caravan in Chertsey.

At 3 p.m. on 16/12/58 I called at 42 Percival Road and did not obtain any response for some minutes and, when just about to leave, grandmother Gloria called out from a ground floor room, saying she was in bed with a cold and could not see me, that mother was out visiting friends in Bedfont with Willson and she was not likely to be back for some time. I told grandmother I would visit again the next day. I enquired about Willson and she replied, "He is doing fine".

I called again at 11 a.m. on 17/12/58 and found the place clean and tidy with Willson very happy, a bundle of energy, mischievous and something of a handful. I also saw half-brother David Gardener, born 11/9/58, a healthy looking, well cared for baby. Both mother and grandmother were clean and tidy and, although grandmother did not appear to be suffering from a cold, she did not look too well as she suffers from asthma. It was apparent to me that relations between mother and grandmother were strained but I was able to see mother alone for a short time during which she told me some of her difficulties, saying she had much to tell me but would prefer to see me at maternal aunt Isabel's place where she could speak more freely, and I made tentative arrangements to see her there before Christmas (but owing to pressure of other work I was not able to do so).

A further discussion took place in the grandmother's presence; Gloria Sherman said that she and the grandfather are very fond of Willson but it was up to his mother to decide his future. Mother was not very happy about him staying there. Mother said this was so and wanted to know if we would accept both of her infants to enable her to make a fresh start away from Feltham, as it seemed we should not be able to assist with Willson's passage money should she decide to allow the putative father to send him to his people. I pointed out that I had understood her to tell me there was a chance of her going back to her husband, when it would be natural for her to have baby David: she then said that chance was extremely remote as she had summoned him at Feltham Court on 22/10/58 for desertion. The question was then raised about her returning to Mr Gardener and, as she then said she did not wish to do so – he had not offered to take her back – the summons was dismissed but she was granted a Court Order in respect of the baby and Mr Gardener has to pay 15 shillings per week. He had not paid regularly and has since disappeared from his home address. Grandmother's attitude suggested she was not in favour of mother going back to him even if he were willing.

I told them I should be visiting again within a week or two, expressing the hope things would work out satisfactorily, although I had some doubts as to this, seeing there was such underlying antagonism between mother and grandmother, conflict that was rather deep seated but controlled in my presence.

As stated, I was unable to call and see mother at Chertsey before Christmas yet I intended to do so on 2/1/59 as mother visits on Fridays but on 29/12/58 she telephoned me at Headquarters to tell me that she and baby David were being sheltered by maternal aunt Isabel as grandmother had turned her out on 23/12/58 following another heated quarrel. Willson was left with grandmother and she was not happy at all about this as grandmother liked to go to Public Houses at weekends and would not be able to do so if mother was not there. I arranged to call mother on 30/12/58 telling her I would first call grandmother to see how Willson was getting on.

I duly visited the grandmother at about 2 p.m. on 30/12/58 and she took several minutes answering the door, being a little reluctant to let me in. When Gloria did so, she apologised for the place being untidy and not cleaned up – it did not look too bad to me. She told me a unhappy story and said from the time Willson had been restored there had been ceaseless bickering as Molly was dissatisfied with the set up, not being able to go out to work, nevertheless she had kept the place clean and tidy and was a good mother to the children.

However, on the afternoon of 23/12/58 Molly went out for a short time and when she returned she complained that David was very wet and had not been changed. She also took great exception to grandmother having had a drink (Mrs Sherman admits that she was partaking of one – "The festive season", she said). High words ensued and grandmother told Molly to clear off if she did not like it. Mother then went, taking baby David with her, and had not contacted the grandparents since. Grandmother had not been well since and grandfather has had to do the washing and all things considered, they now felt Willson was too much for them and they could not care for him much longer. During the time I was with Mrs Gloria Sherman this little boy, who was clean and tidy, was certainly very active and quite beyond the control of his grandmother, who seemed content to let him do just whatever he pleased.

It was obvious that the grandmother regretted the mother leaving and intimated she would not be unwilling for her to return – when she would continue to do the housework, etc. – but admitted she would not settle, being under the influence of maternal aunt Isabel, who since leaving the family home had always been at cross purposes with the grandparents. Before Molly left there had been friction between her and grandfather, who would be sorry to see Willson go yet realises that grandmother is unable to cope with the boy by herself.

Later, on 30/12/58 I called at the Caravan Site, No. 1 Mixnan's Lane, Chertsey, Surrey, and saw the mother with half-brother David and maternal Aunt Isabel, who happens to have a baby boy of eight months. Molly had much to tell me that was not favourable to grandmother, whom she condemned as an inveterate drinker who, when under the influence of alcohol, shows her nasty temper, making the atmosphere undesirable for Willson, who is always up to mischief and requires constant supervision.

Mother related the events which led to her leaving home on 23/12/58 and said the position had become intolerable due to grandmother's bad drinking habits and the consequent nasty moods. It was wrong for the grandmother to say Molly had not paid her any money: she gave her 2 pounds and 5 shillings the day before she left home. Maternal aunt Isabel and her husband had taken her and baby David in to provide shelter over Christmas yet they could not stay there indefinitely as the caravan was overcrowded. Furthermore the aunt's husband strongly objected to the presence of Willson – if mother had it in mind taking him – as the little boy was so destructive whereas the caravan is newish, being well furnished and equipped.

At present mother's income is £1 and 5 shillings from the putative father of Willson, 15 shillings from Mr Gardener for David, 8 shillings Family Allowance and £1 and 2 shillings and 6 pence National Assistance Board (N.A.B.). She had been to the Children's and Housing Welfare Officers for Feltham and Chertsey Districts but they were not able to assist, so Molly would like us to readmit Willson on payment by her of £1 and 5 shillings from putative father plus her contribution of 8 shillings, her plan being to place baby David with a foster mother locally and she herself would obtain a room and employment.

Maternal aunt Isabel corroborated all that mother has told me, particularly with regard to grandmother, and said she hoped we would again assist her sister as their caravan was overcrowded (this is quite true) and her husband had made it plain these conditions cannot continue much longer.

So once financial arrangements had been made, particularly Billy's regular weekly contribution of £1 and 5 shillings, Molly Gardener signed the forms agreeing to place me back again into the care of St Mary's Children's Charity on 18

January 1959. In February 1959 a letter was sent to Miss Howarth, the superintendent of Tiny Tots Palace in Madehurst, West Sussex, explaining the circumstances behind the restoration breakdown and asking if there was a vacancy available. Miss Howarth's reply advised a delay in my readmission as there was an outbreak of mumps at Tiny Tots Palace.

In late March 1959, a letter from the chief executive's office at St Mary's headquarters informed Molly Gardener of the quarantine due to mumps at Tiny Tots Palace, advising that if she accepted the risk that I might contract mumps, my readmission would go ahead. Molly approached St Mary's for assistance with travel arrangements to Madehurst due to her poor financial situation. A letter to her from the chief executive's office suggested she approach the NAB with said correspondence in order to obtain a free travel warrant. This letter reminded Molly that all financial arrangements should be in place and concluded with the following paragraph:

> We sincerely hope that Willson will quickly settle down again when he arrives at Tiny Tots Palace and that you will be able to get him there soon. We are not in favour of the idea of Willson's father taking him to our establishment and we cannot agree to such a proposal.

I was eventually readmitted to Tiny Tots Palace on 17 April 1959. At the end of the month, Miss Howarth reported that

> Willson is a well built, nice looking half coloured boy. He is both clean and dry, eats well but sleeps very lightly and does not go to sleep quickly at night. His speech is good for his age and he appears average.

I do not presently think he is ready yet to go to a foster home because he screams with dread whenever any adults approach, whether he knows them or not. Willson is very uncertain of everything, extremely unstable, capricious and unpredictable, and in general a very emotionally disturbed toddler.

His mother brought him here mid April gone, stating that he was growing out of hand, since when she has not written or visited.

chapter v

Dreams are true while they last,
and do we not live in dreams?
—Alfred Lord Tennyson (1809–1892)

On 31 May 1959 Miss Howarth jotted down:

> At this moment in time Willson shows all the symptoms of a thoroughly upset child emotionally – He screams and cries at the sight of strangers – Bangs and hits other children, and is very difficult and wild.
>
> It is quite tricky assessing this situation just now because one feels that as soon as Willson finds his feet again he will become the jolly little boy he was when he was with us last year.

Months later, November 1959, Miss Howarth again wrote:

> He has passed as being medically fit for boarding out, dark soft curly hair, small muddy brown eyes, very well made and altogether an attractive looking child.
>
> Willson is very friendly and sociable both with adults and children. He is sporting in his play and for the most part is very amenable and easy going. He is very popular with both staff and

children. He appears well up to average for his age. Speech is good.

No letters, visitors or enquiries. No brothers or sisters at Tiny Tots Palace. Willson has a warm outgoing personality and should fit into a foster home very well indeed. He is very friendly now with adults – whom he distrusted on his return here in May – and he is altogether a charming child.

By presenting as a stable and no longer emotionally insecure toddler, I met the criteria for being boarded out. Having recently turned three, I was visited by prospective foster parents, Mr and Mrs Jeffers, in March 1960 and both seemed delighted with me. I was described as "instantly at home" with them and within moments was calling them both Daddy and Mummy and sitting on Mrs Jeffers's knee. Later that week I was still talking excitably about the Jeffers's visit and looking forward to seeing them again.

The Jeffers felt they would not be able to visit again as they had such a difficult journey to make, but they told an official they felt sure they would take me into their home. On 21 April 1960 Mr and Mrs Jeffers of Broadstairs, Kent became my foster parents. Two months later, 21 June 1960, the placement was terminated and I was once again readmitted to Tiny Tots Palace, the reason given being the ill health of the foster mother.

A Tiny Tots Palace report of 1 September 1960 stated:

Willson can be rather difficult to handle at times as he is most strong willed and determined. At other times he can be charming – if things are going his way. He is an affectionate boy.

Willson returned to us in June this year after his fostering had broken down. He has settled down fairly well, but still talks about his "real home" and his "mummy and daddy". No relation has been in touch since his re-admission here in May 1959.

A case review of 15 November 1960 commented:

> The reasons why it was necessary for Willson to be re-admitted to our care were briefly reviewed and it was apparent that his mother had lost all interest in Willson. In fact her present whereabouts are unknown to us.
>
> It was most unfortunate that Willson's recent placement in a foster home broke down so quickly through the foster mother's ill health and he had to return to Tiny Tots Palace. He would possibly be suitable for fostering again. He is a happy loveable little boy but would need firm handling. He is physically strong and could easily dominate a foster mother if she did not take care.
>
> Regular payments, through the Courts, are being received from the putative father – Mr Garnett Willson Vimikh (a West Indian), and Miss Radclyffe felt that the possibility of getting him interested might be explored. If we have not got up to date information about him, we could perhaps approach the Court to see if they would give us his address or else let him know we would like to contact him.
>
> Action should be taken along these lines.

All was looking promising – it appeared that my sojourn within the care system was to end with restitution to my father, Billy. On 16 December 1960 an official recorded:

> Willson was recently discussed at Stepney and it was felt that the possibility of the putative father's interest might be explored. It was known that Mr Vimikh visited regularly at one time but it appears that he has not visited since December

1959 and may not have visited for some time prior to that date. He did propose at one time that Willson should be flown to Antigua where he would be looked after by the putative father's parents but this fell through.

The mother, in 1959, was said to be on quite friendly terms with the putative father but as far as is known has never cohabited with him. Payments made by Mr Vimikh via the Collecting Officer at Isleworth Magistrates Court have been very regular. Could a Welfare Officer please visit the putative father, Mr Billy Vimikh, last known address, 21, Alma Road, S.W.18 and discuss the matter with him to ascertain if he still has any interest in Willson? If he is not at the address stated perhaps an enquiry at Isleworth Magistrates Court might bring to light some up to date information about him and his present whereabouts.

Mr Walsh, the welfare officer, was given the task of enquiring at the court, with the result that Billy was confirmed as still residing at 21 Alma Road. Mr Walsh wrote to Billy and subsequently met with him at this address by appointment on 29 December 1960. Mr Walsh wrote of this meeting:

I found him to be a pleasant, intelligent little man of 25, occupying a large front room on the upper floor of a smallish, clean looking house in a somewhat drab neighbourhood. Mr Vimikh told me he has been living there about three years and pays £2 and 15 shillings per week rent for the room and use of the kitchen. At present he is attending a Hairdressing School near Piccadilly daily from 10 a.m. to 5 p.m.: the Course will end in February, when he hopes to obtain employment as a Ladies Hairdresser. In the meantime he is sustaining himself by part time evening work as a chef. He has not seen Willson's mother since Christmas 1958 and has no knowledge of her present address or circumstances.

The putative father said that he had maintained an interest in Willson by visiting him when he was with the grandparents in the hope that he would be allowed to send the boy to relations in Antigua but when mother indicated she was opposed to this he was discouraged and he discontinued contact. I explained the present set up with regard to Willson and he was quite enthusiastic about resuming interest, saying he would like to visit one Sunday in January and thereafter occasionally on Sundays: he would make a formal application through Headquarters in the first instance to do so.

Mr Vimikh went on to say that he still has in his mind the possibility of sending the boy to his married sister in Antigua and he gave me the following details about her: her name is Esme Grimes, aged 30: she has a daughter of 12 and a son aged 10. She is expecting another child in March so she would not be able to have Willson for some time. This is just as well from our point of view and it was agreed the matter would be left in abeyance and he will raise it again after he has become better acquainted with Willson and when he feels his sister would be able to cope. I was shown photographs of the sister, with her husband, also a West Indian, and their two children, and they appear to be quite good types.

The putative father went on to say he is friendly with a West Indian girl who is a trainee nurse at a hospital in Winchester. She is aware of Willson's existence but the boy has no place in their future plans: he is not yet planning in terms of marriage: he may go back to Antigua later on, when he may go into business as a Ladies Hairdresser.

There was renewed optimism in the New Year as my father's idea of sending me to reside with his sister Esme in Antigua received further attention from St Mary's Children's Charity. The chief executive officer for the southern area, Miss L. M. Radclyffe, in putting pen to paper on 20 January 1961 to a Tiny Tots Palace official stated:

> You will remember on your recent visit to Stepney for a case discussion that the suggestion was made in Willson's case that the extent of the putative father's interest should be explored. Our Welfare Officer, Mr Walsh, has now visited Mr Vimikh and I attach a copy of his report for your information.
>
> You will see that Mr Vimikh was enthusiastic about resuming interest and would be making an application to us at Richmond Head Office to make a visit this month. So far we have heard nothing more about this and of course, should he ask for permission, this will be given. If we do hear nothing within the next few weeks, the matter will be given fresh consideration.

On 9 February 1961 Miss Radclyffe wrote:

> Jean Willson Sherman is waiting for a foster home – he has been baptised in the Church of England. Mother's present whereabouts are unknown and she was last heard of in Surrey.
>
> Willson is a sturdy little boy, bright and light brown. He is a very likeable child, who is very affectionate. He is especially determined, though, and at times needs a firm hand. He is well liked by other children in his group and plays well with them. He appears to be of average intelligence. The putative father did say he was interested and

may like to visit, but so far has not done so. No other relatives have been in touch.

On 17 February Tiny Tots Palace wrote to Miss Radclyffe:

> Mr Vimikh visited Willson this afternoon and the visit went very well indeed. Before he left, Willson told him he liked him, which pleased him very much.
> Mr Vimikh hopes to pay another visit in about three weeks time, when he would like to discuss Willson's future.

Months passed by, and in August 1961 Tiny Tots Palace recorded my particulars on a form for a child over two years for whom boarding out is required. I was passed for boarding out. That October an official wrote:

> Willson is still in need of a foster home and, therefore, would you please make a special effort to find suitable foster parents for him. On the latest 'Boarding Out' Form he is described as 'very sturdy, strong looking, broad shoulders, light brown skin and dark curly hair. Is lively and boisterous and enjoys plenty of rough play. He is very friendly and is not bashful with strangers. He gets on well with other children, particularly boys. Is very affectionate but does need firmness as he is extremely determined. He appears to be of average intelligence.
> Willson's father has visited him twice this year but since April he has not written or sent gifts. We look forward to receiving any suggestions you can make for this little boy.

A welfare officer named Mrs Millward was allocated the case. She would, over the forthcoming years, become one of the most consistent adult figures in my childhood, aside from my "putative" father in London. She corresponded with Miss Radclyffe about a potential foster placement:

> As you know I saw Willson when I visited Tiny Tots Palace earlier this year. Mrs Collier has recently approached me in the hope that they might be able to have another little coloured boy, especially now that her son is married and there is a spare bedroom, but I hesitated owing to their ages. They have been wonderful foster parents for Martin and I wonder ...
>
> I have made my own study of coloured children in Plymouth and find that the majority of parents feel unable to accept them because of being unable to cope with the children's unhappiness and their colour, and of course Willson is practically the same age as Martin.

In November 1961 Mrs Millward received a letter in reply:

> Thank you for the deep thought you have put in to suggestions that Martin might well accept as a companion and "brother" Willson from Tiny Tots Palace. I too have thought a lot about this and it seems suitable apart from the fact that Willson is only 5 months younger than Martin and I wonder if we dare risk the competition between boys that this closeness of age is likely to produce. Worked out on a logical basis I realise that unless we can place a boy almost the same age as Martin we cannot place at all because for a younger child it would not be fair to have foster parents the Collier's age and to place an older child in hope would be quite unfair to the child and to Martin.
>
> It would seem, therefore, to be Willson or nobody and I am, therefore, wondering if we could make an exception to our usual rule and consider this. There is no doubt that Willson needs a home

where he can settle down and feel a sense of belonging. Do you think a chap as described in the Boarding Out Form would be acceptable to Martin, because unless the two boys become very good friends such a placement would be doomed from the start.

All I can suggest at present is that you try and plan a visit to Tiny Tots Palace again so that you can talk the whole thing through with the staff who know Willson best, prior to seeing if we can arrange a holiday for Willson with the Colliers in the true sense of a holiday so that he knows he is going back to Tiny Tots Palace and Martin knows he will be going again and their first contact would, therefore, be less of a strain than if Martin thought he was coming for good. From the photograph of Martin one wonders if he would be overwhelmed by Willson but perhaps he is more boisterous than he looks. It would, of course, be lovely for Willson if this proved a good plan but I think we must consider it from the start as not very hopeful and only press on with each step when we are all as assured as we can be that it seems a good idea.

A week's holiday went ahead as planned in mid December and proved a success with "both boys bonding well". On 23 January 1962 I was transferred from Tiny Tots Palace to the foster home of Mr and Mrs Collier in Tamerton Foliot, Plymouth. A week later Mrs Millward wrote:

I am completing the usual routine report on Willson for the end of the month but in the meantime am writing to tell you that all is well with this dear little boy and the foster home – Martin is so very thrilled that Willson is going to live with him and very happy that Willson has commenced school. The foster mother has been able to rearrange accommodation and I have seen the bedroom and find the new plan very satisfactory. She has had to purchase a divan bed – cost £5 and I did say – without permission – that I knew we would help. Willson is extremely happy and has fitted exceptionally well into the family life here and I know we have found the ideal home for him.

Mrs Millward's February report concluded:

Willson is delightful – he was busy playing around outside on his bicycle. He and Martin are so very different but are perfect pals. They play with each other very well indeed. Willson is always ready for bed at 6pm and asks for his bath as soon as the foster father returns from work. He loves school and has settled down perfectly.

Her April report ended similarly:

Willson was full of life again! The foster parent's son, daughter in law and new baby were here today and Willson is a great favourite with them. He is really thrilled with the new baby and wants to hold her all the time. He was very anxious to know if she loved him and was full of pride and most pleased when he was reassured.

As the welfare officer's detailed reports continued throughout autumn 1962, disquieting comments began to appear among the favourable. In October of that year, with reference to my personality, Mrs Millward penned;

Affectionate – cheeky – destructive – easily led – loves an audience.

It was noted that:

> The foster mother was rather distressed as Willson had come home from school with his trouser seat all torn and told her he had been sliding down the wall, and only laughed when she had told him he was a naughty boy. He is quite unimpressed at the immaculate appearance of Martin.

The winter of 1962 – 1963 was one of the coldest ever recorded in the UK. A deep weather depression had set in, bringing months of Siberian-like, sub-zero temperatures. Some likened it to a mini ice age as the nation's transport system plunged into gridlocked chaos and the River Thames at Windsor froze over. As Christmas 1962 approached, Mrs Millward wrote:

> Willson's foster mother had been telling him the story of the first Christmas and the boy was full of awe and wonder, and retold it to me. Again there is this vexing problem of his clothing and only last week she had to ask her husband for another two pounds to replace shoes only worn twice and now torn at the toe – and they were expensive. I suggested she purchase really strong ones with heavy soles.
>
> He went out to play when the foster mother was talking to me and I saw him when he walked to the car with me. Willson was so full of the coming events at school that I did not speak to him about his clothes and I also felt that Mrs Collier had said quite a lot about his shoes and the woollies that he sits and unpicks. He is not serious for very long and soon seems to forget.

As my sixth birthday approached, Mrs Millward recorded:

> Willson's personality is exuberant, noisy, willing, easily led and very free in his ways.
>
> The foster mother was again rather upset as the boy had again been destructive with his clothes and had made several holes in his jerseys. She says that when he knows he is being observed Willson stops almost at once and gives her a most angelic smile but then "away" he goes again. She told me this usually happens when they are watching TV and I did say that I thought it was because Willson became so engrossed, and perhaps tense with the story, that it was what my daughter describes as being a defence action as her child did this when recently watching a Charles Dickens story.
>
> I think the choice of viewing has to be watched carefully but Mrs Collier felt that "drama" does not leave too great an impression on him as on Martin as Willson discusses things afterwards but I tried to explain that perhaps this is his way of thinking about things and a sign of expression.
>
> Willson was thrilled today about his birthday and all the lovely presents. He proclaimed "I am a lucky thing." and asked "I don't need anything more do I?" He has, however, been very destructive with his toys and although Martin has kept his perfect and intact since Christmas Willson's are ruined, and he did not seem to care. He very soon tires of one subject and commences to wander aimlessly around and then starts to destroy things. The foster mother and I decided to try to occupy him at all times and with various things as it was useless expecting him to concentrate for very long and even maintain interest as Martin does. I did remind her they are so very different although the same age and we can see their

different "breeds" which she says is fascinating as they have such set ways.

In April 1963 I appeared to Mrs Millward as:

> ... very robust, enjoyed attending church every Sunday, had interests in painting, Art, everything in bright colours, music, jigsaws and outdoor games. Personality: loveable, full of vitality, noisy, all outward show, airy fairy, emotional and mercurial.
>
> Willson was laughing at the antics of the baby; he has a delightful sense of humour. He looked fit and strong and has a most attractive smile. He did look very tidy and quite clean. He was trying to pull along a truck and I watched him become very angry when he found it wouldn't work and was on the point of flying into a real rage and picked it up with the intention of throwing it across the path but one of the boys grabbed it and showed Willson how to work it and at once he was all smiles again, and I felt he needs a patient "Mum".
>
> Mrs Millward, along with another welfare officer called Miss Howe, paid a visit to the foster home in August 1963. Unbeknown to both officers, the effete Martin had recently, while being cuddled, whispered into Mrs Collier's ear that he was indeed overawed and fearful of this boisterous rival competing with him daily for her affections. "Willson's a real golliwog, he is. He's not nice, and he scares me at night!" This era was the tail end of the British Empire and the time of much venerated author Enid Blyton (1897–1968), whose novels made her one of the most popular children's writers ever. Blyton's golliwog characters – akin to America's Jim Crow, black-faced Daddy Rice caricatures – were often

childishly whimsical yet equally villainous, churlish fibbers and darkly impish fellows.

Miss Howe later wrote:

> Willson is a most attractive coloured boy with an appealing mischievous smile, quite frank and friendly but a wee bit shy with any strangers; he was playing outside with Martin and a few other local children when we arrived.
>
> Foster mother, Mrs Collier, had changed remarkably little since I saw her about six years ago. A calm, motherly, understanding person who one would expect to make a child feel secure if anyone could, but in discussing Willson I did sense a concern, possibly even fear, that he might get beyond them. Mrs Collier asked if we did not think that he might need more discipline that they could not give as he got older. I think Mrs Millward and I both felt that there was just a hint of trepidation that this coloured lad might become too much for them in his teens. We stressed that consistent firm but loving handling is what is required.
>
> At a first meeting Willson strikes one as a perfectly natural child but we were enumerating his various habits and were concerned to find that it adds up to a rather disturbed picture. He is extremely destructive of his clothing, even abnormally so, and he is very greedy of food. He seems unable to tell the truth, he cannot concentrate on anything for long at a time and is also very destructive of his toys.
>
> Although Martin and Willson get on very well together they are rather close in age perhaps and, as Martin is so very secure in this foster home, we both wondered whether Willson's disturbance is not perhaps an expression of his still very much

feeling a newcomer as well as a legacy from his insecure past.

In September 1963 I was "growing awfully tall, had very strong teeth and walked well, almost with a swagger". The welfare official's tentative suggestions to take me away from the Colliers due to my misbehaviour and perceived menace were to become more concrete plans. Mrs Millward reported to Miss Howe of her September visit and the final straw:

> I called to see this home this week end and the foster mother was exceedingly upset and said that it was not her wish that Willson should go but that her husband was adamant. Mr Collier has been cross for some time about Willson's behaviour and feels strongly that he is not responding to the love and affection that he is receiving, and he cannot tolerate it any longer.
>
> Apparently two weeks ago they were entertaining a few relatives at a party in their home when her son went to peep at the two boys asleep in their bedroom and he then discovered that Willson was missing from his bed. After an indoor search lasting for a long time which resulted in Mrs Collier becoming ill family members, believing some terrible fate such as abduction had befallen the boy, decided to call the police but at that precise moment Willson was discovered lying across two chairs beneath the dining room table concealed by the overhanging tablecloth. The sense of relief was too much for the foster mother who broke down, and the foster father later told the family that this had to come to an end; Willson must go as he could not contemplate another distressing scene like this.
>
> I then had all Willson's faults relayed to me and when I told the foster mother they were the

actions of a very insecure little boy she could not accept this. Mrs Collier said that they loved Willson as much as Martin, in fact considered him more as they realised he needed greater affection owing to his past and because he has not had the security that Martin has had from an early age. I did feel unable to convey my thoughts to her as I know she feels that they have both done everything in their power for him. I do think that she would continue as his foster mother but her husband is afraid to do so. I have told her she will have to help us settle Willson for his future when a plan has been made for him.

I talked to Willson in her company as he had been told that I would be calling and they would tell me about the things that had happened. I found him a very truthful little boy and complimented the foster mother later on this as he always fibbed his way out of anything in the beginning. He told me that he wanted to stay where he was with Mr and Mrs Colliers and I did feel that too much had been said to him. Apparently Willson had been hungry so silently tiptoed downstairs to get some food and panicked, then hid, when he thought the Aunt would glimpse him and give him a telling off. He has just commenced soiling his bed and I impressed upon her that this was not bone idle laziness but a very great disturbance.

Willson told me that he is a very good boy at school and had a been awarded a gold star for his hand writing this week. I was unable to see Mr Collier this week but will visit again. In the meantime the foster mother will give him all the love she can and I left him laughing with other children at play and he waved goodbye holding Mrs Collier's arm – one would have said a very natural and happy picture.

I then called on Mrs Dodd, however she had gone to a Whist Drive but the boys, who were painting a birdcage, almost pounced on me and asked if I was thinking of bringing a new boy to live with them. I asked them if they would like a coloured boy and their reply was "Yes and we'd care for him 'cos he'd be dark". I told Maureen I would call again when her mother was in. I should like to know what you think about this possibility before I see Mrs Dodd.

chapter VI

*Do not forget the things your eyes have seen
or let them slip from your heart as long as you live.
Teach them to your children and your children's
children.*
—Deuteronomy 4: 9

M y vanishing act on the night of the family party, only
to be detected feasting hungrily on dry slices of bread
raided from the kitchen parlour, was indeed the breaking
point for the Colliers. Mrs Millward hastily arranged for
me to visit the Plymouth home of Mr and Mrs Dodd on 25
September 1963. The Dodd family was made up of Mr and
Mrs Dodd, their daughter Maureen, and her two children,
Ian and Anne, and another foster child called Dennis. The
Dodd household welcomed me, and the fleeting visit was
deemed satisfactory by welfare officials, who decided I
could be transferred to live there in one week's time. Mrs
Collier was informed on 27 September. She reportedly
could not be consoled and was distraught at my pending
departure. After all, I had been in her care for one year and
nine months.

On 2 October 1963 I was taken by St Mary's welfare
officers to live with the new foster parents. Roughly about
this time, my biological father, Garnett Willson (Billy)
Vimikh, quit his Harrods job for night shift work at a food
processing factory in West Kensington called Cadby
Hall so as to fulfil his long-held ambition to qualify as a
hairdresser. Billy had been enrolled for a couple of years

at the prestigious London Institute and Morris School of Hairdressing in Shaftsbury Avenue, near Piccadilly, and was soon to graduate.

Mrs Millward made one of her routine welfare visits at the year's end to the Dodds' house in the district of Leigham, Plymouth. Driving downhill she pulled to a stop on Plymbridge Road outside the foster home in her iconic 1963 bottle green Mini Cooper S. After locking the car, she daintily removed her fine black leather driving gloves as she approached their front door. The welfare officer was herself the grandmother of two girls aged six and eight, close in age to myself. She was a happily married, stoutly proportioned lady, always stylish and neatly groomed, and had driven that morning from the picturesque village of Newton St Cyres, Exeter, roughly thirty-five miles away, where she lived in a comfortable, detached cottage with whitewashed walls and a water reed, thatched roof common to many such West Country period properties. Typical of many affluent, middle class, career-minded English women in the swinging sixties, Mrs Millward preferred to look professional and smartly adorned. For welfare visits she always wore fashionable, knee-length, semi-fitted woollen suits, preferably coffee-coloured, blue or green, purchased from Dorothy Perkins. Her most favoured suits had collars trimmed with mink or beaver and matching fur hats that were complimented by a similarly toned three-quarter-length coat. After this December 1963, visit Mrs Millward concluded her report:

> Willson has settled down incredibly quickly in his new foster home and Dennis has taken him under his wing. He has his own bed but shares a room with Dennis and Ian Dodd. He has a vivid imagination and has told the older boys that where he lived previously huge rats used to run about over his bed at night. He has settled acceptably at Leigham Infants School and appears to be reading quite well. At times he tears his clothes

and the foster mother despairs of his footwear! The foster father says Willson talks incessantly to every member of the family except for himself; he gives Mr Dodd and the corner of the front room where he permanently sits a wide berth.

At the Dodds' I recommended weekly Christian worship at Sunday School in nearby St Jude's Church of England and come the new year continued attending Leigham Infants School where, in February 1964, the teacher recorded that:

He will not always try – has to be encouraged. He seems to have a chip on his shoulder.

Mrs Millward stated that:

Willson has been wetting the bed at nights and the foster mother had taken him to the Doctor. Mrs Dodd thinks that he should be circumcised but the Doctor does not consider this necessary. He has had spots again but they disappear for weeks and then return and Mrs Dodd now thinks it is "some form of acid" and she keeps an eye on his diet.

I was seven years old in June 1964 and the transcribed six-month review read:

The foster mother is a good manager. The foster father is on permanent sick-list and the foster mother does not work. The Welfare Officer says the foster father is definitely the boss, even though he may not at first appear to be.

There has been no family contact. Of maintenance payments; Willson's father's payments are clear to January 1964.

Leigham Infants School is very pleased with him. His teacher told the Welfare Officer that he was teased about his colour in the beginning, but he was soon up with his fists and could now hold his own. The teacher describes him as a typical little negro boy, rather cheeky, fond of jazz music and boxing.

Willson is still very destructive of his clothing and the foster mother cannot manage on the clothing allowance. He still picks at his pullovers and is extremely heavy on his shoes. He has settled into this foster home very well and has not mentioned his previous foster home for some time. He is an incredibly happy little boy, relaxed, boisterous, is very interested in nature study, well accepted into the foster family. The foster father says Willson looks at him and laughs, but does not say anything.

Mrs Millward's August 1964 report made reference to my continued progress at Leigham Infants School:

His reading is only average and yet his composition is very good - he had 22 out of 25, and for Dictation 26 out of 30. His Arithmetic is good as he had 23 out of 30 and 15 out of 20 for Mental Maths and his class teacher was most pleased with him.

Willson had been very thrilled as the foster mother and her daughter Maureen had taken them all out to various haunts and they were planning a picnic to Cornwall very soon. He is rather envious of Dennis who has been to Camp but we promised him that he would be able to go with the school when he was old enough. He has joined the Cubs - he says their base is a long way away but he thinks he will like them.

The foster mother's daughter says he has been using profane language but when I talked to Willson alone he denied this and said it was all the boys joking together but Maureen had told the foster mother and he alone had been blamed.

He seems less rough on his clothes now that it is summer but he always kicks out the toes of his shoes. Mrs Dodd spends twice as much on his footwear as she does on the other children but Willson told her he could not help climbing trees or kicking stones along the road.

The autumn school term of 1964 saw me move up into Leigham Junior School. Despite having had a bad cold and chill that winter, which would eventually require a tonsillectomy, and losing a tooth, I seemed very strong. Mrs Millward wrote:

Willson told me that he does not think he will like the new school as the Headmaster has instructed him that he must behave himself. The foster mother's daughter was full of complaints about him but I told her that she must give him a great deal of love as he had had frequent moves in his life and he had not felt secure like the other children here in this home. She complained that he was very rough again with his clothing and that, although her mum had knitted him a cardigan along with the rest, his was already in holes while the others were still good.

I had a long talk with the foster mother after this and she does realise that this little boy needs all the love and affection that she can give him, and she confessed that she gave him an extra special hug when others were not around.

Willson is very fond of Mrs Dodd's little granddaughter here who is quite a tomboy and in his own way seems to want to protect her. He told me he had great fun with the fireworks party last night. The foster mother says he is a real boy and is always climbing trees so no wonder his clothes are the worse for wear.

The stoked coals and chopped logs in the fireplace exuded a picture of much warmth on Saturday, 30 January 1965 as all adults and children in the Dodd household gathered before the television to watch the BBC's coverage of Sir Winston Churchill's state funeral. To the masses he was the heroic leader of victorious British forces in World War II. However, a few voices would never forgive nor forget his much earlier responsibility in World War I for the ill-conceived and ineptly led Dardanelles (Gallipoli) campaign in 1915. Mrs Millward had just conveyed her findings to her colleague Miss Howe:

Mrs Dodd sent for me last week. You will be sorry to hear that she was bedbound and feeling very ill. The doctor was called in on Monday and said that he considers she has ulcers and is in a pretty bad way, but will send her to hospital for observation. She now tells me that she had this trouble a long time ago but has managed to fight it all these years except for occasional bouts of sickness after eating certain foods. I told her that if she had to go into hospital for treatment that we could help with Willson, that we would care for him if she thought it necessary and also that Maureen wouldn't be able to manage or even Mr Dodd. I was surprised at Mrs Dodd's reaction, although on looking back I feel it was just Mrs Dodd being herself, who said to me "You certainly won't help by taking him away from here and what's more, he would not go." Willson then came up to Mrs Dodd's bedroom to ask if she required anything and she told me afterwards that Dennis, although he loved her very much was not awfully sympathetic when anybody was sick and apart from the morning kiss before he goes to school and his goodnight one, he doesn't seem bothered to see her much at other times. Willson on the other hand has been constantly going to her and asking her if she requires anything.

I then took Willson out in order to buy Mrs Dodd some fruit and it was on his orders that I purchased some black grapes as he informed me that apples and oranges were very ordinary for people who were poorly and confined to bed. During the time I was out with him I talked to him about his foster mother and he told me that he was very happy there but I think he does feel a little apprehensive in case anything should happen to take Mrs Dodd away from the house.

Later while I was in the house, and we had been talking about Willson going to the cubs, Mrs Dodd said he didn't go in the very dark evenings, and when I asked why Maureen told me because it was some distance away and Willson was frightened of the dark. As it was night while we were going shopping, I asked him about this and he said he didn't like going in the darkness because he had heard Maureen talking about thieves who come round the houses at night and therefore he was afraid. I wondered if this is one reason why he doesn't like going up to bed first although the foster mother has told me in the past that he is always ready to go upstairs and is fast asleep when the others go up to bed.

I promised to visit Mrs Dodd again early this coming week and shall report accordingly when I have done this. I did not tell her on this occasion that I would be bringing Mrs Woodward as I felt she was in a rather distressed state of mind and any mention of a change might not have been very welcome just at the moment. She asked me if she was admitted into hospital would I visit her and I promised to do this.

Of her visit in early February Mrs Millward wrote:

I called again yesterday and was very pleased to see that Mrs Dodd seemed to be much brighter in spirit although her physical condition remains the same. The doctor had been visiting her each day and is allowing her to go downstairs for a few hours daily. Naturally she will still have to attend the hospital for observation and x-rays. Maureen met me at the front door with the news that they had just received a letter from Freedom Fields Hospital requesting them to take Willson on Sunday for his tonsillectomy for which Mrs Dodd had had to wait a year. Maureen's little girl, Anne, who was playing near the kitchen came running through on hearing this news and started to cry saying "Oh it's not our Willson that has to go into hospital is it?" and that little scene told me quite a lot because it is very obvious that this little child is very fond of Willson, and I did gather that the whole family are very concerned because he has to be away from them for some days.

Mrs Dodd herself told me that she had made arrangements with her son, who has a car, to take Willson to Freedom Fields on Sunday. I am visiting this home again tomorrow and will take Willson on Sunday myself should these arrangements fall through but the foster mother, with her usual show of independence, informed me that she had told the doctor only that morning that she wanted to see Willson safely installed in the hospital. They had not told Willson then that he was going in on Sunday but I asked Mrs Dodd to have a quiet time with him in the evening and to explain to him so as to prepare him for going in the children's ward, and what would take place because I know Willson will be able to cope with this.

I then saw Willson, who had been playing with another boy on his skates, and immediately he rushed upstairs again to see how Gran (Mrs Dodd) was, to give her a big hug and to inform me that Gran had received ever such a lot of grapes, and some of them were bigger bunches than the ones I had brought last week. I shall of course be visiting Willson next week in hospital and also make arrangements with Mrs Dodd for his safe return home.

Mrs Millward's post-hospital report read:

Willson told me that he did not like school so much this term as his teacher had left and her replacement was very strict. She had already sent him to the Head Teacher who had been rather cross with him as he had been rude to one of the kitchen staff serving dinner. I find Willson very truthful at all times and he always owns up to any misdemeanour.

The foster mother has been ill for weeks and has been confined to bed. The Doctor has diagnosed ulcers and will send her to hospital for observation. Willson has been the one who has been most affected by her illness and has been the most helpful child here. Mrs Dodd says he seems apprehensive about her condition, and he no doubt feels quite insecure with the foster mother being in bed.

Willson went into hospital on 31 January and had the operation the following afternoon. I visited him in the morning and the Ward Sister said what a fine boy he was although he had been in a fight with one of the other small patients but he told the Sister that the boy had commenced the scrap first after calling Willson horrible names and he merely retaliated so she forgave him. He seemed fond of two girls awaiting the same operation and had learnt all about them in a very short time.

While I was there he read from a book lent to him by Sister and I was agreeably surprised to see how easily he can read, and from a strange book. He can build or do "look and say" with new words and I feel he can practically read anything if he will only persevere. Willson soon tired of reading and wanted to play – I can imagine he likes his own way very much and without doubt a certain firmness is required here although he does need a great deal of love.

I saw him at home after the operation and he said he enjoyed the hospital but was naughty once or twice and wouldn't do what the nurse told him. His throat was still rather sore and he had to see the Dr before returning to school.

The foster mother told me that he did not wet his bed at all during the stay in hospital and he is "good" at home except when he sneaks out to get a drink after he has been put to bed at night.

Mrs Millward explained in March 1965:

The current teacher reported to me that Willson had been somewhat naughty this term as his new teacher last term in the new school had left at Christmas thus making yet another change for him and she thinks that he has had to take so many in his short life. She says he can do some very good work if he will only put his mind to it and settle down. She thinks that he feels he is different but there is one other coloured child in this school and he will be able to accept his colour. She thinks Willson requires firm handling but also a great deal of love, and she confided that she can appreciate his position as she was an orphan herself and often moved around like some parcel without any real roots.

The June 1965 report read:

The foster mother says he has been fighting quite a lot with some of the local boys and on one occasion rushed indoors in an uncontrollable rage to get a knife to one of the boys but she checked his conduct and told him that this was not the attitude to adopt. Mrs Dodd counselled him "Sticks and stones will break your bones but names will never ..." She feels that Willson cannot accept the fact that he is very often in the wrong and not others.

On this visit he spoke very nervously and was not very interested in conversation but kept going off on a tangent to something else. He told us that he was given the cane once again by the Head Teacher for throwing stones but he seemed more concerned with the Head's manner when he was in the process of being caned and told us, with an amused smile, that the Head Teacher always closed his eyes when he used the cane on him.

Willson is now a member of the choir and enjoys this very much. He has commenced going to the Cubs again and I think is very keen if only he will take an interest in them. He is swimming in the baths at school and likes this, and we think he will be very proficient. The foster mother was going to take the boys on the moors next week if it will be fine.

Mrs Woodward came with me on this visit to meet all the family.

Mrs Millward wrote to Miss Howe in July:

> I had an occasion to call at this foster home today. As a result of Mrs Dodd still insisting to the Doctor that all was not "quite right with Willson's bed wetting" she had received a letter from the hospital stating he would receive an examination tomorrow. She told me the Doctor said they would probably "telescope" the bladder.
>
> I telephoned Mrs Woodward when I arrived home tonight as I introduced her in May and she would be making the routine visit in early August but she asked me to continue visiting at present and so I will call in again today and report accordingly.

At Leigham Junior School I continued to make good progress in every subject with all teachers very pleased with my change in attitude to work in the classroom and general behaviour. Following the tonsillectomy, I succumbed to a further throat infection, caught the chicken pox, and my enuresis was still a problem. Mrs Millward's August review went on:

> He had two days in hospital recently as he still wets the bed at times although the foster mother says she thinks it might be laziness. The Ward Sister told her there was a little sediment in his water which would be the "cause of the dribbling".
>
> Willson has been much happier in his home and is less tense. I was very pleased to hear the foster mother defend him the other week when she was describing how Alan – the 16 year old newcomer – had called Willson a "Gorilla" and Mrs Dodd said "Don't you call my Willson names." and the "my" spoke volumes to me as I thought that Mrs Dodd would never get around to this form

of endearment towards Willson, and it has been very noticeable when she has been discussing the boy with other members of her family.

He is very fond of Ian Dodd and they were busy making a tent together in the back garden and were sleeping in it that evening. He had also been fishing on Plymouth Hoe with Ian, and Ian had taken and collected him from the cubs the previous week.

Mrs Millward had no inclination, never mentioned in her detailed reports, that my play with Ian often meant hours upon hours, sometimes a whole day from dawn to dusk (at least that's how I remembered it), away from the Dodd household. Such occasions saw us ferret around in nearby secluded forests and even explore the dangerous coastal areas near the Hoe in pursuit of our hobby, ornithology. The study of birds was a passion of Ian and myself, but something never spoken of and strangely kept secret, as if taboo, from the enquiring Mrs Millward. During the colder winter months indoors, we would spend hours drawing pictures of our favourite birds from books, noting the adult male or female plumage, colour and pattern of their eggs, their food sources, habitat, and so on.

With the emergence of springtime, our adventures led us into the nearby countryside in pursuit of birds' eggs – a pastime now illegal. The eggs and even the chicks of various English birdlife we considered fair game. Feathered inhabitants of nearby hedgerows and woodland, from linnets, chaffinches, tree creepers, and wrens to sparrows, blackbirds, and song thrushes fell prey to our childish destruction. Royal Society for the Protection of Birds (RSPB) supporters would have been up in arms had they witnessed such destructive behaviour.

Being the more accomplished climber, and physically far smaller than Ian, I was nimble enough, coupled with a degree of recklessness, to climb the tallest, most densely foliaged trees or scale rocky nooks and crannies for treasured eggs. Very often the only way to retrieve an egg from a nest without cracking it, especially having scaled a height, entailed placing it safely in one's mouth while triumphantly descending to safe ground. Newly laid eggs are noticeably more buoyant in water than an egg with the weight of a growing chick's embryo therein, and once back at the house, we would carefully prick either end of the egg with a pin so as to blow out the yolk. Suffice to say, many plundered nests and eggs were destroyed as we mastered this skill. In the garden shed, our collection of blown eggs was displayed in cardboard boxes on top of a layer of sawdust, neatly labelled with details of the bird species the egg was from.

Mrs Millward continued:

> The foster father says that the child is still as cheeky as ever and quite a young rip.

The foster father, Mr Dodd, was well into his dotage and, to my childish imagination, appeared forever cemented to his armchair. Day after day Dodd sat immobile apart from piercing, bluish green eyes whose alert gaze tracked my every movement whenever I entered the sparsely furnished front room. With a large head and pudgy face reminiscent of Coronation Street character Albert Tatlock, Dodd's double chin fused with a neck of extraordinary proportions that sat upon broad shoulders. In his prime he had been a bull of a man. Always wearing a grandad shirt soiled by the week's food stains, his bloated, engorged belly was covered by well-worn greasy trousers he was unable to fasten at the waist, hitched up to his swollen crotch by braces. I would often gawk at the huge balloon-like swelling in Mr Dodd's groin region, a debilitating ailment that was in fact an inguinal hernia, hence his indolence.

Mrs Millward's transcription went on:

> He still tears his clothes but says he doesn't do any more climbing. Willson looked very fit and well and is quite self assured. I was pleased to see how he could hold his own with John, a child previously fostered by the Dodds, who was here on holiday.
>
> There has been no present contact with either the putative father or birth mother. The putative father's maintenance is clear to 31/03/65 and is paid through Isleworth Magistrates Court. The foster mother knows something of the history. Willson told nurses in the hospital that his parents are dead and that the foster mother is "Mum". He has made no enquiries re; his colour yet but shows interest in coloured babies.
>
> Future plans and action needs to commence with a letter to the Area Office re: arranging for a Welfare Officer to trace the putative father, make tactful enquiries and visit him if it seems wise.

Sometime during 1964, Billy found decent paid employment at Fulham Power Station, just a short walk north across Wandsworth Bridge, which was a stone's throw from his Alma Road address. With its straight line of four cream-coloured, towering concrete chimneys, this huge industrial complex sat on the bank of the Thames in a part of Fulham known as Sands End. Originally built in 1901, it was a major employer in South West London, and was expanded when the Central Electricity Generating Board (CEGB) opened the B station in 1936. Billy would work a rotating weekly shift pattern of mornings, afternoons, and then nights, and there was always ample overtime available. Billy was ever industrious, and these hours enabled him to also cut hair in a popular West Indian Barbershop called Rico's Hairdressing Salon on Clapham High Street.

Fulham Power Station Power was not to be confused with the Lots Road Power Station located a mile further down river in the royal borough of Kensington and Chelsea. In the streets spreading northwards from the gates of the Fulham station, and on the southern, Wandsworth side of the river, were row upon row of compact Victorian terraced properties whose working class occupants had endearing nicknames for that which most dominated their daily vista: "the Four Sisters" or "Matthew, Mark, Luke, and John". Such lovely, benign terms for industrial sites that for decades spewed out upon local inhabitants lung-damaging smoke, the fine dust particles of which would ruin many a diligent housewife's laundry, hung out to dry on clothes lines in their tiny back gardens.

Miss Howe wrote a letter to St Mary's Children's Charity's Thames area office dated 23 August 1965, stating:

> Billy Vimikh makes regular child maintenance payments towards Willson's keep via the Magistrates Court in Isleworth. A Mr Smith is the Collecting Officer for the Court and he forwards [**sic**] the money on to us.
>
> The question has arisen at the last review on this child (copy enclosed) as to whether it might be advisable to establish at least a first contact with the putative father. With this in mind, we would be grateful if you could ask a Welfare Officer to call and see Mr Smith and ascertain the present circumstances of the putative father. It may be, of course, that Mr Smith will not divulge any information but it is felt that an approach should at least be made. If the Welfare Officer obtains the address of the putative father from Mr Smith and also feels, in the light of any information which may be given, that a visit to the putative father is wise and practicable, we would be glad if a tentative contact could be established.

On 24 September 1965, Miss Howe received the following reply from a Mrs Lovell:

I have been given Mr Vimikh's address which is 21, Halmer Road, Wandsworth, London, S.W.18. The Collecting Officer was not able to give me any other information at all, as Mr Vimikh has always paid very regularly, and they have never had any cause to seek him out, and thus know nothing at all of his present circumstances.

I shall wait to hear from you as to whether it is felt it would be wise to make an approach to Mr Vimikh without knowing anything of his circumstances; and I would be glad to contact him if you wish.

Mrs Millward reported on her November 1965 visit to the Dodd's house:

Willson was out with Ian Dodd as they were collecting for the Guy and had already constructed the beginnings of a very fine bonfire across the road ready for Guy Fawkes night on the 5th.

He had been in trouble at school because he had cheeked the Games Master that very afternoon but Willson said that this teacher did not make him miss football as he was one of the team's best players and they had too much to lose as it was. The boy is reading very well and his spelling is excellent. I observed him trying to teach Ian Dodd to read but he got impatient with him and commenced showing off. The foster mother told him not to be such a big head, to which he replied, while smiling brightly at his own cleverness, "Well I've cause to because he's much older than me."

The home was very cosy and full of warmth and there was a very special high tea in preparation for all the family. Mr Dodd was not well, looked very pale and said he had had chest trouble but hoped he wouldn't have to go to bed.

Willson was chosen to go to Ballads Centre on Saturday to compete in a swimming Gala. He is very good at this. He is also very fond of football and is always chosen to play a match.

The choir has had to be suspended at present at St Jude's Church as not enough children were interested in applying for the audition. The boys said the Vicar is trying again after Christmas.

I found him relaxed on this visit and quite cheeky towards the foster father.

In early December Miss Howe responded to Mrs Lovell's September letter:

It is felt that it would be helpful if you could make a very tentative visit to Willson's father, Mr Garnett Willson Vimikh domiciled at 21, Halmer Road, Wandsworth, S.W.6, to give him news of Willson if an opportunity should arise and to get an up to date picture of the father's present circumstances. We are not, of course, aware as to whether his wife knows of Willson's existence. We would not wish Mr Vimikh to feel that he had to do anything at this particular juncture, but no doubt a Christmas card or some gesture of that nature would please Willson and not be amiss.

Willson is now nearly nine. He leads a very active life in his foster home with plenty of outside activities – Cubs, fishing, swimming, and camping in the garden at night in the summer. He is doing quite well at school and has been described by the teacher as a reliable, helpful member of his class who has an angelic voice – Willson recently sang solo the hymn "Morning has Broken" by Eleanor Farjeon in school assembly. His last school report showed good average results and gave the impression of an alert and enthusiastic pupil. There are two other foster children living in this foster home. In general, Willson seems a well adjusted, normally active and happy boy according to present reports.

On 17 January 1966, Mrs Lovell updated Miss Howe:

I am sorry to be so long in replying to your last letter dated 6 December, but I had some difficulty in contacting Mr Vimikh due to an error of address – he resides at Alma Road not Halmer Road.

Mr Vimikh called to see me by appointment this morning. He appears to be a pleasant person with a boyish cheerful face. He wears his hair cut very short and on the whole presents a very neat exterior. Until six months ago he and a friend shared a hairdressing business in Shepherds Bush, but he says he let this go as the friend was inclined to be lazy and things were not going too well. Now he is employed in some form of engineering and does shift work. His time off varies from 1 or 2 days per week. Mr Vimikh comes from Antigua and has been in England since 1954. He has never been home since, and tells me that his mother is now quite ill.

About one year ago Mr Vimikh married a Jamaican girl who has been in this country five years. She is employed as a dress machinist. She knows about Willson, and Mr Vimikh says that they both feel they would like to have Willson come to live with them one day. His wife is herself barren and unable to have any children. However, they are not thinking of having him before they have larger accommodation – at present they are in a one bedroom flat. Financially they could get a larger place now, but intend to continue on as they are and save something for a while.

How much of these thoughts of having Willson have been in their minds for the past year, or if they are prompted by the arrival of my letter, I do not know. I gave Mr Vimikh up to date news of Willson, telling him that he was in a foster home in Devon. I said we were not asking or expecting him to do anything, but that we just wanted to know his feelings concerning Willson; also pointing out that Willson was without any family contacts, and we felt that such contact might be good for him. As he expressed a desire to have Willson eventually, I said, should this come about, it would require his getting to know Willson again and getting Willson used to him and his wife. He didn't seem too convinced of the point of this, and feels that Willson would of course fit in naturally and easy with their pattern of life; yet I got the impression that he would cooperate with us to a certain extent with gradual visiting if things did come to restoration. He has the usual casual attitude of the West Indian parent, that Willson would be able to look after himself after school and would not mind being on his own until he and his wife were home from work. I did point out that legally his hold on Willson was nil, and said that I didn't know just what the position was with regard to his eventually having the boy.

Mr Vimikh feels that Devon is a long way off, but certainly talked as though he would be willing to visit Willson there. He did ask how the foster parents felt and if they would object to his writing or visiting? I told him that I would discuss the matter more thoroughly with you now that we know his feelings, and would be getting in touch with him and his wife again.

The last contact Mr Vimikh had with Willson was when he was with the maternal grandparents. Since then he has had no news of them or the mother. (Have we?) He told me that he was engaged to a girl after that, but it fell through – and the general impression given is that if he had a wife before this time, he would have considered having Willson also.

Miss Howe replied in the second week of February 1966:

Dear Mrs Lovell,

I have now had a discussion with Mrs Millward, Willson's Welfare Officer, about the possibility of contact being made between Willson, his putative father and his putative father's wife.

I see from your report that Mr Vimikh said that the last contact he had had with Willson, was when Willson was with the maternal grandparents. I think Mr Vimikh's memory is a bit at fault here as he did visit Willson twice in 1961 when he was at Tiny Tots Palace. According to a memo in the file, he visited Willson twice briefly in the early part of that year, the second time being in April. Mrs Duncan, the Superintendent of Tiny Tots Palace, said that both visits were flying affairs of about one hour in which Mr Vimikh said hello to Willson, cut his hair and departed! Mr Vimikh has, however, faithfully sent his maintenance through the years. I think the time Mr Vimikh was referring to, was when he saw Willson with the maternal grandparents, which must have been during the brief disastrous restoration, prior to 1959, when he went to his mother, Mrs Molly Gardener, at the home of the maternal grandparents. It could be, of course, that Mr Vimikh's casual attitude that you describe, is the reason for his apparent inability to sustain contact with Willson through the years.

I am encouraged by the fact that Mr Vimikh is now married and that his wife knows about Willson, although as you say, we have yet to know exactly how deep the present interest will go. Mrs Millward and I feel, therefore, that if you could possibly find time to visit Mr and Mrs Vimikh quite shortly and suggest that they should send Willson a Birthday Card in the first instance, this would be a good beginning. If this can reach the office by 12 or 13 February, Mrs Millward will make a point of taking it personally to Willson. Mrs Millward says that Willson does mention his mother from time to time, but it is quite impossible to know whether he is talking about his foster mother (past or present) or his biological mother. If the Birthday Card materialises, Mrs Millward will be able to use it as a means of communicating with Willson about his father.

Mrs Millward has recently seen Willson's Headmaster again and he considers that he is of very good average intelligence. Mrs Millward thinks that this is certainly no underestimate. Willson has recently been seen by a specialist on account of persistent enuresis, but no physical reason had been found. We hope very much that Mr Vimikh will be willing to cooperate in this awfully small way, so that Mrs Millward may have an opportunity of helping Willson to talk about his background.

chapter VII

No Viet Cong ever called me nigger.
Protesting black US servicemen on
returning home from Vietnam (1967)

In March 1966, Mrs Howe sat at her desk, completing the final draft of my six-month review in which she described the poor physical health of my housebound foster father, Mr Dodd. He had recently suffered a slight stroke, and for many weeks had been very poorly with chest and stomach problems but had somewhat recovered. Mrs Dodd's health was to some extent improved, though she was still under the doctor. Mrs Howe described my reaction to recent correspondence from Billy:

> Willson was understandably rather overawed by the birthday card from his putative father and asked "Is he coloured?" and when told "Yes" exclaimed excitedly "Oh, good show!" He then asked where his father lived and was told a town in London called Wandsworth. Mrs Dodd suggested that he write a letter to his father and Willson said "Yes, if you'll help". The Welfare Officer told Willson that his father's wife was the same colour. The foster mother has accepted this contact happily. He ran out to play quite naturally after this.

Mrs Howe then wrote to Mrs Lovell in London:

When Willson was seen by the specialist about his enuresis, it was felt that his foster home was not meeting his needs and the specialist then wrote to the Plymouth Children's Department not having realised at the time that the boy was in our care. Mrs Millward has now discussed the whole situation with the specialist. Mrs Millward does feel, however, that Willson's level of intelligence is probably higher than that of the foster home and other members of the household, apart from Dennis. To put you a little more fully in the picture of this rather "mixed bag" I should explain that Mr and Mrs Dodd, though humble, are the type of accepting people one turns to in emergencies.

They were first accepted as foster parents for John, now in his twenties, and Dennis, still there, who were placed with them by their respective mothers. They were received into full care and left with the Dodds on boarding out terms. Maureen Dodd is Mr and Mrs Dodd's youngest daughter and Ian and Anne are her two children. They are fairly normal children, as far as can be seen, and the home's maternal standard of care is good. Alan, aged 17, is an After Care boy placed there temporarily in an emergency when his other lodgings broke down, who has stayed on. Michael is the lodger of such long standing that he passes almost unnoticed, but he occupies a single room and seems to cause no trouble.

Willson was placed in this outwardly strange medley when his other foster home in Plymouth broke down, in part because we had no other suggestion to make at the time but also partly because we felt that Mrs Dodd's maternal warmth would help the boy. I feel that the placement has been justified and Willson has been helped by his acceptance into this family group, but I agree with Mrs Millward that he will probably grow beyond it in the not too distant future and we shall have to give some serious thought to any further move. If it appeared that there was likely to be sustained contact now with his own father, I think this would be of enormous value to Willson, but it would be pretty disastrous for the child if Mr Vimikh started off in a burst of enthusism and then let it drop, so anything you can do to interpret and clarify things would be most welcome.

That April in London Miss J. Sanders, a welfare officer, visited Billy's home on Alma Road and reported back to Miss Howe:

I have been to call on Mr Garnett Vimikh, Willson's father as you requested. I found him a very pleasant man, neatly dressed and clean. He seems genuinely interested in Willson, and re-affirmed his desire to have Willson home with him. He has discussed this with his wife and she is in agreement with him.

Unfortunately I did not meet Mrs Vimikh as she was at work when I called. She is a dressmaker. Their flat was beautifully fresh and tidy, at least the part of it I saw, but judging by what I witnessed I should think the rest was as nicely kept. The lounge was very tastefully decorated and furnished. I see in Mrs Lovell's report she says they had a one room flat but Mr Vimikh tells me they have now three rooms, and are thinking of buying the flat.

I told Mr Vimikh that Willson was pleased with his birthday card. Mr Vimikh asked if Willson could possibly write back to him. I explained to him that if he was going to take an interest in Willson it would have to be constant otherwise it would do more harm than good. I think he understood this and remains keen to have contact with Willson.

As it is now four months since Mrs Lovell first saw Mr Vimikh and he still feels the same way about getting in touch with Willson perhaps there are grounds for thinking he means what he says.

I wonder if at this stage you would like me to arrange to see Mrs Vimikh to ascertain what her reaction is given that so far we have only got Mr Vimikh's word for it that she is in agreement.

Mrs Millward's May 1966 commentary read:

Willson has been very pleased to hear that his father has been enquiring about him. He was also thrilled to receive his birthday card from Mr Vimikh and wanted to write and thank him for it, and indeed made two attempts after asking the foster mother for her help and support.

He remains extremely hard on his clothes and in particular his shoes, but Mrs Dodd does accept that he is growing rapidly and also that he is such an energetically robust boy. At times when he is reproved he cries very easily but on other occasions he can be extremely arrogant and defy both of the foster parents. Strangely enough it is Dennis and the Lodger who tell me in front of the foster parents that he is quite a good all rounder on the whole, and Mrs Dodd has to laughingly agree.

Last week he went to Plymouth Zoo with the Church outing and was seen on the Westward Television programme feeding the monkeys. Willson says that the rhinoceros was his favourite as it reminded him of somebody – the portly Mr Dodd I guessed but he would not say who!

At present he is better about his nocturnal enuresis and the foster mother did wonder if it were because the weather had become warmer. She is trying to cure it herself and she is working on her own theory about this and will let me know the results. I rather think she is showing him more love than the others especially now that she feels she has to help him with what might be an important contact with his father.

Willson has won three further certificates for sports, for "roll racing", swimming and the long jump. Nobody seems to know what the first one means. He seems to be very much happier when talking about school and, surprisingly, still has been able to keep clear of the cane.

Meanwhile Miss Sanders had met up with Mrs Vimikh in early June 1966 and described their meeting for Mrs Howe:

I found her a most affable person. She is in full agreement with her husband over Willson. They would love to have him live at home with them.

Mr Vimikh finds it difficult to understand why things are moving so slowly and I tried to explain that in these matters one could not rush, and that it would also take time for Willson to get to know his father again. Mr Vimikh feels that as it is merely four years since he saw Willson the boy should remember him. I tried to explain that although four years may not seem long to an adult, to Willson it is half his life. Mrs Vimikh understood this and said that like all men Mr Vimikh had far too little patience and may well not understand why he could not have Willson now.

Mr Vimikh also feels a tad bitter because he has paid maintenance for so long, and yet the boy's mother (Molly) might just take Willson if she so wished, as I believe she did on one occasion. He asked how long it would take to adopt a child, as he thinks that this would be more easily accomplished than getting his own son back. I told him that this also takes a long time.

I liked this couple very much and feel sure that Willson would have a good home with them. I have suggested to Mr Vimikh that he write to Willson and send the letter to your office.

If you feel that a meeting between Mr and Mrs Vimikh and Willson would be a good idea, I would be especially pleased to help in any way. As it is such a long way to Devon perhaps a meeting place could be arranged half way between here and Plymouth. I would be very pleased to help with transport.

Mrs Vimikh, who works as a dressmaker, told me that she was prepared to work part-time should Willson go to live with them. She seems to be a very sensible woman and I think quite intelligent. She appreciates the difficulties regarding Willson's future more readily than her husband.

I wonder if Willson could perhaps write to Mr and Mrs Vimikh so that they would have a more tangible sign of contact with Willson. I feel that if this contact is to be established something should be done fairly soon, as we have been in touch with Mr Vimikh now since January and seem to have made so little progress towards this end. I am concerned that Mr Vimikh may become exasperated with the slowness of these things and wash his hands of the whole affair and this would be a great shame for all concerned.

I do hope that I haven't been too gushing about this young couple, but I really was most impressed by them.

I was encouraged to write to my father. Just over a fortnight passed when Miss Sanders recounted:

> I delivered Willson's letter personally the other evening and found Victoria Vimikh in the house alone. I was glad of the chance of seeing her alone so that I could ascertain if she really was as keen as her husband to have Willson live with them. I am very pleased to say that she is. I feel that she has definitely a mind of her own and is not just going along with her husband's wishes.
>
> Mrs Vimikh was thrilled with the correspondence from Willson as much for the letter itself as for the anticipated pleasure it would give Mr Vimikh when he saw it. She told me that they had only been discussing Willson that very morning over breakfast and she told her husband that everything would turn out well
>
> I was so pleased to hear that Mr Vimikh had written to Willson and sent a photograph, and hopefully now he will really think that things are moving and not feel so despondent. I am sure that Mrs Vimikh will be able to convince him of the need for patience in this matter as she strikes me as being a woman of good sense.
>
> I look forward to hearing from you regarding the plans for meeting with Willson and Mr and Mrs Vimikh.

June turned to July and still no concrete plans were in place. St Mary's officials made attempts to trace my mother, Molly, at her last known address in Chertsey, Surrey because she had signed the original agreement form back in January 1959 handing me back again into their care. The charity desperately sought out her consent to give legality to their plans for me to be placed with my now married father and his wife Victoria. Now, however, seven years later, it was no real surprise to learn that Molly had vanished without a trace, her whereabouts unknown.

The ever-present figure of Mrs Millward paid the Dodds an August visit. She found:

> The household was the same as normal, with everyone engrossed in their own activities, and it presented the usual "rough cosy" picture. All the children had been to the swimming pool and Ian Dodd had told the foster father that "our Willson" was the very best swimmer and had been praised by everybody present. Willson was awfully pleased with this praise and told Ian to go with him to buy an ice cream.
>
> The foster mother said that he had been a little better lately and she had only one or two wet beds but he remained extremely heavy on his clothes, although he is well aware how to take care of them as he was very careful to tell her to keep his new clothes in a safe place for his proposed visit to London.
>
> Willson borrows Dennis' ties at times which he allows now as he remarked that at least the child returns them in good condition.
>
> We had a further talk about the forthcoming visit to London and he asked numerous questions about his father and his wife again. He wants to come home to the Dodds after the weekend however, and said we should make other arrangements for the next holiday if he enjoyed this meeting his father.
>
> He seemed much more relaxed on this visit and I did feel that he is aware that he may now have two homes to go to and that he can choose. He told the foster mother in front of me, "Don't worry, I shall be back soon." Mr Dodd says he is quite "cheeky and can be very argumentative",

but Willson just laughed and then went happily out to play.

The September welfare visit to the Dodds reported that I had received the cane for cheeking teachers. Then on 14 October 1966, Miss Sanders wrote to Miss Howe:

I think it would be very beneficial for Willson to spend his half term with Mr and Mrs Vimikh. They really enjoyed the last meeting with Willson and are looking forward to their next meeting. As I think I have told you before, Mr and Mrs Vimikh occupy the ground floor of the house. There is a good size lounge, a smaller bedroom with a double bed, and a large kitchen, bathroom and outside toilet beyond this. In the lounge there is a sizeable settee where Willson could sleep, but Mrs Vimikh said that they were going to get a folding bed if Willson was going to be a frequent visitor. I think the settee would be quite adequate for a night or two – it is one of the long, fairly modern types. If you are not happy about Willson sleeping on the settee, I could perhaps borrow a camp bed from somewhere for the weekend.

In the flat upstairs there is a lad who is about 10 years old and from my observations of him he is a very nice boy, so Willson would have some company to play with.

Mr Vimikh told me that so far they have not heard from Willson, thanking them for his new Raleigh bicycle, and I wonder if he could write to them. They are not upset about this really but would like to hear from him. As Mr Vimikh said, perhaps he has been very busy learning to ride, and has not had time to think about writing letters.

If Mrs Millward is coming to London by train I would be happy to meet her when she arrives at Paddington Station and take her and Willson to

Mr and Mrs Vimikh's. When things are arranged I can let the Vimikh's know what time to expect us.

I am looking forward to meeting both Mrs Millward and Willson.

On 3 November 1966, Mrs Millward's testimony to Miss Howe read:

As arranged I collected Willson for the journey up to London on Friday 28 October to stay with his father and step mother until Monday morning, 31, this being his half term from school.

I had discussed the plan with his foster mother who told me a few days previously that while Willson agreed to this visit, he wanted to return to Plymouth before commencing school so that he would be able to enjoy riding his new bicycle. He also told me that he hoped he would be back before Bonfire night.

Mrs Dodd brought him to the station and saw us off on our trip to London, and I was very touched by his parting gesture to her. He hugged and kissed her rather warmly and told her not to fret as he would be back very soon. When we boarded the train Willson said that he wished his foster mother could have journeyed with us and met his father and step mother, as he was sure that they would have all liked each other.

We had a most interesting train journey, being entertained by two sailors and a WREN who were seated in our carriage. Willson was extraordinarily outgoing, loquacious, chattering confidently with them throughout, laughing at their jokes, and joining in singing their sea shanties. I was quite surprised to find how many of these songs he knew – Blow the Man Down and Drunken Sailor among them – clapping in time, and what an awfully fine voice he had. Once the enlisted trio alighted at Taunton Willson couldn't sit still for very long – he was constantly out in the corridor, on the toilet, and wanting to go to the buffet for lemonade, and thoughtfully brought me a drink along with his from pocket money that his foster mother had given him before his departure. He thoroughly enjoyed having tea on the train and nattered freely with a young couple sitting opposite to us.

We were met at Paddington Station by Miss Sanders who drove us to Wandsworth where the Vimikh's live. Willson soon made himself at home again, and he was joined by Raphael, the boy who lived in the flat upstairs, who had been eagerly awaiting his arrival. Both boys quickly made friends again and commenced playing together. Mr Vimikh was not yet home from work, but the stepmother gave us a very warm welcome, and after agreeing arrangements for our return journey Miss Sanders and I left their home.

Miss Sanders and I then deliberated on the possible future with his parents. She feels that the Vimikhs want Willson to stay and live with them especially if this visit proves successful. Miss Sanders thinks that they would be very good parents, Mrs Vimikh in particular as she seems to know and understand the needs of this boy and has carefully thought about his future with them and all that this implies.

I met both parents on the Monday morning and we discussed the visit before leaving. They all appeared to have enjoyed themselves over the weekend. Both parents are convinced that Willson's place is now with them and they will do all they can to make him happy and secure, and to let him feel that he is among his own kindred although I did remind them that he had a mother. They are now going to write to ask if he may come for a vacation with them at Christmas and perhaps stay with them after that. Miss Sanders and I did wonder for a time whether they should become foster parents for us for Willson, and I think this might be the best solution.

On the return journey Willson described in full detail his weekend in Wandsworth. He said he did not care for the meals that his stepmother provided but said if he was told it was West Indian food he supposed he simply would have to get used to it, although he enjoyed a chicken dinner on Saturday. On Saturday afternoon when his father returned to work a late shift he and Mrs Vimikh went shopping which he thoroughly enjoyed especially as she bought him a new pale grey pullover and jeans so that he could play in the local park. Later he played with Raphael on Wandsworth Common, and that evening went to the cinema with Victoria to watch "Fantastic Voyage", a science fiction adventure about a shrunken submarine injected into the human bloodstream.

On the Sunday morning he went for a walk with Raphael and afterwards in the early afternoon with both parents, and then later in the evening played games. He confided to me that he did not like his father's remarks about the length of his hair of which he is quite proud. Mr Vimikh apparently told him that when he eventually goes to live in Wandsworth he would cut it short like his own, and Willson took exception to this, such is his pride in his own dark curly hair, and did not like his father's style.

He is not too sure, he says, whether he will stay in Wandsworth after Christmas as he would like to pass the Eleven Plus examinations at Leigham Junior school and then go on to the senior school. This observation I found most intriguing as he had already been in hot water twice this term and as a result on each occasion was caned by the Headmaster. Willson also said that he must be able to ride his bike properly before he goes to live in Wandsworth as there appears to be more space than in Plymouth. He did not seem unduly worried about his return to his foster mother and warmly greeted her when she came to meet us at the station. He told her that he enjoyed himself and would like to go and visit his father again when he next had a holiday.

Mrs Vimikh did tell me that she thought he was a very typical sporty boy, who needed a lot of love but also that one had to be quite firm with him. I think she found that he would be very hard on his clothing, and I told her that the foster mother had found this also.

It will be very interesting to hear from Miss Sanders how the Vimikh's feel about future visits and the possibility of Willson perhaps coming to live with them at some stage.

Miss Howe's letter on 25 November 1966 to Miss Sanders reflected upon the legal position:

I am sorry at what may seem rather a delay in writing to you further about the plans for Willson. We have been considering it in the office here and I have today discussed the scenario with our Regional Executive Officer, Miss Hodges. The consensus is as follows: -

Our original Agreement was made with Willson's mother but she has failed to maintain contact and, although we have visited her last known address, we have not been able to ascertain her present whereabouts. At the time of Willson's 1959 re-admission, Mrs Gardener was agreeable for Mr Vimikh to keep in touch.

We think that if Mr Vimikh now wants to take full responsibility of Willson he can be advised to apply for custody under the Guardian of Children Act. If he was successful in this application, Willson could then, with Mr and Mrs Vimikh's cooperation, be placed with them and restored. We could maintain our contact by regularly visiting and helping with advice, if necessary, and of course, should difficulties arise, receive Willson back into our care. We have also considered the possibility of Mr and Mrs Vimikh applying to be foster parents to Willson and for him to be placed by us with them as a boarded out child but this sort of arrangement can lead to complications and, Mr Vimikh, being Willson's natural father, would possibly not be so ready to accept this position as a foster parent. It also seems likely that Mr and Mrs Vimikh are now in a position to maintain Willson without boarding out allowances and would probably prefer to do this.

You will have noticed from Mrs Millward's report of 3 November, that Willson still has somewhat mixed feelings about going permanently to live with Mr and Mrs Vimikh. Perhaps the reasons he has put to Mrs Millward indicate a certain awareness that he would be living in a very different world from that in which he has been brought up so far. It may be, of course, that if he goes to Mr and Mrs Vimikh for the forthcoming Christmas holidays his bond with them will be strengthened, and he will feel more eager to go and live with them permanently. From what you say I think that Mrs Vimikh would understand these mixed feelings of Willson's and do her best to help Mr Vimikh accept them. Do you think that if and when he goes to live with them permanently, that if Willson shows a desire to return to Mrs Dodd for some holiday periods that his father and Mrs Vimikh would be sympathetic to this. Mrs Dodd has already told Mrs Millward that should he leave her care Willson will always be welcome to return for holidays if he so wishes.

Will you be able to visit Mr and Mrs Vimikh in the fairly near future to discuss these various points? If Mr Vimikh decides to apply for custody, I expect that you would be able to obtain the necessary information to enable him to do this or to advise him where to apply for it himself. In the meantime, I think it would be as well for me to have the maternal grandparents' last known address visited in case they are there. I should be most interested to hear from you about your discussion with Mr and Mrs Vimikh.

Meanwhile yet another six-month review was concluded:

Nocturnal enuresis had re-occurred. Willson's contact with his putative father and step-mother seems to have deepened his relationship with Mrs Dodd as he is able to confide in her. Willson has got mixed feelings about going to live with the Vimikh's permanently – all linked with the different foods and environment. He has learnt to ride the new bicycle bought by his father. A good swimmer, keen on judo and boxing, goes to Cubs. The foster father says he is cheeky, the foster mother says not. He now accepts admonishment and correction without crying. Not a spiteful child or boastful, and shows affection. He recently hit a girl in his class at school after she called him "Nigger!" ...

Race remained an incendiary issue in 1960s England. Far right groups in the Midlands circulated posters declaring "If you want a n***** for a neighbour vote Labour", and soon demagogue Conservative Member of Parliament Enoch

Powell would speak of "rivers of blood". Early on I learnt that a coordinated flurry of fists wielded without warning with the possibility of inflicting tooth loss, a bloody nose, and more, was oft a deterrent to such name-callers, a lesson I held in good stead into my early adult years.

If a lexicon of racial slurs existed, then the adjective deployed by this young girl would have utter supremacy, pre-eminence. It would be in a class of its own due to its sheer power to inflict the most acute, painful, and agonizing wounds. In terms of etymology, it originates from the Latin word for the colour black: **niger**. No studies precisely pinpoint when "niger" became the pejorative, noxious racial epithet "nigger" (R. Kennedy, 2003; see also www.aaregistry.com and search for the word **nigger**). But by the early nineteenth century in the English speaking Americas, the term had become a prominent and common slight, designed to deeply injure. Since then this merciless put-down, this most supreme epithet of all epithets, has additionally been deployed when insulting other racial groups: the Irish, for example, being called the "niggers of Europe" and Arabs "sand niggers".

... and Willson told Mrs Dodd that the girl's mother came to school to complain to the Headmaster however when given the reason, actually apologised for her child's behaviour and said the incident would not be repeated. He can be most honest and truthful, and the foster mother says that contact with his natural father seems to have enhanced his good qualities.

A long holiday is to be arranged for the approaching Christmas period.

chapter VIII

All tragedies are finished by death,
All comedies are ended by marriage.
—George Gordon Lord Byron (1788–1824), **Don Juan**

Following a lengthy discussion with my father and stepmother, Miss Sanders replied to Miss Howe's letter of November 1966:

> Mr Vimikh is most anxious to apply for custody of Willson, and I have agreed to help in any way that I can. I have been in touch with Wansdworth Children's Department and they have advised us to get in touch with the local Probation Officer. I haven't yet done this, but I am hoping to do so before the end of the week, and arrange for Mr Vimikh to see them. I don't know all the ins and outs of a case such as this, but I deem that the fact that Mr Vimikh has assiduously paid maintenance for so long, should at the very least be a point in his favour.
>
> Both Mr and Mrs Vimikh are agreeable to Willson going to them under F.A.S. [**sic**] Restoration and I explained to them that this would mean that I would have to visit quite often in the first instance. They both said that they would be pleased to see me anytime and hoped that I would keep in touch even when it was no longer necessary.

I was quite frank with Mr and Mrs Vimikh about Willson's mixed feelings. I judge that they have together got enough understanding to realise that when a child gets to Willson's age he is bound to have opinions of his own. They both took this very well, although they are going to be bitterly disappointed if Willson decides not to go to live with them. Both Mr and Mrs Vimikh are looking forward to the Christmas holidays, when Willson can join them. They asked for details as to when he finishes school and when he could come to them for the vacation. I promised to let them know. I have thought that if it would be of any help to Mrs Millward I could meet them about halfway between London and Exeter. This would save her having too long a journey. I could only do this, however, if Willson came to London before Christmas, as I have made plans to be away Christmas week.

Mr and Mrs Vimikh were quite agreeable to Willson visiting Mrs Dodd if he should come to live with them.

I explained to Mr Vimikh that we were trying to contact Willson's mother as she had originally signed our agreement form. He said that he did not know where she resided, but that he had an address for the maternal grandparents and if we needed it he would let us have it.

I mentioned to Mr Vimikh Willson's remark about his hair, and the hope that if he came home he would not have to have it cut. This caused some amusement as apparently Mrs Vimikh had said the same thing to him before my visit. She told me that Mr Vimikh only keeps his hair shorn so low because he is going bald. Personally I think it is really because of the nature of his work in an industrial building, as by keeping his hair short it is easier to keep clean.

I do hope that this letter answers most of your questions. There is one more factor that perhaps you would like to know. It has no actual bearing on the case, but it is interesting. Mrs Vimikh told me that she was studying Spanish at night school. She did do a college course in design when she first arrived in this country – she showed me her sketch book and her drawings and designs were extremely good. I was quite impressed. I told her that I was surprised she did not continue as she really seemed to have a flair for both drawing and design. She said that she preferred to stick to plain dressmaking. Before she came to England she had run her own dressmaking business, and had only really come to this country to learn design, but that she had met Mr Vimikh and they got married, so she went back to dressmaking. Mrs Vimikh said she hopes that one day they will return to the West Indies, although Mr Vimikh is not too keen. He said that after one monotonous week on his own island you will have seen all there was to see.

If you could make me aware of when Willson will be coming for Christmas I will let the Vimikh's know so that they can be prepared.

Mrs Millward transcribed the details of my Christmas holiday of 1966:

As planned I collected Willson from his foster home on 20 December and brought him to Exeter to stay overnight with me, so that we could leave early from Torquay the following day. He settled in very well during the evening and enjoyed his supper although he refused a hot drink with my grandchildren when it came to bedtime.

He was an exceedingly happy companion, enjoyed crayoning a picture and quiz games, and was very interested in the pet white mice, making the suggestion of a playing a practical joke with them. Willson had my bed for the night and there was no nocturnal enuresis. In the morning he remarked on this and said that he had been extra careful. He was quite at home with all the family, very self assured, but behaved incredibly well and sensibly. I found that he was reading comics in bed until quite late, and asked him to turn out the light which he immediately did.

After a hearty breakfast we departed for London and during that long journey, 183 miles as the crow flies, Willson told me that he did not mind going home for Christmas but hoped that I would make it quite clear to Miss Sanders when we met her at Paddington that he would be returning to Plymouth in about two weeks time. He said that he liked his father and Victoria (his step-mother) but that he thought he enjoyed living with white people in Plymouth better, although he did know that sometimes white children, and some adults, did not altogether like him. I think the boy was working through a recent episode where a child called him a nigger – this slur was to Willson the most hurtful ethnophaulism among the litany he'd endured since birth – blackie, coon, darkie, golliwog, half breed, half caste, him with a chip on his shoulder, jigaboo, jungle bunny, kaffir, monkey, nig nog, rastus, rubber lips, sambo, sooty, sunshine, tar baby, wog, et al – and she had been unsmilingly reprimanded by her mother as well as Willson's foster mother Mrs Dodd.

He still described his indignation at his father wanting to cut off his frizzy curls, although we had previously talked about this. He mentioned again that he was not very keen on the type of meals that Victoria prepared, but he felt that if he stayed there he would be able to describe to her his tastes in food.

Having been nurtured in English households, my palate was used to staple foods such as bread spread with butter, margarine, jam, lemon curd, golden syrup, even beef dripping or pork lard. The norm for breakfast at the Dodds' was soft-boiled eggs or Scots porridge oats, occasionally with demerara sugar as a luxury, faggots (traditional British meatballs made with pig's offal) and mashed potato or fish 'n' chips for Friday dinner, with the additional treat of jam tarts or iced buns, and always an indulgent Sunday roast dinner. Billy and Victoria usually prepared meals with strangely exotic flavours: spicy neck of lamb soup with Caribbean style dumplings, rice and peas with curried chicken, minced beef meat balls, fried liver with onions, corned beef and rice, or well-done scrambled eggs cooked with crispy pieces of fried, chopped bacon. However, I devoured with relish slices of tinned peaches served with Carnation milk.

Mrs Millward continued:

I do find Willson a little condescending at times when he is discussing people but this is probably some form of defence that he has set around himself. He continued to say that Mrs Dodd had told him that he must live wherever he wanted, and that both she, and his father and stepmother, would help him to decide if necessary about his future. He said that his foster mother knows all about the different kinds of foods that he likes, and perhaps she herself would be able to tell Victoria about this. I did mention to him on this occasion that if he decided that he wanted to go and live with his father, it would be arranged that he could go and stay with the Dodds for his holiday, and he told me that he knew that his father had agreed to this.

We had a good lunch on the train, as by this time we knew that we should be arriving very late at Paddington station.

Miss Sanders was waiting for us, but I had only the briefest time to say goodbye to Willson before I had to meet another child who was being returned to Plymouth. Miss Sanders and I made arrangements for the homeward journey, which I said I would confirm the evening she returned from her Christmas holiday.

On 3 January Miss Sanders brought Willson to where I was staying in London and we were able to discuss the holiday. Apparently Willson had had quite a pleasurable time with both his parents and also the people upstairs. I think Mrs Vimikh had found him rather cheeky on one or two occasions and he had been reprimanded very slightly for this.

On the journey home Willson told me that he had enjoyed his holiday. He found the food on this occasion ever so much better, enjoyed playing with his Christmas presents and especially his friend Raphael, the boy from upstairs. He went on to say that he could confide in Victoria, as he was able to talk to her much better than he thought he could with his father. I can quite see the reason for this, as I find Mrs Vimikh very understanding, and probably more patient than her husband.

Willson continued to say that his father had asked him if he wanted to come home and live with them, but that he, Willson, had replied that he hadn't quite made up his mind.

We stopped for some time for tea on the journey home and he divulged to me that he felt torn between his two homes. He said that he was very used to Mr and Mrs Dodd and the children, and indeed he loved Mrs Dodd and "felt safe" with her particularly, although he did not care for Mr Dodd very much but said that he did not worry him. He said he liked his father and Victoria, particularly Victoria, but he did feel that he had more open space to play in his foster home. He said that he did not want to go to any other school at present except Leigham Junior, and I believe he told Mr and Mrs Vimikh that he wants to get through his examinations. He told me that he did not think he would like to go to school in London, and I had to explain that there were some very fine schools there, probably every bit as good as the Leigham one.

I am sure, however, that Willson is undecided at present where to live, and to quote him, he hasn't yet made up his mind. He did tell me, however, that for the present he would like to remain in his foster home, but go as often as possible at half-terms and holidays to his parents, and I feel for the next few months that this should be the plan.

As before, we stopped for a meal and he asked if he may go and buy Mrs Dodd a present from the pocket money that Mrs Vimikh had given him. On this occasion he bought two boxes of chocolates, one for Maureen as well as his foster mother.

When we arrived at the foster home, he went straight to Mrs Dodd and kissed her, saying "Hello" to the other children, but I noticed that he did not greet Mr Dodd. He then started to describe his vacation with his parents, but finished up by saying that he decided that he would visit London again on his next holiday, emphasising that he had not yet made up his mind whether to live with them for good. Mrs Dodd embraced him warmly and was very touched by his gift. In next to no time Willson had been received again into this family, and it was as though the fortnight had never been.

Miss Sanders will no doubt be reporting on the holiday from the parents' angle, but I do feel that we have to consider Willson's wishes very much in this case, and suggest that each holiday time if he is willing that he should visit the Vimikh's, but return to the foster home until a decision can be made.

On 7 February 1967, Mrs Millward paid another visit to the Dodds' home and reported:

The foster mother says Willson has talked an awful lot about his father and she has the feeling that he prefers his stepmother, but after further discussion Mrs Dodd gathered that he usually spends the time with Mrs Vimikh, was "more used to her" and she seemed to be very understanding. He told Mrs Dodd that his own mother was white. The foster father says he is still very cheeky but the foster mother seems to take his part always.

The foster mother has been very happy lately now that the nocturnal enuresis appears to be much better – she insists that Willson is lazy and will not go to the toilet before going to bed, but has been attending to this each night now for some time and feels that they "are over the worst now". She has much more confidence in her own methods than the Doctor's, so she tells me.

I told her that no doubt arrangements would be made for him to see his father at Easter and she thoroughly agreed.

A couple of weeks later, Miss Howe wrote to Miss Sanders in London:

Mrs Millward and I have today been discussing the next step for Willson. We feel that he is going to need help to work through this situation and that, if a holiday can be arranged at Easter, we should be able to decide between us then, even if Willson has not finally done so, whether or not we would make a plan for him to go to his father and stepmother. It is not possible, of course, to know exactly what is behind Willson's indecision. Mrs Millward feels that his reluctance may be partly due to the food and also that he probably feels that he has not, as yet, formed any great relationship with his father and stepmother. On Mr Vimikh's side too, perhaps while being very fond of Willson in theory he needs time to deepen the relationship. As far as we know there has been no correspondence between Mr and Mrs Vimikh and Willson since the Christmas holidays and I should be grateful if you could fit in a visit to them fairly soon to discuss the possibility of an Easter holiday. Mrs Millward suggests bringing him up to London on Wednesday 22 March, if so.

Mrs Dodd, Willson's foster mother, has discussed with him the home that he could have with his dad and stepmother and Willson's indecision seems largely to centre around comparisons between life on the council estate on which he lives at present and the more urban surroundings of Wandsworth. He seems for instance to feel worried that he may not be able to ride his bicycle so freely and also gives as a reason the question of his staying on at his present school to sit his Eleven-Plus tests. It seems likely, doesn't it, that Willson is feeling fearful of starting a new life and is expressing it in this way.

On the other hand, perhaps it is asking too much of a boy of ten to make his own decisions about so important an issue and, if Mr and Mrs Vimikh do genuinely want him and if they are prepared to have him for yet another holiday, perhaps we shall ourselves then have to make the decision for Willson. You are better able than we are to assess the depth of Mr and Mrs Vimikh's feelings and, if you feel they are to be depended on, I think we must seriously consider Willson going to live with them, perhaps in the summer holidays.

During the 1967 Easter holidays I vacationed with Billy and Victoria, and one evening Miss Sanders paid an impromptu visit just to see how things were going. Of my appearance, she observed that I looked to be in fine fettle, very fit, and even appeared to have put on weight. I told her that I was having a good time. Billy informed her that he had had to smack me on one occasion because he had discovered me playing astride a motorcycle that was parked outside nearby Wandsworth Town Train Station, near Wandsworth Bridge. Before she left, Miss Sanders advised Mr Vimikh on a course of action through the local magistrates court to kick-start the custody application process.

Mrs Millward again summarised the situation:

Willson said that he enjoyed the holiday very much but does not think that he wants to go and live with his parents, and put the usual obstacles in the way.

I have since visited Leigham Junior School and had a lengthy conversation with the Head Teacher. He thinks that Willson most certainly should live in London with someone who belongs to him. He says that this boy is very arrogant yet quite cute and enjoys asserting himself in school, and he feels that such an important decision on his future should be made for him. He continued to say that he has noticed that Willson enjoys "people dancing to his tune" in other things and providing there is a comprehensive school that he can be admitted to in London there should be no fear of his present type of education being interrupted. The Head Teacher said that he cannot promise if the boy stayed in Leigham that he would get an A pass although he is top of the B stream, can be quite good if only he would concentrate more, though in class is often prone to be a lazybones. He said he is quite fond of the boy but he is a handful.

When Miss Sanders brought Willson from London to Plymouth he was rather naughty on one instance in the train, and the foster mother says he has to be watched continuously.

The foster parents have suggested that he should go and live at home, and he then commenced to weep but I have a feeling he plays on Mrs Dodd's sympathy.

I do sense now that he should go to London at the commencement of the summer holidays and remain there, otherwise he will never settle at home. He has told the foster mother that he will run away if he has to stay in Wandsworth, and of course Alan, the seventeen year old Aftercare boy, had "to chip in" and mischievously tell him that I cannot force him to go, that Willson can live wherever he chooses and if he returns to Plymouth there's absolutely nothing we can do.

Miss Sanders wrote to Miss Howe:

I called in on Mr and Mrs Vimikh on Monday 10 July. Unfortunately Mr Vimikh was at work in the power station but Mrs Vimikh told me that her husband had been to the Children's Department in Wandsworth, and they told him that they would make enquiries and get in touch with him. Mrs Vimikh said that since that time they had heard nothing. However I visited Mr Vimikh the next day while he was at home from work, and he told me that he had in fact been to the local Magistrates Court as he had been advised to do by the Children's Department. They had then referred him to the Probation Department, who in turn told him to see the Children's Department. Mr Vimikh had been to see them all in turn and was patiently waiting to hear from someone. As Wandsworth Children's Department seem to have passed his enquiry back to us, we are back to square one.

After this interview with Mr Vimikh I went myself directly to see the Probation Officer at the Wandsworth Court. After a rather irritable interview with a Probation Officer who seemed loathe to pass on to me any information about how Mr Vimikh should start the proceedings for getting the custody of Willson, I eventually managed to pin him down – he told me that the best thing Mr Vimikh could do was to see a solicitor who would advise him. I then went back to see Mr Vimikh again, and as he does not have a solicitor I advised him to go to the Battersea Citizens Advice Bureau. They could arrange for him to see a solicitor, and he promised to let me know what the outcome of this is. I also informed Mr Vimikh to ask for Legal Aid so that his fee for the solicitor's advice will not be too large.

On 27 July Mrs Millward along with Mrs Paget, another Welfare Officer, visited the Dodd household. Mrs Dodd took Mrs Millward aside and disclosed to her that she had recently learnt that Alan had, while she was ill, asked Willson to "hold him". Another child later informed Mrs Millward that Alan had been doing similar things with other local boys. Alarm bells were sounding and Mrs Millward said that she desperately wanted Alan to leave the Dodd's house. On 1 August both Welfare Officers visited once again:

> We met up with Mrs Dodd and Willson outside a clothing store called Costers to shop with an extra grant which had been provided to smarten Willson up for his father.
>
> Willson was looking very well-dressed in his school mackintosh and grey trousers. He rolled his eyes and smiled whenever Mrs Dodd spoke to him. Otherwise he was silent and seemed preoccupied and distant. He occasionally joined in the conversation by volunteering information – e.g. in the shoe shop he remarked that he had seen similar sandals marked at a cheaper price in another shop.
>
> Willson was provided with a new blazer, a pair of sandals and a pair of Danny Kaye Boots – plimsolls with instep support and ankle protection.

On the Sunday, 6 August 1967, Mrs Millward collected me from the Dodds' for my summer break with Billy and Victoria. This time she drove all the way to London in her beloved green Mini Cooper and afterwards transcribed the following:

> Willson was very happy on the long journey, and during the two stops that we had he conversed incessantly and seemed extremely pleased that he was again going to London. At tea time,

however, he asked when he would be returning to Plymouth. When I reminded him that we had discussed the possibility of him staying with his father, he became very annoyed and said that he did not realise that he would not be returning to Plymouth after this holiday, and that I had not specifically told him of these arrangements when I met him last week. I reminded Willson that he knew about this, and that I only saw him for a few seconds before the foster mother and Mrs Paget went off with him to buy his new clothes. He soon recognised the Wandsworth area when we approached and pointed out quite a few landmarks, and it was obvious that his last holidays here had been full of interest.

When we arrived at his father's home, I noticed how warmly he greeted the stepmother Victoria, but he did not kiss his father.

While we were sitting in the living room Mr Vimikh told me what had transpired in the last fortnight concerning his application for Willson to live with them permanently. Willson showed interest at this but then asked if he would be remaining in Wandsworth when the holidays came to an end and when Mrs Vimikh told him that she hoped and thought that this was possible he burst into tears and commenced to bawl and holler at them.

He put the usual reasons forward for his preference for living in Plymouth such as 1/ School, 2/ District, 3/ Lack of country facilities and hobbies, 4/ Friends, 5/ Lack of freedom, but one by one the stepmother explained how all of these points could be surmounted. The father very calmly and sensibly said that some of these issues were rather petty, and that when Willson had settled down in Wandsworth he would find that the above obstacles could be easily overcome.

I would like to record here, that I thought the Vimikh's handling of Willson's bad tempered behaviour, and possible distress in this case, was admirable. Both of them, while hiding their disappointment at seeing Willson so upset and rude, showed their self discipline, and never once raised their voices or showed their own torment.

There was a family friend present who also spoke very calmly and carefully to Willson, and told him to give everything a chance, and try and settle down. He went further to say that if things could not be altered then they would all have to think again.

Willson was very, very rude to me and refused to say goodbye, even when his step-mother came to the door to see me off.

I told Mrs Vimikh that if she had any serious trouble to telephone the office at once, as Miss Sanders had given her the number, but Mrs Vimikh very wisely thought that after the passage of a few days Willson would probably settle down.

The next morning I telephoned Miss Sanders the Welfare Officer, to ask if it were possible for her to make one last visit owing to the unfortunate happenings yesterday, although we both realised that he would probably quieten down in the next 72 hours.

When I returned to the foster home this last week and told the foster parents about our visit and arrival, Mrs Dodd stated that she did not think Willson would remain permanently with the Vimikhs and she felt that he would run away, as she did not believe that he was quite ready to live with his parents. She rather irritated me when she said that she thought he would not be staying after this holiday.

As if spurred on by the worrying issues of alleged sexual abuse in the Dodds' home that had surfaced late in July, Miss Howe confirmed their intentions on 9 August 1967 in a letter to Miss E. Hodgkinson, a St Mary's regional executive officer based in London:

> We have decided that Willson should remain with Mr and Mrs Vimikh and not return to his foster home in Plymouth at the end of the summer holiday. I have given a great deal of anxious thought to this and Miss Sanders, the Welfare Officer, who has been visiting the Vimikhs regularly, has also gone into it very thoroughly.

On 9 August, Miss Sanders made a follow-up visit to 21 Alma Road, as requested by Mrs Millward.

> Willson looked much happier than I had expected he would. Mrs Vimikh told me that he had cried quite a bit on the Sunday, but since then he had begun to cheer up. He talked quite happily about going to school in Wandsworth and about having his bike sent up from Plymouth. Of course it might be a different tale when the time comes for him to actually start school and I suppose it seems such a long way ahead in the future to Willson.
>
> Mr Vimikh told me that he had seen a solicitor at the Citizens Advice Bureau, and he has advised Mr Vimikh to adopt Willson. Mr Vimikh had the adoption forms at home and showed them to me. He has to sign them and take them to the court in Battersea. In the forms they asked the court to waive the mother's consent on the grounds that she has never shown any interest in Willson, and also because no one knows where she is. The solicitor gave Mr Vimikh to believe that the adoption would not take very long, and he was

surprised to find that it was so simple! I am pleased now that things are beginning to move, after so many abortive attempts to set the ball rolling.

As I shall be moving up to Warwickshire this next week, I shall be handing over this case to Miss J Farmer who is the Welfare Officer in the Wandsworth area.

On 16 August 1967, Miss Howe sent a final letter to my foster parents, Mr and Mrs Dodd:

I know that you will be most pleased to learn that an encouraging report has been received from the Welfare Officer who has been to see Willson. It sounds as if Willson is feeling happier now at the prospect of going to school in Wandsworth and is looking forward to having his bike sent eventually. The Welfare Officer will be visiting again, of course, but it does look as if Willson will be able to remain with his father and step-mother and make his home with them now.

Although I do realise that this is going to be a wrench for all concerned, I feel sure that you will be happy if it means that Willson is able to live with his own father. All that you have done for him in the time since Mrs Millward first brought him to you in October 1963 has made this plan possible, and you have the thanks of us all.

Mrs Millward will be in touch with you about the financial details of his bike and any other personal belongings – and I trust that Willson will write to you. St Mary's Children's Charity will be visiting him for some time to come I expect, so there will be news to pass on.

I do hope you and Mr Dodd are both keeping well – with renewed thanks, and every good wish.

Change, my restitution to blood relatives, had indeed been a long time coming. Up to this point in my life, I had been called Jean Willson Sherman, but now my parents, through a solicitor, had my surname legally changed to Vimikh. In September 1967, the start of the autumn term witnessed me commence attending year six at High View Primary School, located off Plough Lane near Clapham Junction. I settled incredibly quickly into the school, with its diverse mix of students, and soon made friends with James "Guinness" McLean (from Jamaica), Carlton Peters (from Grenada), Sean O'Connor (from Ireland), and Dimitrios Charalombos (from Cyprus). Each day I'd travel to High View from East Hill on a red No. 37 Routemaster bus, and loved nothing more than alighting from the moving bus's platform onto the pavement before it halted at the bus stop outside the Granada Cinema on St John's Hill. Miss Farmer, the Wandsworth Welfare Officer, visited monthly, and I appeared relaxed. She reported in October 1967:

> Willson looks very well indeed and says he is enjoying his new school. Mrs Vimikh had just made him a very gay dressing gown and was in the middle of altering a new school suit for him.

In early December Miss Farmer again wrote:

> Unfortunately I have missed the Hearing of Mr and Mrs Vimikh's application to adopt Willson, as the Case was heard on the 13 November, and not as I understood on the 30 November. I think the mistake has arisen because both Mr and Mrs Vimikh have quite strong accents, and like many West Indians do not pronounce the words thirteenth and thirtieth with a 'th' but only the 't'.
> Mrs Vimikh stated that the hearing was very short and no complications arose as a result of it. The ever industrious Mr and Mrs Vimikh were

busy working, Mr Vimikh painting, and Mrs Vimikh making Willson a pair of pyjamas. Willson said that he was very well and that school was simply fine. Indeed they seem an incredibly happy little trio.

chapter IX

*If there is no struggle there is no progress.
Those who profess to favour freedom and yet
deprecate agitation, are men who want crops
without thunder and lightning. They want
the ocean without the awful roar of its many
waters. This struggle may be a moral one, or
it may be a physical one, and it may be both
moral and physical, but it must be a struggle.*
—Frederick Douglas (1818–1895)

My art history tutor at the London University's Camberwell campus in 1980 was atypical, a youthful-looking man, clean cut, bespectacled, and probably no older than thirty years of age. Always smartly dressed, this academic favoured loafer type, soft leather shoes, neutral-coloured contemporary tailored linen suits, and simple, plain long-sleeved T-shirts. Ajit Gupta was of elfin, slender stature, a South African exile of Indian origin who had the vastest of intellects and title professor of art history and theory. Ajit's immense knowledge base was grounded in Sanskrit, the language of the Vedas and other Hindu scriptures, the classical literature of James Joyce, and other areas of scientific, philosophical, and religious scholarship. He was also fluent in several languages including Hindi, Urdu, Afrikaans, Zulu, and Xhosa.

Lectures and seminars were considered an irrelevance, a dull waste of time by some of my learned peers, but Ajit's delivery in these forums was mesmeric. His terminology and articulation of the English language was a revelation as he informed assembled fine art students on the context and meaning underpinning the works of intellectual giants such as linguist Ferdinand de Saussure, philosophers Jacques Derrida and Michel Foucault, and anthropologist Claude Levi Straus. Ajit was a great mentor, coaxing and coaching me in private tutorials. He provided me with the rigorous theoretical platform essential to defend my blossoming artistic concepts and written work against more critical Eurocentric-minded art tutors, academics, and fellow students.

In June 1982 much consternation and tongue wagging was caused at the Final Year Fine Art Degree Show by one of my exhibits: a six feet by four feet painting of a black man and white woman in intimate sexual embrace, derived in part from erotic imagery found in Japanese art. My exhibition juxtaposed "The Lovers" alongside linocuts, woodcuts, etchings, and silk screen prints. These images were further bolstered by black and white photographs of Ghana taken the previous summer and of the Black People's Day of Action, when 20,000 people gathered to peacefully demonstrate, marching from New Cross to Hyde Park Corner following the deaths in an arson attack of thirteen young black people at a house party in New Cross on 2 March 1981. That work in combination with my final year dissertation on "Elmina Castle and the Coastal Fortress System" helped me gain a bachelor of arts upper second class honours degree in fine art.

The invitation to attend a London University degree awards presentation ceremony for fine art students, with all of its pomp and pageantry, at Senate House, the administrative centre in Bloomsbury, held minimal interest for me. To my knowledge I had no kindred aside from Billy, now living several thousand miles across the Atlantic Ocean in St Croix, United States Virgin Islands, with whom to celebrate my achievements. Instead I elected for my degree certificate to arrive by royal mail recorded delivery in a sturdy A4 Manila envelope. Ajit, meanwhile, divulged that my 2:1 grade had required some fierce negotiating for on his part given that the decision-making assessment panel from the Council for National Academic Awards were most keen to give me a third class degree. My tutor knew my intellectual limitations, that I was no art prodigy. However, these custodians of aesthetic standards had struggled to comprehend the underlying messages and validity behind my artwork, creativity they assessed as meritless. Nor were they remotely sympathetic to the central thrust of my thesis.

With the degree course successfully concluded and no obvious career path in mind, completing a PGCE teacher training course beckoned. David Pendlebury, head of the college's fine art department, endorsed my place on the course, writing in an open testimonial:

> He was one of those exceptional cases where we backed our judgement of character and ability against the fact that he was without any academic qualifications. Willson took the chance offered and proved to be an outstanding student.
>
> He has the rare quality of combining good humour with good judgement which allowed him to be critically rigorous without generating hostility. This is important in that his art work did challenge the persuasive central thrust of Western European art history and seek instead African roots. I have seen this phenomenon before but I have not seen it pursued, argued or presented in such intelligent and eloquent form.
>
> The images were at their most compelling in his prints. He became a very accomplished printmaker using screen, litho, etching and block printing.
>
> Willson's secondary education was a disaster, he has climbed above that without recrimination. He will be, I am sure, an excellent teacher

and valued member of any teaching team. I recommend him without reserve.

With completion of the one-year PGCE course in July 1983 fast approaching and a successful teaching practice placement at the Archbishop Michael Ramsey Secondary School, located off the Camberwell New Road, behind me, my thoughts turned to employment. All trainee teachers concluded the PGCE year by mounting an exhibition: a juxtaposition of their own creative efforts alongside the artwork produced by their school pupils. The show was a headhunting forum, where senior teaching professionals recruited fresh blood to their institutions. One such departmental head, Peter Chadwick, encouraged my immediate application for a vacant position. After attending the one interview, I was offered a full-time teaching post in the London Borough of Hackney, subject to receipt of satisfactory references. In September 1983 the former high school dropout grabbed this golden opportunity, signed a contract, and proudly began employment as a newly qualified teacher. The establishment I joined was a large secondary school off the Kingsland Road, Hackney, where I successfully taught art, film and photography to boys and girls aged eleven to seventeen years until December 1985.

For two years and one term, I held this teaching position with some success. I resigned to pursue a bohemian lifestyle: the idealistic, noble aspiration of pursuing an artistic dream by surviving on the proceeds of my art and photography, supplemented by part-time paid community work. From January 1986 to July 1994 I worked for the London Borough of Kensington and Chelsea's Leisure and Recreation department at the Harrow Road Centre, which proved a wonderful, almost perfect job. The centre manager there, Nick Padmore, was this soft-spoken middle-aged white guy with a passion for Blue Note Records, John Coltrane, Charlie "Bird" Parker, and all things Jazz. Nick gave me free reign, having first recruited me to the role of temporary play leader, to help him run a successful summer play scheme five years earlier. I would return to that job year after year each summer and Easter holiday, even after I started teaching. Nick became a trusted friend, took early retirement in 1987, and then migrated to the Antipodes with his Aussie partner Ruth, where he continued to develop local community arts resources.

Because I had neither a rich benefactor nor family, this part-time neighbourhood work eventually became full-time out of economic necessity. Soon I taught daytime and evening beginners and intermediate classes in black and white photography to adults. Over time I expanded the centre's photographic facilities from one to three community darkrooms, all hireable at reasonable prices to aspiring photographers. The darkrooms were named with plaques in honour of three renowned photographers: Jo Spence (England), Peter Magubane (South Africa) and Sebastiao Salgado (Brazil). I coordinated a weekly old age pensioner's group for local seniors whose activities included indoor bowls, pool, darts, tea and coffee mornings, theatre visits, seasonal day trips to the south coast, and an annual free Christmas party and dinner where at the end of the celebrations I would drive a small twenty-five-seat coach dressed as Santa Claus, dropping folks safely off at their doorstep.

At the Harrow Road Centre, I played a lead role in organising, planning, and delivering the pioneering school holiday play scheme for ninety local children. This provision catered for five- to eleven-year-olds; ran from 08.00–18.00 each weekday throughout every summer, Easter, and half-term holiday; and integrated disabled with able-bodied children. In 1987 I founded and coached a successful young men's soccer team, Harrow Road FC, which competed in the Senior Sunday Amateur Football League. The team won promotion and divisional titles year after year, eventually doing so in the Senior Sunday's highest division. My players were renowned for their levels of fitness and played the beautiful game with

Brazilian strength, panache, and supreme standards of sportsmanship. I organised several successful tours to Holland. The team was renamed and registered as N. R. Mandela FC in 1990, a tribute to Nelson Rolihlahla Mandela, following his long-awaited release from prison in apartheid South Africa, triggering alarm and dismay among Senior Sunday's league officials.

These were halcyon days, an idyllic employment period that simply could not last. Foreboding news of wholesale local government departmental restructuring filtered out during the summer of 1993 and gathered pace. Kensington and Chelsea Council began the process of **rationalisation** as local trade unions were consulted. Numerous non-statutory posts were in the frame to be lost, and invitations were extended to eligible employees wishing to opt for voluntary redundancy. The following spring austere public sector cuts kicked in. I learnt that an exemplary track record and history of zero days sickness stood for absolutely nothing. Those cold, calculating, unseen staff in human resources had identified the posts to be culled, and I joined many workers hit with severance in July 1994.

Redundancy struck at the time my common law wife was four months pregnant. The first time I had encountered Claudia was one gloriously bright spring afternoon back in 1980 as she travelled home from the Kings College's Waterloo Campus where she worked. Having got off her train at Clapham Junction Station, she was strolling home to her parents' house in the East Hill area of Wandsworth in brilliant April sunshine – her perfect, beautiful Afro glistening proudly – just as I happened to be cycling home from the Camberwell site of London University's School of Art. Having previously surveyed Claudia only from a distance in and around Wandsworth, on that day I overcame my timidity and summoned up the confidence, then gracefully dismounted, bringing my bike to a smooth halt beside her. Gazing into her dark ebony eyes and beaming a disarming smile, I said hello before politely asking to accompany her as she walked.

Claudia fitted my ideal definition of female attractiveness: an independent mind, feisty, defiantly unwilling to act subserviently to any man, a modest yet vibrantly colourful dress sense, hair worn natural, either braided in cane rows (cornrows) or an Afro, with a fine, petite sylph-like figure, and (crucially) healthy, smooth skin of the darkest hue, moisturized by cocoa butter. She was, though, rightfully wary of me in that early period of our courtship. Both of her parents, Mable and Hubert Morrison, actually knew my father, Billy, and being good protective parents they forewarned their daughter of her love interest's earlier turbulent teenage years. "Im was," they emphasised, "a bad bwoy!" Despite this disapproval, our love flourished. After all, I had long since put my misspent youth behind me, and in time her people welcomed me into their ranks. Ever since 1976, when Billy departed English shores for the Caribbean, the presence of kinfolk had been absent from my life. Claudia's folks filled this void, satisfied my soul, and from 1983 I would spend every Christmas embraced by her family's warm hospitality.

The following event from early in our blossoming relationship remains a vivid indicator of my ardour for this slender, graceful Jamaican beauty. One evening when working as a youth worker for ILEA in a youth club off Trinity Road, Wandsworth, I became aware of the presence of Royston, a guy around my age from the nearby Earlsfield housing estate. Royston, Claudia's former Grenadian boyfriend, was lurking around the club's pool and table tennis hall where the tuck shop was being manned by two volunteers, namely Claudia and a female friend. While I was out of sight performing my duties, Royston saw an opportunity and boldly made an amorous advance towards her that she rebuffed. He made his brash approach despite knowing I had been dating her for several months and that I was in the immediate vicinity in my role as a staff member. Harsh words were exchanged between Royston and Claudia, which I caught the tail end of, and shortly afterwards she confided to me that he had rudely approached her, declaring: "Claudia, me wan fuck you." Carrying on with my youth worker duties as if untroubled, I weighed up my course of action as inwardly I seethed.

Silent calculations concluded, my response, when it came, was fleet. Upon closing time, when the majority of those youths attending had left the premises, I encountered Royston lingering with a few stragglers in the narrow, ill-lit corridor leading towards the building's exit, so I beckoned him over. Looking him cold in the eye, I unleashed in a flash, without warning, a Mae Geri – Japanese karate terminology for a front snap kick, knee raised to point at the target and then *bang!* the sudden extension of the kicking leg with the ball of the foot striking the said target – making full contact with his solar plexus. Executed correctly, a Mae Geri is quite a brutal technique. At the time I was a student of Shotokan karate under seventh dan sensei Ichiro Nakamura and had trained at his dojo in Garratt Lane, Wandsworth, for a couple of years. There I had practised repetitious physical exercises, various blocks, punches, and kicking techniques to the sensei's count: *ichi, ni, san ... hachi, kyuu, juu,* over and over again but never, ever making full contact, even when sparring with an opponent. This sudden violent deed was no act of self-defence, though, as I was under no imminent threat of physical harm. Such actions contravened every tenet of self-control and discipline that underpinned the bushido spirit of my martial arts training. Royston collapsed like an imploding, high-rise tower block under demolition, gasping painfully, hands clutching his abdomen as I stood over him and growled, "I'll give you some real brimstone and fire if you ever, ever speak to Claudia like that again!"

Claudia and I courted for a few years then travelled to Ghana in the summer of 1985 – the trip a kind of unofficial honeymoon. On returning to London, we began cohabiting, domiciled together at the East Hill flat which we had purchased from Wandsworth Council under Prime Minister Margaret Thatcher's controversial Right to Buy scheme, offered to long-standing tenants. In 1987 our daughter

Afua was born, followed in 1989 by a son, Kwesi. When the gloomy news of redundancy was first announced in July 1993, we had just moved to a new home, having taken on a substantial mortgage to purchase a three-bedroom house in the outer West London borough of Hillingdon, and Claudia shortly miscarried. One year later my post as activities coordinator at the Harrow Road Centre was deleted – I had become supernumerate, surplus to requirements – and, distressingly, faced unemployment for the very first time since expulsion from Southfields Boys High School at the age of fifteen. To compound matters further, Claudia had fallen pregnant once again. During the months that followed, I searched in vain for employment, and then our beautiful second daughter Ayo was born.

To all intents and purposes, Claudia appeared to have made a sound choice of partner and lifelong soulmate by selecting Billy's son. Stories abound of incompetent, feckless, absent adult males, irresponsible men with behaviours akin to the foulest-smelling ram goat. My father could so easily have followed this misogynistic trend and disappeared out of my life when faced with seemingly omnipotent adversity. Yet he proved heroic, committed, and an impressive example of manhood. Against the odds I would somehow prove to be decent father material, a family provider, and ever-present protector, contradicting the chances many would have given to one raised as a nomadic orphan in the difficult regimes of the British social care system during the 1950s and 1960s.

Each of my children's first hospital scans were amazing events, and only death would have prevented my presence in the delivery room throughout their births. Fatherhood proved a kind of salvation, never failing to instil joyous exhilaration in my heart and frequent, overpowering thoughts of warm, tender love. Each infant's innocent voice was, to my ears, a sound sweeter than the finest vocals on any jazz, reggae, or soul record. In next to no time, I evolved into an affectionate, consistent, hands-on, stay-at-home dad for whom bachelor pursuits and career aspirations occupied the back seat. Morphing into a modern househusband, I became an expert at bedtime storytelling and dab hand at domestic chores like pots of perfectly cooked basmati rice, school runs, neatly ironed uniforms, and DIY tasks. This was not the result of being henpecked, but crucially through being intuitive, attentive, perceptive, and first rate in some "feminine" and "masculine" roles. Childcare experts would define this parenting style as authoritative, and underpinning my raison d'être was an indomitable determination that our offspring's formative years would never mirror my own.

If a magus or distinguished scholar were asked "What is in a name?" the reply might well be "Everything!" Hence, following careful research and much deliberation, we gave each beautiful infant a strong-sounding, meaningful African name in recognition of their ancestral origins and heritage.

Claudia's mother, a wonderfully devout, churchgoing, no-nonsense matriarch, initially queried our choice of given names. "Why not good English-sounding Christian names?" Mrs Morrison grumbled.

"Our children," I would respectfully retort, "already possess this within the full names of Claudia and myself as recorded on their birth certificates. And your very own beloved, eldest daughter Carol," I quietly reminded Mrs Morrison, "after much investigation, proudly changed her given name by deed poll ten years ago to Ada."

Carol's findings, which could easily have been the wise words of a griot, revealed that Ada (pronounced *Aye*-dah) is an Igbo, also spelt Ibo, name meaning "first born daughter". Igbo is a major language of southeastern Nigeria. A variant of Ada is Adah, a Hebrew name from the Old Testament meaning "beautiful ornament" - Adah was the first wife of Lamech and mother of Jabal and Jubal (Genesis 4:19-23), and also the first wife of Esau (Genesis 36:2). This biblical link appealed to Mrs Morrison's Christian sentiments.

When our first child arrived at Hammersmith and West London Hospital, we proudly named her Afua (pronounced Ah-**fwah**), a Twi name meaning "a female child born on a Friday". Twi is one of several Akan languages, including Asante, Ewe, Fanti, and Ga, spoken in regions of République de Côte d'Ivoire (Ivory Coast), Ghana, and Togo. One Sunday a little over two years later, in the very same maternity ward (Annie Zunz), our son was born. Immediately adjacent to Claudia's bed lay a woman, yet to deliver her baby, from Kumasi, the capital of Ashanti region in Ghana, so it proved fitting to name our new baby boy Kwesi (pronounced **Kway**-see), spelt as in the Ghanaian Asante language, meaning a "male child born on a Monday".

Kwesi was fortunate enough to attend a great voluntary sector nursery before moving on to mainstream primary education. This twenty-five-place, under-fives care facility was called New Dawn Community Day Nursery. It provided low cost, quality day care from Mondays to Fridays, 08.00–18.00, for children aged two to five years, with priority given to children of African or African–Caribbean origin, though not exclusively so. New Dawn was located in a large Victorian house behind the Harding and Hobbs department store in Clapham Junction. After our family moved to Hillingdon in 1993, Kwesi continued attending – Claudia and I sharing the commitment of a tortuous daily commute – as he received excellent early years care there. Each day on dropping Kwesi off before work or picking him up afterwards, the nursery coordinator, Susan Barratt, would merrily cajole and lobby me to join other volunteers – parents or former parents – on the management committee. I eventually signed up in mid 1992. By late spring 1993, I was elected as the chairperson of the nursery and became the "registered fit person".

During my two-year tenure as chairperson, New Dawn continued to thrive and develop in all areas of its work. For the fiscal year ending 31 March 1995, Battersea chartered accountants and registered auditor Terry Collins reported sound housekeeping, with an income of £132,078 from a local authority voluntary sector grant and £51,000 from parental fees, enabling the employment of twelve full- and part-time staff. My proudest achievement as chairperson was being at the helm through a process of constitutional changes, inspections, and audit reports that led to an application in November 1994 to the Charity Commission for charity status. Written confirmation of success was received on 9 December 1994, and New Dawn Community Day Nursery's name was entered on the Central Register of Charities. I stepped down as chairperson at the annual general meeting on 6 June 1995, by which time my son Kwesi had advanced to primary school.

Five years after Kwesi's birth, our second daughter, Ayo (pronounced E*ye*-yoh) arrived. The name Ayo is of Yoruba origin, can be feminine or masculine, and means "joy", "happiness", and "delight". The language has been spoken for over 1500 years in South West Nigeria and Benin. The CIA's **World Factbook** estimates Nigeria's current population as close to 180 million people, of whom Yoruba is one of most populous ethnolinguistic groups at 21 per cent. This unique name, Ayo, celebrates her parents' delight at the girl's safe passage into the world following the tragic loss of our third, miscarried child the year before.

Refusing to endure the indignity of dole queues or claiming welfare benefits after being laid off by Wandsworth Council, I opted to survive on my redundancy package, which, by early 1995, had all but vanished. Still unemployed despite months of fruitless job applications and interviews, my destiny turned a corner come March when I accepted an offer of permanent employment with a national children's charity at one of their central London projects, working with children and families in temporary accommodation. It was challenging, demanding work in some of London's poorest, most deprived boroughs – Lambeth, Lewisham, Southwark and Tower Hamlets – providing advocacy and support services to destitute, homeless children and their carers.

In my first week, I joined other new employees attending a staff induction day at the children's charity's quaint villa, sited amidst several leafy, green acres in Richmond upon Thames, which is now the charity's national headquarters. Lo and behold, long-forgotten, suppressed memories of my upbringing under the auspices of St Mary's Children's Charity were resurrected. Driven by a deep impulse, I tentatively commenced taking the first of countless steps towards unearthing the many obscure facts about my past. Billy, my father, had always remained guarded, loath to speak about my childhood years in foster homes, and until the catalyst provided by this new employment, and fatherhood itself, I had never felt remotely inclined to investigate.

On April Fool's Day 1995, in glorious midday sunshine, I arrived punctually for my wedding at Wandsworth Town Hall's Registry Office attired in a navy blue double-breasted suit over a Bob Marley T-shirt. For many years a wedlock sceptic, marriage had since come to signify the permanence of my unwavering commitment to Claudia, and so, witnessed by a handful of close friends, Claudia's family, and our three children, we recited our vows while serenaded by Al Green's love song, "Simply Beautiful". My wife would support what was now my irrepressible desire to hunt, to unearth what could no longer be suppressed or ignored, and yield for my children facts about that unspoken side of their ancestral origins.

Approaching my fortieth year in 1996, I guardedly contacted St Mary's Children's Charity's After Care Section, formally requesting in writing access to the records of my lost years in their care. I was put in touch with Penelope Devine, an unassuming, soft-spoken white lady about my age, who proved to be non-judgemental and a skilled listener when faced with my story's weighty emotional baggage. The process was no instant fix, as accessing the annals of my childhood would prove painstakingly slow and last several years.

Within months I'd taken a morning off work for my first appointment with Penelope at the villa in Richmond. From the onset I made it emphatically clear that I desired no direct contact with my mother, Molly Sherman, should she still be living, but was prepared, through therapist Penelope Devine acting as intermediary, to let her know I was alive and well. On the train journey to work afterwards, I scrutinised the assorted Caucasian faces sat about my carriage and pondered: *Could you be my relative? My mother? Perhaps my brother?* Back at the Central London project I remained totally composed, wearing an impassive mask of cool that gave colleagues no inkling of my earlier steps on such a monumental emotional journey. However, upon returning home that evening to my beloved wife, Claudia, I flew into an uncontrollable rage, hurled the TV across the front room, and wept inconsolably.

Finding resolution and acceptance that wounds from one's infancy are often more than skin deep seemed straightforward, easy to live with at the time. I had no realisation that this revolving door would simply never just close. Internally, psychologically, such cathartic healing was beyond me.

As the days and months went by, the dust settled. Yet periodically, when without company, I often found myself daydreaming, reflecting trance-like upon the circumstances that might have surrounded Molly's despondent deed. From my line of work I understood all too well that the long-term consequences of maternal deprivation and the theory of attachment (as postulated by Bowlby, Rutter, et al.) could explain my impulsive adolescent delinquency and increased aggression when acting on a whim with scant regard for any consequences. Aided, abetted, and officially sanctioned, Molly's breaking of the critical bond between infant and primary caregiver, her withdrawal of a mother's sacrosanct nurturing embrace, and her act of maternal rejection would remain permanently lodged in the deepest recesses of my memory forty years later. This discharge also influenced my adult aversion to dating

European women – a fundamental question of trust – though in the years before meeting Claudia I had the odd short-lived romantic liaison.

In the jobs section pages of **The Voice** newspaper of 25 June 1996, an advertisement placed by a London council caught my eye. Featuring a photograph of a weathered baseball bat lying amidst shards of broken glass, it solicited candidates for the post of care officer at a secure children's home. This flagship facility was developing a nationwide reputation for excellence in the provision of secure care for the country's most difficult teenagers, understanding their problems, assessing their needs, and providing them with education and training in order to assist them in breaking free from their problems. To help achieve these objectives, the secure children's home had a full range of professional support services: teams of in-house educators, consultant psychiatrists and psychologists, and a comprehensive training programme for all staff, among whom there was an extremely low turnover, and a good ethnicity and gender balance.

Feeling a craving for this fascinating position, I requested an application pack, believing my blend of experience, interpersonal and communication skills, organisational flair, and problem-solving abilities were perfectly suited to succeed in the role. Meticulously completing my submission and honestly declaring my juvenile criminal convictions as I'd done to all previous employers, I submitted the application. The gruelling recruitment process comprised visiting an assessment centre, taking psychometric tests, and giving a panel interview followed by a Warner Interview (a social services safeguarding and vetting tool). Character and employer references were sought, and an enhanced police criminal records bureau check. At long last three months of recruitment red tape concluded in December 1996 when I received a contract, thus enabling me to hand my employers the required notice period. I'd landed a job at Lederer Manor, a secure children's home for adolescent boys run by Redbridge Council. Full of optimism, my new employ was a pristine, purpose-built, superbly equipped twenty-four-bed facility, financed by money from UK taxpayers – several million pounds from the Department of Health – scheduled to open in the spring of 1997.

Epilogue

The wave of new Lederer Manor recruits in mid January 1997 received three weeks of induction. It would be no mistruth to say that these weeks of training were a serious financial investment on the part of Redbridge Social Services. Areas covered included child and adolescent development, criminal legislation and the youth justice system, education, substance misuse, mental health, child sex offenders, social learning theory, race awareness, and policies and procedures. Induction concluded with five days of control and restraint – a phrase used to describe the legally permissible and safe forms of physical management deployed when overpowering a child – as the nature of the work meant that aggressive, dangerous incidents were inherent, routine, and a daily occurrence. After numerous security-focused dry runs and team building sessions, the three staff teams of Endeavour, Mayflower, and Victory (my unit) were ultimately as prepared as they could be for the imminent admission of troubled youngsters, youths with a history of serious offending or disturbed behaviour, and all deemed by either criminal or civil courts to be a serious risk to the public, to property, or themselves.

Further appointments with the aftercare counsellor Penelope continued, slotted in between my busy work schedule at Lederer Manor, married life, and the raising of three children. Sometimes, on days she did not attend nursery, I'd take Ayo, aged about three, with me from Uxbridge to the villa in Richmond upon Thames. There, in a nicely furnished meeting room, my daughter contented herself in a child-friendly, carpeted corner well stocked with lovely toys, oblivious to the sensitive subject under discussion. Ayo played on in childish innocence as the counsellor directed my painful journey through past revelations. In time Penelope passed on to me Molly's correspondence of many years, a few black and white family photographs, and copies of records from St Mary's detailing their communication with Molly before she vanished from West London.

The written documentation of my childhood years in St Mary's Children's Charity had been preserved for posterity on microfilm. Before being granted full access to peruse, take notes, and ultimately be given any requested paper copies from my microscopic records, all named third party individuals had to be carefully deleted. So monumentally onerous was this task that St Mary's could not, and indeed did not, thoroughly delete every third party. I acquired, quite literally, hundreds of pages of meticulously kept data, either handwritten or typed, descriptive facts about my sojourn in the care system.

Scrutinising these manuscripts repeatedly to fully digest their contents, I occasionally paused to pass a comment, but my voice cracked mid sentence as I fought back gathering tears, inhaled, then exhaled the deepest of breaths, in an effort to remain poised. The hidden evidence that detailed my early years was no longer mysterious, the conjecture of flashbacks or daydreams, but now fully divulged in writing and in my possession. It is as a result of acquiring these documents that I was enabled to narrate for the reader such unexaggerated, truthful accounts of those events in the 1950s and 1960s from my decade in children's homes.

Forty years after Molly's decision to surrender me up into their guardianship, St Mary's received a rueful international telephone call. In May 1997, staff at their aftercare department transcribed the extensive phone conversation with the caller, who said she was Molly

Sherman, now a resident of Hamilton in the province of Ontario, Canada.

This was a long, poignant call and Ms Sherman became quite emotional at intervals – for which she profusely apologised. She was very talkative, and awfully eager to express how she feels about Willson.

She rang because, although she accepts Willson's absolute right to refuse any contact with her, and understands fully why he would make this choice, she feels that "life is too short", and her own health is not too good – she is on medication for asthma and for an irregular heartbeat. She wants Willson to know certain things about the circumstances which led to her giving him up (see below), and she thinks he may need to know about the family's medical history. She does not wish to use her health as any kind of emotional blackmail.

Ms Sherman wants Willson to know that he was always loved, by her and by her parents too – particularly her father – he was given the first name Jean after her father's middle name. If she could have found a way to keep Willson she would have done so, but felt she was up against powerful social pressures because he was black, which she could have borne, but she felt inadequate to protect him. She mentioned friends, neighbours and unknown people sneering, making threats, spitting or throwing stones at her in the streets whenever she walked out with Willson. Neither of her two husbands were prepared to take Willson in, though she pleaded with them both to do so, and this was because Willson was black.

Although she tried to have Willson home at her parent's house, this proved impossible because both her parents were invalids and she was trying to work to keep them all, which was very demanding as she was so young. When she finally gave up Willson to St Mary's she hoped that his father would soon be able to take him on himself and return back to Antigua, and she felt this would be right for Willson.

Ms Sherman spoke with respect for Willson's father. She described him as "a wonderful man" who had always behaved honourably towards her and towards Willson; she had not accepted his proposals of marriage because she was influenced by some family members and friends to believe that it would be impossible to make an inter-racial marriage work. Her two daughters in Canada would very much like to have contact with Willson; they were all thrilled to hear that he was alive and well. One of her grandsons was called Willson after him. She also has a sister in Canada who has a son of the same age: she too would like to have contact.

Over many, many years Ms Sherman has been trying to get in contact with Willson: she wrote two or three times a year to the Registrar's office on the island of Antigua in the hope that they could help her trace him. She never received a response.

Ms Sherman described herself as "a bit psychic", and says she has a feeling that something bad has happened to him in his life. She wondered if he feels "bothered" about his colour, and if so would like him to know that her father's mother was black – from Buenos Aires (I asked her to be more specific and she said that her grandmother was probably a South American Indian).

Most of all, she wants Willson to know that he was, and is loved, and that it is not for selfish reasons that she wants contact i.e. not that she is sick or lonely, or fearing old age, as she has a close family, a full life and lots of friends. It is simply that there is still a space in her life left vacant by losing Willson; she doesn't want either of them to regret not making contact later on.

In addition to the above, which she stated explicitly that she would want Willson to know, Ms Sherman also shared other information:

She had a second child (a boy), by Adrian Gardener, her first husband. As their marriage ended before this child was born, she was persuaded by the authorities to have this child adopted. She has no further knowledge of him.

Her second marriage, to the father of her two daughters, lasted until 1981, despite the fact that her husband was physically and mentally abusive to her. She stuck the marriage out for fear of losing her two daughters as she had lost her sons.

She feels glad in some ways that her husband didn't agree to accept Willson into the family, as she now believes Willson would have been physically abused by her husband such was his level of intolerance of Willson's blackness.

I reconfirmed what she already understood – that I could tell her nothing about Willson's life. I did let her know that he had approached us for information about his background.

I said I would let Counsellor Penelope Devine know she had called, and expected that Penelope would be back in touch with her. I also said that Penelope would be likely to inform Willson in some way that she had called again.

At Lederer Manor each secure unit staff team consisted of a manager, three group leaders, eight senior care officers, four care officers and two night care officers. All were drawn from diverse racial and cultural backgrounds, with equally diverse professional qualifications and experiences in areas such as social work, clinical psychology, psychotherapy, teaching, and youth and community work. There was even a world champion aikido champion and a magician. The wider organisational framework included two ten-bed open units, and specialist teams in the following; mental health, primary health, education, finance, administration, and data and referrals.

Lederer Manor was a soundly managed establishment, had a child to staff ratio of two to one, with aspirations of becoming a centre of excellence despite the ever-present prospect of violent altercations erupting out of the blue whenever a boy or boys "kicked off". This meant that daily life was compelling, often punctuated by spontaneous brutality and instability that would be a dramatic scriptwriter's paradise. Key to Lederer Manor's success was a busy, individually tailored programme for each youth, underpinned by a points-based token economy system, grounded in Bandura's (1965) social learning theory that rewarded pro-social behaviour, and the implementation of a daily routine of some rigour, which all of the young people had to follow. A typical day on each secure unit went something like this:

07.30	Bedroom doors unlocked. Wake-up call, shower, get dressed, clean and tidy your room, and complete a designated daily morning chore.
08.15	Go to breakfast in the unit's dining room. All bedroom doors are locked as are doors to the lounge and corridor. Metal cutlery unlocked, counted out and then counted back in and locked away. Return to the unit.
09.00	Daily morning orientation meeting in the lounge. A brief summary and feedback on every boy's behaviour from the previous evening and all appointments for the day ahead announced.
09.15	Attend national curriculum-based education classes – pupil to teacher ratios of four to one with additional one on one support available.

11.15	Mid morning break in the unit's dining room – hot or cold drinks and biscuits served.
11.30	Attend education classes.
12.30	Lunch time in dining room. Metal cutlery unlocked, counted out and back in, washed, then locked away. Return to the unit.
13.45	Attend education classes.
15.45	Return to the unit. Homework hour in bedroom or lounge.
17.00	Dinner time. Metal cutlery unlocked, counted out and counted back in and then locked away. One young person assisting staff with washing up as per an alternating daily rota. Return to the unit.
18.00	Daily evening orientation meeting, feedback on the day's events and individual behavioural points earned.
18.30	Participation in the evening activity programme – one of the following examples: football, basketball, badminton, table tennis, pool, superstars competition, fitness room, group discussion, bingo, higher and lower (play your cards right), music or general knowledge quiz, board games, and movie night.
20.00	Showers. Telephone calls to family members.
21.00	Suppertime – Cutlery counted out and back in.
21.30	Bedtime – locked in bedroom for the night with access to a TV or radio for one hour if enough points have been earned during the day for good conduct and full participation in individual programme.
22.30	TV or radio removed for the night.

I resigned from Lederer Manor in November 1998 for the improved position of senior practitioner at Hammersmith & Fulham's secure facility, Stamford House, the very same Stamford House where I had endured incarceration as a thirteen-year-old. On Victory Secure Unit I'd been happy and successful. The twenty-two months there proved a major learning curve as I discovered that my own troubled childhood and adolescence made empathy with, and understanding for those in my care second nature. My reason for leaving rested solely with the geographical distance involved in the stressful daily commute from Uxbridge in West London to Redbridge in North East London, and its impact on Claudia and the children. Some Lederer Manor colleagues intimated that my decision to leave was flawed. They opined that I would regret the move. Yet what could they know? None of them had ever visited or worked at Stamford House. They must be jealous, I surmised, ignoring their counsel.

Stamford House Secure Children's Home was in transition, undergoing a facelift. The old Victorian secure unit was scheduled for closure in early 1999, pending the new-purpose-built building, financed by UK tax payers – £7 million from the Department of Health – and staff teams passing a series of social services inspections. I arrived there at this time, my sound experience in a well-run secure establishment welcomed by senior managers.

However, my first day at Stamford House proved horrific. At 08.00 hours that Monday morning, I arrived and met another freshly recruited colleague, Jeff Bridgeman, who had recently moved house to London from the midlands upon securing his new position. Fifteen minutes later, after collecting our keys, we were ushered to the first floor of House One by Rachel, only one week in the job herself, to a staff locker area where we could leave personal effects. The dimly lit building was poorly ventilated and reeked of stale air, an aged musty smell – part urine, part adolescent sweat – and ancient, ill-maintained decor. Rachel then departed for House Two, saying other colleagues were due shortly. There was no handover from night staff – they had furtively disappeared home.

Minutes ticked by and no other staff arrived. Jeff and I realised we were alone, dropped into the deep end on this floor with no other experienced staff members in sight. Soon a couple of teenage boys commenced banging on their locked room doors, hollering to be let out with a torrent of verbal abuse. Both of us advised the boys to calm down, cease swearing, and that they would be let out shortly. Our response appeared to further incense these youths, who took absolutely no notice. They continued thumping, kicking, cursing, and repeatedly pressing their room alarms. An experienced staff member suddenly appeared from nowhere, unlocked their doors, proffered no introductions, advised both Jeff and me that the remaining five boys would be "having a lie-in, so keep their room doors locked", and then disappeared into thin air.

Sensing my skin crawl, the hairs on the back of my neck stand up, and a nauseous feeling in the pit of my stomach, I gave Jeff a knowing glance. We were both flabbergasted and fearfully apprehensive in equal measure, and instinctively knew that this volatile situation was unsafe. We had entered a snake pit. The two unknown youths, now out of their rooms, aggressively and profanely demanded the electricity be put on in the lounge so that they could watch TV. When told firmly but politely no and then to please stop swearing, they became more crazed and threatening. They attempted to kick in the cupboard door where the power was controlled from.

I pressed the panic alarm obscurely located on the wall at the end of the dingy corridor, and we waited anxiously, with bated breath, in the shadows for response staff to arrive. Meanwhile, the two youths entered the lounge area and commenced vandalising whatever could be trashed: cushions on seats, chairs, plastic bins, and a large television, which they threw across the floor. Nigh on five minutes passed before support arrived in the form of several experienced staff. The boys, later said to be high on contraband, were directed to their rooms, conceding compliance only if the electricity in their rooms was turned on so they could listen to their radios or watch their televisions. Our "experienced" colleagues agreed, and the vandals got their way, their negative behaviours reinforced, rewarded by the very adults who were meant to know better. The following week one of these two youths would abscond over the perimeter fence while en route to play football, ably assisted by his peers who menacingly blocked off his escape route from approaching staff.

Welcome to the absolute chaos, the nightmare of Stamford House Secure Accommodation, an utterly shambolic regime where, sadly, it was routine for adolescent boys to physically attack other boys and the care and teaching staff with impunity. These youths thought nothing of using contraband drugs flagrantly or seriously assaulting female domestic staff serving their meals. They dictated when they would attend education, often preferring to remain in bed all day. Astonishingly, amidst all this daily turmoil, Hammersmith & Fulham Social Services, central government's Department of Health, and the Youth Justice Board for England and Wales were planning and would shortly sanction the housing of a girls' unit alongside two boys' units within the yet-to-be commissioned new building. This baptism of fire, which began within my very first half an hour – how unlike Lederer Manor – continued unabated each day. By Friday of that dreadful, roller coaster first week, an exasperated Jeff Bridgeman had walked out after handing in his letter of resignation and avowing: "To hell with working a period of notice for these jokers."

Stamford House's failings were so rife, its besmirched reputation so notorious, that many a London social services department boycotted the provision. Wholesale root and branch treatment was required for any redemption: closing down temporarily, getting rid of the 80 per cent or more temporary agency staff, rigorous recruitment and training of new staff, and reconstruction afresh. However, to Hammersmith & Fulham Council, the fiscal benefits derived from "bums on beds" – it cost around four thousand pounds per week per child – was the prevailing mindset, pouring scorn on the much-lauded edict from the Children Act 1989: "The welfare of the child is paramount". Following Jeff's hasty departure, I soldiered on, persevering to play a key role in passing the two inspections – the first being a dismal failure – necessary before the new building and staff teams for the two boys' units were granted a licence to open.

Senior managers were advised of the critical need to ensure that the sterile, new building remain exactly that. I urged effective management and control of this extraordinary situation, this one-off window of opportunity: a robust, methodical approach to preventing the shipment of contraband to the new facility by the youngsters who were to be moved across from the old building. This strategy had to include full clothing searches – the young people retaining only a towel they held open on the left then right side to reveal clear lines of flesh – and room searches conducted by two staff members in the privacy of each young person's bedroom prior to transferring them one at a time to the new building. All young people should stay locked in their rooms while awaiting their turn to be searched, and only after full compliance be transferred. This would minimise the risk and prevent the passing from one young person to another contraband items, which proliferated in the old building.

In January 1999 common sense and good professional practice did not prevail. Senior managers, some with minimal background experience in the secure estate, pathetically refused to sanction the more thorough clothing searches. The simple pat search or a polite request to "turn out your pockets" would have to suffice, they stated. Predictably, the boys triumphed, smuggling their contraband across to Units 1 and 2 – later named Marley and Genesis respectively – in the new building. My reading of the predicament was not good. I was working face-to-face with seriously disturbed and highly volatile young offenders in a poorly managed, deteriorating institution beset by endemic levels of violence, mismanagement, disorganisation, high staff turnover, and sickness.

Each passing day, as I drove to work along the A4 motorway towards Hammersmith, a most powerful sense of apprehension overcame me. I suspected that a dangerous crisis was always imminent, just a hair's breadth away, when an event would arise where I'd receive a mouthful of thick, warm phlegm or a punch full in the face. I prepared myself mentally for a hostile event when I'd find myself isolated from or unsupported by colleagues. In these trenches, I anticipated being left with no other option but resorting to self-defence measures not in the rule book, ending up a pariah, my career in tatters and on the employment scrapheap.

The pristine building's large laundry room was located centrally in an area called the Rotunda, a communal space accessible to all three units. After four weeks the girls' unit was granted official sanction to open – unbelievable given that those charged with licensing, monitoring, and inspecting such institutions knew of Stamford House's routine failings. Within days of the first girls being admitted, I realised the worst would inevitably happen on overhearing several boys bragging about their successful sorties to steal female undergarments from the laundry room in the Rotunda. This was the final straw. In late January I telephoned Ainsley Cameron, centre manager at Lederer Manor, to explain in graphic detail my experiences; of the deep-rooted, unspeakable standards of care and poor practice at Stamford House; and to humbly beseech, plead for my old job back. Ainsley declared that he would welcome me back with open arms, and so on 1 February 1999, three months after keenly arriving at Stamford House, I tendered my resignation.

Before my final day I wrote frankly to my line manager having not received an exit interview:

16 February 1999
Unit Two/Genesis Unit Manager
Stamford House
206 Goldhawk Road
London W12 9PA

Dear ...,

Firstly I enclose, for your attention, a completed form for the two sleep over duties I performed during the month of February 1999.

Secondly on the night of 12/2/99 at 22.45 hours I was verbally abused and threatened with physical violence by OI, one of the young people on Unit 2. This was retribution for switching off the power to his TV as he was on a 24 hour electrical ban for having contraband (cigarettes) in his room. Hours earlier, before bedtime, I had double checked that staff had switched off his power as instructed. Following this OI had somehow been permitted out of his room and broken into his electrical distribution cupboard, switched his power back on and was watching TV at 22.45. Hence, upon discovering this I switched off his power and, through his locked door, reminded him of his ban, which elicited the threatening response.

The following day OI missed breakfast and dinner having refused to get out of bed. Later when up he requested something to eat and was given cereal and yoghurt by myself. His demeanour appeared non threatening as he sat eating his cereal, when suddenly he became verbally abusive and chucked his unopened yoghurt at me. Hitting me on the chest it caused considerable mess to my clothes and the surrounding kitchenette but fortunately no great physical harm. He had carried out his threat of the previous night and was escorted from the dining room by Femi, Dave and Paul – all staff members – and to his room where he targeted me with further threats of violence. I recorded the above on an ABC – antecedents, behaviours and consequences – chart and in the daily log.

Aware of the above antecedents, and knowing that this young person has a history of repetitive violent physical assaults on staff – just two days earlier, from a distance of half a metre, he gathered up and spat out a mouthful of the thickest phlegm into the face of Chris – while at Stamford House, I viewed attending work for the P.M shift on 14/2/99 with much trepidation and dread. I did not wish to again be targeted with violence, risk being hospitalised or find myself responding unprofessionally. I felt it in the best interest of myself, and the young person concerned, that I stay off work.

You are aware that I have resigned from the post of Senior Practitioner after only three month's service. Violent assaults on staff, many recorded yet many unrecorded, typical of the above examples highlights one of the main reasons for my departure. Consequences following such anti social behaviour for residents at Stamford House is minimal. Such behaviour is, therefore, reinforced as acceptable. All staff working in secure accommodation need to feel a degree of safety, upheld and endorsed by management. They can then provide appropriate responses to children likely to suffer significant harm, to injure themselves or others.

I wish yourself and all my former colleagues every future success.

Yours sincerely
Willson Vimikh
Cc. S. S. at Social Services Personnel

A major inspiration for my work was the formation of attitudes, identity, and beliefs shaped by my underprivileged childhood and teenage history. My personal risk factors were plentiful: (1) Family factors: low income, harsh discipline, physical abuse, and parental conflict. (2) School factors: low educational achievement, aggressive and disruptive behaviour in school, and non-attendance. (3) Community factors: availability of illegal drugs, disadvantaged area with a high crime rate, and lack of attachment to neighbourhood. (4) Individual and peer factors: mixed parentage, history in the care system, rebelliousness, early involvement in crime, and friends involved in crime or whose attitudes condoned lawbreaking.

Fortunately, opposing these risk factors were enough protective factors – personal characteristics; social bonding; healthy beliefs; and clear standards, opportunities, skills, and recognition – which enabled me to break my offending cycle and ultimately go on to fulfil my potential. Had malignant neglect, emotional, sexual, or physical abuse further compounded my lot, as happened to some of my charges, I could very easily have committed some monstrously psychopathic, unforgivably heinous act like the fifteen-year-old who fatally stabbed headmaster Philip Lawrence in 1996, or the two ten-year-old sadistic killers of toddler James Bulger in 2001.

Come middle March 1999, I was leading shifts again on Victory Secure Unit at Lederer Manor amidst capable, pro-social, trustworthy colleagues and effective managers. It was as if I had never left. Routine assaults on staff were a rarity, and the grim reality of Stamford House soon faded from memory. Within the year I achieved a promotion, acting up in a lower management position (group leader). The majority of boys in our care at Lederer Manor, whether welfare, remanded, or sentenced, came from totally dysfunctional backgrounds. Those under fifteen were legally too young to be sent to a young offenders institution (YOI), and of those over fifteen, many exploited their supposed "vulnerability" to avoid transfer to the harsher regime of a YOI.

Ethnically and culturally, the balance of staff at Lederer Manor was varied and fairly reflective of London's demographic. The number of African-Caribbean staff at the level of group leader, unit manager, and above was more or less equal to that of European staff. At the lower level of senior care officers and care officers, the balance was about 60 per cent African-Caribbean staff to 40 per cent European staff, and the young people on these secure units tended to mirror this diversity.

The crimes committed by many of these boys, when seen through the eyes of the average woman or man, would be utterly shocking. One might well ask: How horrifying could their offences have been to necessitate years of childhood incarceration? What follows, therefore, are some notable examples.

1. Location: North London. Violence erupts at the turn of the millennium when two youths confront another boy over a debt. In the violent fracas that ensues, one of the two, a thirteen-year-old England-born boy of African-Caribbean origin, stabs to death a fifteen-year-old boy of Somali origin with a kitchen knife with one downwards thrust from behind. The victim died simply because he owed £10.00 for a small bag – a couple spliffs – of cannabis. Life sentence imposed.

2. This high profile case made front page headlines in national newspapers. A lone woman returning home from a pub one summer evening accepts an invitation from an eighteen-year-old female and her younger male companion to smoke a joint on the towpath of the Grand Union Canal in Ladbroke Grove. Suddenly the woman is surrounded by a deviant teenage gang of up to fourteen youths – including girls – of diverse racial backgrounds who rifle through her pockets and flick lit cigarettes into her hair before pushing her into the canal. On struggling out of the water, the victim is punched and has her top ripped off by the female assailant, who then helped to pin her to the ground while she is raped by two males, one aged eighteen and the other aged fourteen. The younger youth was held on remand at Lederer Manor until sentenced at a Crown Court to five years imprisonment. The eighteen-year-old male also received five years, and

the eighteen-year old female seven years. Reporting restrictions were lifted and all three placed on the sex offenders register for life.

3. A fourteen-year-old youth with learning difficulties sodomizes a seven-year-old child playing in a field, receives a four-year custodial sentence, and is placed on the sex offenders register for life.

4. With an IQ of 124, no previous criminal history, and described by his English teacher as a model pupil, a fourteen-year-old lover of dark Goth clothing from a stable middle-class background in South East London hatches a fearsome, murderous plan to kill his family members, thus paving the way for his adoption by a rich couple. The lad sets fire to his family home, causing a younger sister to die from smoke inhalation, and also batters the head of a younger brother with an axe, leaving him brain damaged. At London's Central Criminal Court (the Old Bailey to laymen), he was ordered to be detained at Her Majesty's pleasure for a minimum of fifteen years. The judge told the boy he had shown not a "shred of remorse" having committed a crime that "was premeditated to a high degree".

5. A fifteen year old youth, originally from a failed West African state, receives a life sentence for robbing guests at gunpoint at a South London christening celebration. During the offence he, alongside his elder brother, shot and killed a mother and the baby cradled in her arms. Both face deportation at the end of their sentence.

6. To fund his heroin and crack habit, a youth was said to be a "one-man crime wave". Forensic tests and his detailed admissions linked him to 1,400 break-ins during a six-year period in which he stole valuables and cash worth close to an estimated half a million pounds. Using trickery he inveigled his way into the homes of elderly victims whose average age was almost eighty; one was a 101-year-old woman. The

uneducated teenager, said to have commenced stealing at the age of five, was from an itinerant family of some notoriety. His offences were committed in London, Essex, Hampshire, Hertfordshire, Kent, Sussex, and Northamptonshire. One national daily newspaper described him as Britain's most prolific young burglar, following the boy being jailed for eight years in 2005.

A number of the young offenders at Lederer Manor had social histories of persistent offending going back to the tender age of ten, which under British law is the age of criminal responsibility. Even experienced staff sometimes found it unsettling that many of these boys brazenly demonstrated little or no repentance, empathy, or remorse despite receiving the harshest of custodial sentences permitted by the land's judicial system. Pubescent children with absolutely no fear of imprisonment in secure accommodation, and equally no fear of eventual moving on at the age of fifteen to a more punitive, overcrowded regime in a YOI, are chilling to behold.

Many of these youths were themselves child victims of an unrelenting cycle of damage caused by ever-present exposure in their family homes to drugs, alcohol, violence, and sexual abuse. Some were on the Child Protection Register (since 2014 subject to a child protection plan), nurtured by chaotic adults with loose morals, and nourished daily on a diet of junk food. Low educational achievement was typical for the vast majority. Such conditioning meant they had been programmed from a tender age to embrace antisocial behaviour. Displaying coldness and lack of empathy, most had inflicted callous levels of violence towards their rape, buggery, robbery, or murder victims. For many, recidivism would be their fate, a cycle of events seeing them reoffend once released or become tragic victims of crime themselves. The meaning of Tupac Shakur's acronym THUGLIFE – The Hate U Gave Little Infants Fucks Everyone – evokes the much earlier words of W. H. Auden, who was not alluding simply to Hitler when writing in 1939 about God being psychopathic, and that all school boys and girls, and the public at large, quickly learn that recipients of evil mete out evil in return.

Having made it clear to all interested Lederer Manor managers just how entrenched, how institutionalised the poor practice was at Stamford House, I was astounded to hear rumours that Ainsley Cameron planned to assist Hammersmith & Fulham Social Services as a consultant. This was a last-ditch effort to turn the notorious establishment's reputation on its head and save it from closure. Behind the scenes an audit of Stamford House's care practice by Redbridge inspectors was conducted, part of a feasibility study to explore the option of jointly managed Stamford House and Lederer Manor secure facilities. Ainsley repeatedly invited me to revisit Stamford House so as to witness the positive changes taking place there under his auspices, but with reservations influenced by gut instinct and traumatic memories, I respectfully declined each offer.

By this time I had agreed to receive my mother's correspondence, including some aged black and white family photographs, which she'd sent to St Mary's Children's Charity over the many unfruitful years when she sought their help in tracing my whereabouts. Molly Elizabeth Sherman had actually passed away the year before, in March 1998. Since then one of her two daughters, Alexandra, my maternal half-sister, continued to maintain written communication with counsellor Penelope in the hope that I would eventually be discovered and be prepared for contact. In October 1999 I wrote to Alexandra via St Mary's:

Dear Alexandra,

I hope that this letter finds you in the best of health. I am Willson, your maternal half brother. I have just finished reading your letter to me dated

7 February 1999. I have decided to write at last, though I feel uncertain and extremely cautious.

I received your letter, the family photographs and our mother's last letter to me, several months ago. I met with Penelope from St Mary's Aftercare in early September. At this meeting I was given some other correspondence from our mother which had been with St Mary's for several years, but I'd not been prepared to accept it for reasons to numerous to explain. It was but a few years ago that I willingly asked to access my records held at St Mary's for the first time. You see when I made enquiries to St Mary's Children's Charity back in the mid 1990's for information on my past I was uncertain as to whether they would have any details. I was equally uncertain as to what I would do if my enquiries proved fruitful. I am, you will perhaps sense, quite wary as to where this all may lead.

I met with Penelope at St Mary's Aftercare several times in 1996-1997. These meetings enabled me, as I approached my fortieth year, to read up on the accounts of my childhood, the history of which I was only vaguely aware of. There were several hundred pages – all in the social work jargon of the time – of incredibly detailed descriptions of the circumstances that led to my admission to St Mary's, the family circumstances at the time and details of the numerous placements I had during my childhood years. Penelope was perceptive, sensitive, non judgmental and exceedingly patient as I delved through all of this historical data at my own pace.

All of this took me back down memory lane as resurrected from deep down in the abyss of my subconscious mind came to the fore long forgotten moments/flashbacks. I was opening "a can of worms". I knew that emotionally I was deeply scarred by this chapter of my life which I had unearthed from the St Mary's Children's Charity's archives. I wept openly. On one occasion when I had got home at the end of the day I flew into an uncontrollable rage.

I am still coming to terms with those revelations and beginning to understand more fully why I am the person that I am today. At 42 years of age, married and with 3 wonderful children it was events in my own family that triggered the desire to unravel my past. Prior to becoming a father and my own marriage it had not been too significant. Yet having said that it was somehow, always significant. I'd always assumed I was an only child until I delved into those archives. I know that my father has no other children. He has never been prepared to discuss the events that led to my St Mary's decade. It was, and remains, off the agenda, a taboo subject for him.

Happiness now is knowing that my three children have each other as my childhood years were quite lonely. I vowed to myself following the birth of my eldest daughter, now 12 years of age, that she would never go through what I endured as a child – the loneliness and lack of parental nurturing. My wife Claudia is fully aware of my family history, our children less so. She has encouraged me to make contact with you, as has her mother. Claudia, though, has not been over zealous with her encouragement as she knows I am extremely stubborn and will only communicate at my own pace or not at all.

I have many, many things to say and am happy to have 'broken the ice' at last. However, as stated at the beginning of this letter I am cautious. I'm still digesting everything. I'm sorry not to have written sooner, especially when our mother was still alive. However this is a new beginning. I will enclose a recent photo with this letter. Please correspond for the meanwhile with me via St Mary's. Put your letter to me in a sealed envelope with my name on it then place that in another envelope clearly marked:

Personal – Addressee Only
Penelope Devine,
Aftercare Department,
St Mary's Children's Charity
Richmond upon Thames
TW9

Sincerely your brother
Willson Vimikh

In March 2000 I again wrote to my sister in Canada:

Dear Alexandra,

How are you? I hope that you and your family are well! I was pleased to receive your interesting letter dated 3/1/2000. I apologise for the delay in writing but this period in time is extremely busy for me in a variety of ways.

The information about you, your sister Elizabeth, and your families, is most intriguing. My family is similar in so many ways to both of yours. My wife Claudia's birthday is three days before yours and our three children are, remarkably, of a similar age to your three. Afua (pronounced Ah-**fwaah**), my eldest, is 12 years old – her name meaning "a female child born on a Friday". Kwesi (pronounced **Kway**-see), is 10 years old – his name means a "male child born on a Sunday". Our second daughter Ayo (pronounced **Eye**-Yoh), is 5 years old – the name means "Joy", "Happiness" and "Delight". I notice that Elizabeth's son is called Wilson.

I have never been to Canada. Your description of it is beautiful. I obviously know of Niagara Falls. Hamilton, from your description of outdoor life and the post card, appears to be an excellent place to raise a family. I can fully understand why our mother Molly and her sister Isabel migrated there back in the 1960's.

I regularly travel to New York City – roughly every two years – which is, I guess, several hundred miles south east of Ontario. My stepmother has a lovely house in Queens where she has lived for over twenty years. We will probably be visiting her for a couple of weeks this August. She and my father have been divorced for many years, with my father now resident in St Croix, US Virgin Isles.

Going back in time I spent the first ten years of my life in various St Mary's child care establishments or with foster carers after our mother's decision not to look after me. There are many records, which I now possess, which describe in great detail these years in care. Eventually I went to live with my natural father at the age of ten as St Mary's felt, at long last, that this restoration would naturally be the most appropriate place for me to live.

My father had originally requested that I be cared for by his sister Esme in Antigua, West Indies, as early as my second year, 1959. This, I understand from reading our mother's letters, is where she believed I had been placed all along. Why St Mary's Children's Charity failed to facilitate this wish of my father's is not clear. Perhaps it had something to do with the English laws on paternal parental responsibility which failed to recognize a father's rights to decision making unless he was married to the mother at the time of a child's birth. Interestingly St Mary's, via the laws of the land, were happy to take payments from my father Billy every week of every year that I was in their care. He never, ever missed one single payment. This I know from the records that I have in my possession. My father, to this day, finds it too painful to discuss these years.

I have lived in West London since being restored to my father in September 1967. As a teenager I underwent struggles of identity and displayed delinquent anti social behaviour which I now understand relates in part to "maternal deprivation" and the number of moves or placements I experienced. For many years I "hated" the white side of my genetic background to the point of denying its very existence to my teenage peers. My mother, I would explain to friends, was a light skinned "coolie", hence my mixed race or Bi-racial appearance.

From adolescence to adulthood I had no wish to know or trace my maternal family origins because of childhood rejection. I focused instead on my father's ancestry, travelling to the Caribbean and West Africa in my quest for identity, or roots. I read up on my African Caribbean past as part of my education and growth to manhood. It is no coincidence that I now work with youngsters of diverse cultural and racial origins whose backgrounds mirror my early childhood. As the years passed I came to openly accept my origins without denying my English mother's ancestry. Becoming a father obviously triggered in me the impulse to uncover my natural mother's circumstances.

From the records I have in my possession I know that Molly, our mother, had her second child, David Gardener, eighteen months after my birth. His father, Adrian Gardener, whom Molly married in the late summer of 1957, was described by our grandparents, Clifford and Gillian, as a "teddy boy". Apparently they did not approve of him and shortly before David's birth the marriage ended. Molly's sister Isabel had a baby boy of around eight months of age at about this time. Do you know of our brother David, as Molly's letters to me make no mention of him?

I will conclude now. Please correspond with me again via St Mary's. Put your letter to me in a sealed envelope with my name on it then place that in another envelope clearly marked Personal – Addressee Only; Penelope Devine, Aftercare Department, St Mary's Children's Charity, Richmond upon Thames, TW9.

Sincerely Your Brother
Willson Vimikh

A Department of Health report, published after a January 2000 inspection of Stamford House, was downright scathing. Unsurprisingly, the press soon uncovered the depth of the systemic failings, and several months later, reports in local newspapers were published beneath such sordid front page headlines as:

KIDS HOME WAS OUT OF CONTROL
SECURE UNIT'S SEX AND DRUG SHAME

Errant teenage antics at the Shepherds Bush secure facilities included having sex, smoking drugs (reports indicate that cannabis was routinely smuggled in) and watching late-night pornography on televisions in their rooms. Systemic management failure and a recruitment crisis meant that many posts were filled by temporary agency staff acting up beyond their station, resulting in these youths running rings around the responsible adults. The education unit was said to be the main venue for sexual activity as unsupervised young people wandered around freely during and in between lessons. Televisions had been installed in each en suite bedroom, and young people were permitted to watch cable TV until beyond 01.00 hours. This meant that residents as young as twelve, some with criminal histories of violent sexual assaults, had unrestricted access to adult entertainment.

Could such scandalous events really be happening in this secure children's home, giving credibility to the years of scaremongering and off the record rumours well known to many local authorities and Youth Offending Teams? One elected local government councillor highlighted the scale of the problems when stating that it was hard to pick out "any aspect of the report on Stamford House that was not appalling". Hammersmith and Fulham Council said that it had begun to take measures designed to halt the chronic rot, and brought in new managers to overhaul policies and procedures. In June 2000 the new managers who took on this horrifically septic challenge were reported to be Ainsley Blair and Tom Brown of Lederer Manor.

All of which was occurring just as a long-term governmental strategic shift was underway nationally in secure provision for offenders from twelve to fifteen years of age. Driven by the Crime and Disorder Act 1998, the strategy, which would take some ten years to unfold, sought the procurement of secure bed spaces outside greater London where costs were far higher than in the rest of the country. Private companies paying significantly less to their staff began delivering this cheaper option, an example being Medway Secure Training Centre in Rochester, Kent, which opened in 1998 with forty bed spaces that undercut the cost of local authority Lederer Manor's secure care bed spaces by roughly £2000 per week per child.

Thriving Lederer Manor, with twenty-four beds in its secure provision, rarely had voids. Annually its total occupancy was nigh on 100 per cent. In 2000 Lederer Manor was a key tool of the Youth Justice Board (YJB) for England and Wales, whose principle aim was to prevent offending by children and young people. The YJB system was comprised of various agencies including the courts, Young Offender Institutions (YOIs), Local Authority Secure Children's Homes (LASCHs) like Lederer Manor, and Youth Offending Teams (YOTs) represented by practitioners from social services, probation, police, education, and health. Underpinning the youth justice system was a continuously evolving legal framework, including parliamentary legislation such as the Children and Young Persons Act (CYPA) 1933, CYPA 1969, Police and Criminal Evidence (PACE) Act 1984, Children Act 1989, Power of Criminal Courts (Sentencing) Act 2000, and European legislation like the Human Rights Act 1998.

Inspection reports indicated Lederer Manor was a "good" and improving institution. Come January 2002, Ainsley Blair attended an awards ceremony at Buckingham Palace to receive his OBE for services to young offenders. Around this time Lederer Manor's two open units for welfare beds achieved about 50 per cent total occupancy but increasingly less than this over the next few years. Had Lederer Manor's senior management team and Redbridge Council made a strategic blunder by taking on the poisoned chalice of Stamford House and in so doing neglecting their own important service?

In May 2002 I wrote to the St Mary's Counsellor:

Dear Penelope,

How are you? I hope you are in good health. My family, myself and work are thriving.

Thank you for your letter dated 11/4/2002 and the letter therein from my sister Alexandra. I have no idea what happened to the Christmas card you say she sent to me. This should have been forwarded on to me from St Mary's as she does not have my address.

I wish to continue corresponding with Alexandra via yourself as she has done for the past couple of years. This is my preferred method of communication and I shall write to her shortly to reiterate this. It is also no bother if you write to me. Thanks again and take good care.

Yours sincerely

In June 2002 Claudia give birth to our fourth infant, and in keeping with tradition, he was named Kwame, an Akan–Ghanaian name meaning "a boy child born on a Saturday", and the given name of Ghana's leader during the independence struggle from British colonial rule. That October at a hotel somewhere off the M4 motorway to the west of Heathrow I got to meet up with my maternal half sisters, Alexandra and Elizabeth, who were in England to attend the funeral of a relative of one of their husbands. I took along both Afua and Kwesi to this family reunion, which turned out to be a pleasant affair. A couple weeks afterwards, I wrote to Alexandra:

Dear Alexandra,

Hello once again! I hope that Elizabeth and you are in sound health and that you've managed to successfully complete the arrangements that brought you back to England.

Meeting you both on Saturday 19 October was excellent, brilliant. You were both warm, indeed extremely pleasant. Our conversation about our mother Molly, Aunt Isabel, mutually important dates and aspects of our own families' growth and development was truly absorbing. I felt a wonderful sense of accomplishment and happiness after meeting you both. Long missing bits of the family jigsaw had been found. I wish we'd had more time! Thank Aunt Isabel for the information she sent to me in the large envelope.

After our farewells both Afua and Kwesi said you were both "really nice" as we walked to my car. I couldn't resist turning to have a final look and wave. Wow! Words can't describe.

Anyway I enclose for you photocopies of some of the documents from St Mary's Children's Charity. I have three folders, each with 80 plastic sleeves, which contain over 200 pages. I have only managed to copy and post to you documents from the first folder detailing matters from March 1957 – December 1960. The others I'll send to your home address. As I said when we met some of the terminology used is quite dated. Terms like "coloured" and "halfe caste" would be frowned upon now. I agree with the change as I always detested the adjective "half caste" – I am, after all, a whole person. Other terms like P., Pu., Put., Fa, and pf are abbreviations for putative father.

I will keep in touch with you and Elizabeth, as promised, either by post or via the Internet with help from Afua. Have a safe and comfortable flight back to Canada.

Peace and Love
Willson

As a child in care, for reasons beyond my ability to articulate, I always felt positive about my black, African genes. Absent from my mindset were the deep-rooted, subconscious feelings of self-loathing and self-hatred common to many other dual-heritage or biracial children both inside and outside the care system. My father has never, ever spoken of his role in the saga of my St Mary's odyssey; rather the documents did, the countless pages of official written records. When bearing in mind this man's resolute, steadfast, and unwavering commitment, I am overwhelmed by immense sensations of filial respect and pride. My eternal gratitude goes to Garnett Willson "Billy" Vimikh for his gift of true love and stoicism, his resolute and unbowed spirit, for not surrendering and disappearing into the ether as many a man might have done in the face of such undeniable adversity. But for his love, my life's trajectory would have been grave indeed – I would have been exactly like one of those six incarcerated youths I described earlier.

At Lederer Manor, one open unit had closed by 2005, deemed economically unviable, with most of its staff deployed to the three secure units. The remaining open unit, with its full complement of staff, attracted fewer and fewer residents, as the lowest occupancy levels on record due to high fees and a national shift away from using local authority welfare beds continued. The year-on-year fiscal shortfall of the open units was offset by the consistant high occupancy and standards of care delivered by all three secure units. Gossip in the walkways and offices was of the imminent closure of the last open unit, that some staff would be laid off and others redeployed within the secure provision.

Amazingly, talk of Lederer Manor being sold off in its entirety and the privatisation of the secure units became part of the daily corridor tittle-tattle and just would not go away. Strategically and financially the closure of the open unit was common sense as responsible stewardship of taxpayers' money should have witnessed this years before. However, the amoral, unethical idea of philanthropic corporate fat cats profiteering from the legal incarceration of children in the fiscally sound secure units was a different matter. Government civil servants would not let it happen, would they?

Due diligence was undertaken, and the council sold Lederer Manor to a private company, South East Welfare, with expertise in adult mental health. Crucially, they had no experience as child care providers. On 1 April 2006, a middle-aged, clean-cut gentleman wearing a hand-tailored Saville Row suit pressed the entry buzzer to Lederer Manor's secure reception. Imbued with the self-assurance of God's chosen, up to the reception desk a tall philanthropist of sorts strode purposefully, whose aura conveyed wealth and power, benevolence and authority. He had come to see one of the senior management team.

When asked politely by Maisie, the bubbly, friendly, yet highly efficient concierge to sign in using the signing-in log, as was the protocol for all visitors, the man remarked aloofly, with a most disdainful look and matching tone that was not overtly aggressive but implicitly menacing, "Do you know who I am? I don't need to sign in!" This was the new owner. Within the month many staff would scornfully christen the corporation "Welfare? What Welfare?".

Daily life carried on normally in the secure units as the last open unit closed a few weeks after privatisation. But some staff – and the boys too – became aware of subtle changes that became ever more tangible. Over the coming months we witnessed the initial slow motion drip of change turn staccato before evolving to a steady trickle of worsening qualitative changes that became routine. Attendees at team meetings were shown commissioned architectural drawings of proposed building developments that would double the bed capacity of Lederer Manor yet everyone's confidence and belief in the hollow promises of investment and expansion slowly evaporated. Among the employees, few brave souls were prepared to speak out candidly. Some of those responsible for safeguarding Lederer Manor's standards of care – group leaders (my job) and above – adopted a blinkered "Please don't rock my boat" approach. A few managers ignored or branded as unprofessional the litany of concerns regularly highlighted each day in the early-morning senior management team meetings, in unit team meetings, and in supervision sessions with hardworking shop floor staff. Many witnessed Lederer Manor's demise in abject silence, toothless souls fearful of what speaking out might mean for their regular overtime or career prospects under "Welfare? What Welfare?".

Repairs to building defects like faulty corridor lights, old paintwork, or criminal damage by the young people took longer and longer to rectify. The four floodlights that illuminated the five-a-side football pitch became three, then two and finally one. Even the entry panel buzzer to the secure garage remained out of order, unrepaired, in such a state of obvious, lopsided dilapidation that drivers and escorts respectfully joked about it daily when collecting boys for or returning them from court appearances. Plans for the rolling programme of staff training at NVQ Level 3 and 4 were stalled, then failed to materialise. The comprehensive list of mandatory training according to grade, and other training contained within the staff training manual for 2006–07 was unceremoniously scrapped. The Mental Health Team (MHT), with its direct connection to the East London and Essex NHS Trust, was dismantled. Ironically, such was the demise of the MHT provision that one year post privatisation, a Lederer Manor court report by its replacement MHT was embarrassingly rejected as inadequate by a central criminal court (Old Bailey) judge, who then issued instructions to one of the ousted former MHT professionals to write a fresh report.

In households in every street, village, town, and city, all half-decent parents know and fully appreciate just how ravenous the appetites of growing adolescent boys are. Parsimonious cost-cutting by the new owners was relentless, the squeeze soon evident by shrinking cooked food portions sent down to the units on heated catering trolleys each mealtime. Such skimping also hit food staples like milk, breakfast cereals, bread, and fruit. As less and less food became the norm, this miserly action brought about an increase in complaints and ever more frequent incidents of violence – angry outbursts directed towards unit staff by hungry teenagers.

Domestic staff hours were reduced. Noticeably in Division Two – the office area for unit management – where staff records were filed and their supervision took place, bins ceased being emptied and overflowed, carpeted floors never saw a vacuum cleaner, and the single toilet ran out of loo roll and was rarely cleaned. Lederer Manor's vehicles were changed for older models and, even though used for escorting clients to and from medical appointments or court, were not serviced. On one occasion, two colleagues and I were escorting a sentenced asthmatic boy with a heart murmur to the King George Hospital in Redbridge when smoke began filtering through the vehicle's air ducts, causing us to make an emergency stop at a garage as the nauseous boy became distressed.

I was exasperated by the disgustingly unclean state of the windowless staff toilet in Division Two. Enough was enough when its specially sealed light fitting remained faulty for well over a month despite being reported for repair. I could no longer remain a circumspect flunky so voiced my discontent at the filthy sanitation in a tongue-in-cheek email to everyone at Lederer Manor:

Sent: 08 May 2007 09.36

To: Endeavour Unit; Mayflower Unit; Victory Unit; Senior Management Team; Group Leaders; Unit Managers; MHT; Concierge; Education Staff; Kitchen; Admin; Data Referrals; Technician; Testboy; Teststaff; Testteach;

Subject: Division Two Loo

Salutations All,

Congratulations to everyone who toils in Division Two as, during the month of April 2007, male and female managers alike passed a unique social skills training programme and new element of our Work Plans. We are now all masters in the art of urinating, defecating and other essential personal hygiene routines in the total darkness of the Division Two Toilet.

Cheers
Willson V

I sent another email to South East Welfare's head office requesting reading materials for the bare shelves of Endeavour Unit's lounge, where I now worked:

J. W. Vimikh

Sent: 08 July 2007 16.15

To: Head Office

Cc: Endeavour Unit; Group Leaders; Unit Managers;

Subject: Books for Endeavour Unit
Hi Head Office,

Endeavour Unit are desperately in need of books, none having been purchased for the unit in the past 18 months to two years – our book shelves are bare. This despite all the evidence that poor literacy is a key factor influencing the offending behaviour of the young people we care for.

The following is a list of books – they are not expensive – plus their product code and price, all of which can be acquired from:

A *reputable book company*. **Address and telephone number supplied**.

or

Online www.***a_reputable_book_company***.co.uk

Terrible Tyranny History Series £12.99

Car Racing/Stunts/Motorbike Racing £4.99

Great War Voices That Were Forgotten£4.99

2007 School Atlas £3.99

Don Palmer Trilogy including "A Teen Called Thing" £6.99

Secondary School Musical Stories – 4 books £4.99

Romans & Greek Myths Collection – 8 books £6.99

Grimm's Teenage Collection – 10 books £12.99

Merlin Wizard Master Merlin £4.99

Freddie's Further Adventures – 3 books£4.99

Why Walter? The Great Treasure Hunt! £2.99

TOTAL£71.89

If all are not available then any will suffice!!!

Cheers

After a couple days a reply came from the Saville Row-suited owner's son:

From: **Owner's Son** [mailto: **Owner's.Son@ Welfare.What.Welfare**.com]

To: Willson Vimikh

Sent: 10 July 2007 09.28

Cc: Senior Management Team; Education Staff;

Subject: RE: Books for Endeavour Unit

Dear Willson

Head Office has forwarded me your email regarding the purchase of books for Endeavour Unit.

I am very keen to see this move forward, however I wish to make you aware that I have recently been speaking with the Heads of Education regarding the purchasing of books which the boys can access while in the Learning Centre and on the Units.

I raised this matter with the Senior Management Team yesterday afternoon and we are in agreement that a collaborative working approach should be adopted to identify a comprehensive list of books that need to be sourced for the Centre which we can then take steps to purchase.

I would therefore like to suggest that you raise this matter with the Heads of Education upon the commencement of the school term so that this piece of work can commence.

I welcome your thoughts on this proposal.

Kind regards
Owner's Son

Frustrated and disappointed by this reply, I responded hastily the next day:

From: Willson Vimikh [mailto:willsonv@lederermanor.org.uk]

Sent: 11 July 2007 16.22

To: **Owner's Son**

Cc: Senior Management Team; Education Staff; Endeavour Unit; Jaywvee@hotmail.com; Subject: RE: Books for Endeavour Unit

Hi **Owner's Son**,

Just some thoughts!

1) With respect the Heads of Education are overwhelmed with specific education tasks for the start of the new term and it was not my intention to engage in a marathon red tape exercise for a mere £70 worth of children's books.

2) I requested these books for Endeavour Unit for social reading as opposed to education reading in a school library context.

3) I have spent in excess of 25 years as a child care professional in various settings, including the raising of my own four very high achieving children, and 18 years in the Care System as a child. I therefore struggle to see that the Heads of Education or even Senior Management Team are more knowledgeable than I re: suitable reading material for the lounge book shelf on Endeavour. And after all the education, rehabilitation and care of our young people is why I'm employed here.

4) Children should "have access to, and a choice in the selection of, newspapers, books and magazines subject to their suitability" – Children's Homes National Minimum Standards 15.7 – as part of their leisure activities. What we have on Endeavor Unit does not meet this requirement.

Cheers
Willson V

This elicited a suspicious reply – I had absentmindedly included my then home email address among those copied in.

From:**Owner's.Son**.[mailto: **Owner's.Son**@ **Welfare.What.Welfare**. com]

Sent: 12 July 2007 09.27

To: Willson Vimikh

Subject: RE: Books for Endeavour Unit

Dear Willson

Thank you for your email.

Before responding to your email, I am keen to ascertain the identity of the individual copied into your previous email using the email address Jaywvee@hotmail.com which is clearly not an internal email address.

Kind regards
Owner's Son

You will of course realise that Welfare? What Welfare? never did purchase any children's books and the festering decay continued unabated. Two years post privatisation – April 2008 – I accepted redundancy terms, becoming one of the few lucky staff members to receive remuneration for many years of service. The following summer Lederer Manor closed permanently, leaving the disgraceful scenario of dozens of long-serving staff members receiving no redundancy payouts and left pursuing redress via industrial tribunals. All of which begs the question: Why were millions of pounds from the public purse and more than a decade's investment in assembling and training numerous experienced youth justice professionals written off with the closure of London's last "state of the art" secure children's facility?

Bibliography

Achebe, Chinua. ***Things Fall Apart***. Oxford: Heinemann Educational Publishers, 1986.

Agbodeka, Francis. ***African Politics and British Policy in the Gold Coast 1868–1900***. London: Longman Group, 1971.

Bandura, Albert. ***Social Learning and Personality Development.*** New York: Holt, Rinehart & Winston, 1965.

Blake, John. ***European Beginnings in West Africa 1454–1578***. London: Longmans, Green and Co., 1937.

Bowlby, John. ***Child Care and the Growth of Love***. Middlesex: Pelican Books. 1973.

Bradford, Ernle. ***Southward the Caravels***. London: Hutchinson and Co. Ltd., 1961.

Las Casas, Bartolome de. ***The Devastation of the Indies: A Brief Account***. New York: The Seabury Press, 1974.

Claridge, William Walton. ***History of the Gold Coast and Ashanti, Vol. 1***. London: Barnes and Noble, 1964.

Cleaver, Eldridge. ***Soul On Ice***. New York: Dell Publishing Co., Inc., 1968.

Colombo, C. **The Four Voyages of Christopher Columbus**. Penguin Books, 1969.

Crone, G. R. **The Discovery of America**. London: Hamish Hamilton Ltd., 1969.

Crowder, Michael. **West African Resistance: the Military Response to Colonial Occupation**. London: Hutchinson & Co. Ltd., 1971.

Davidson, Basil Risbridger. **Black Mother**. Pelican Books, 1980.

—— **Africa in History**. Paladin Books, 1978.

Diop, Cheikh Anta. **The African Origin of Civilisation**. Westport: Lawrence Hill & Co., 1974.

Dixon, Bob. **Catching Them Young[1]: Sex, Race and Class in Children's Fiction.** London: Pluto Press Ltd., 1977

Du Bois, William Edward Burghardt. **The Negro**. London: Oxford University Press, 1970.

Ellison, Ralph. **Invisible Man**. Harmondsworth, Middlesex: Penguin Books, 1969.

Fage, John Donnelly. **Ghana**. University of Wisconsin Press, 1959.

Fanon, Frantz. **Black Skin White Masks**. London: Paladin Books, 1970.

—— **The Wretched of the Earth**. Harmondsworth, Middlesex: Penguin Books, 1976.

—— **Toward the African Revolution**. London: Writers and Readers Pub. Co, 1980.

Garvey, Amy Jacques. *Garvey and Garveyism*. London: Collier Macmillan Ltd., 1970.

Haley, Alex. *The Autobiography of Malcolm X.* New York: The Balantine Publishing Group, 1965.

Humphrey, Derek. and Tindall, David. *False Messiah: The Story of Michael X*. London: Hart-Davis, MacGibbon Ltd., 1977.

Jackson, George. *Soledad Brother*. Harmondsworth, Middlesex: Penguin Books, 1973.

—— *Blood in My Eye*. Harmondsworth, Middlesex: Penguin Books, 1975.

James, Cyril Lionel Robert. *Nkrumah and the Ghana Revolution*. London: Allison & Busby, 1977.

—— *The Black Jacobins*. London: Allison and Busby, 1980.

Kennedy, Randall. *Nigger: The Strange Career of a Troublesome Word*. New York: Vintage Books, 2003.

Koning, Hans. *Columbus: His Enterprise.* New York and London: Monthly Review Press, 1976.

Landstrom, Bjorn. *The Quest for India*. London: Allen & Unwin, 1964.

Lawrence, Andrew Walter. *Fortified Trade Posts*. London: Jonathon Cape, 1969.

Levi Straus, Claude. *The Savage Mind*. London: Weidenfeld and Nicolson, 1966.

Lips, Julius Ernst. *The Savage Hits Back*. New Haven: Steven Austin & Sons Ltd., 1937.

J. W. Vimikh

Ling Roth, Henry. **Great Benin**. New York: Routledge & Kegan Paul Ltd., 1968.

Mandela, Nelson. **No Easy Walk to Freedom**. London: Heinemann Educational Books, 1965.

Marable, Manning. **Malcolm X: A Life of Reinvention**. London: Allen Lane, 2011.

Ngugi, Wa Thiong'o. **Petals of Blood**. London: Heinemann Educational Books Ltd., 1977.

Newton, Huey Pierce. **Revolutionary Suicide**. London: Wildwood House Ltd., 1974.

Onyeka. **Blackamoores: Africans in Tudor England, Their Presence, Status, and Origins**. London: Narrative Eye and The Circle with a Dot, 2013.

Phillips, Mike. and Phillips, Trevor. **Windrush: The Irresistible Rise of Multi-Racial Britain**. London: Harper Collins, 1998.

Plaidy, Jean. **The Spanish Inquisition**. London: Book Club Associates, 1978.

Rodney, Walter. **A History of the Upper Guinea Coast 1545–1800**. New York and London: Monthly Review Press, 1970.

—— **How Europe Underdeveloped Africa**. London: Bogle-L'Ouverture Publications, 1972.

Rogers, J. A. **Africa's Gift to America**. New York: Helga M. Rogers, 1961.

—— **Sex & Race – Vol. I**. New York: Helga M. Rogers, 1967.

—— **From "Superman" to Man**. New York: Helga M. Rogers, 1968.

Schama, Simon. ***Rough Crossings: Britain, The Slaves and The American Revolution***. London: BBC Books, 2005.

Seale, Bobby. ***Seize the Time: The Story of the Black Panther Party***. London: Arrow Books Ltd., 1970.

Strickland, William. ***Malcolm X: Make It Plain***. New York: Penguin Books, 1995.

Welsing, Frances Cress. ***The Isis Papers: The Keys to the Colors***. Chicago: Third World Press, 1991.

Williams, Eric. ***Capitalism and Slavery***. London: Andre Deutsch Ltd., 1975.

Wright, Richard. ***Native Son***. Penguin Books, 1972.

Encyclopaedic Volumes

The British Empire, Volumes 1–6. London: Ferndale Editions, 1981.

UNESCO General History of Africa, Volumes 1 and 2. Heinemann, 1981.

Lightning Source UK Ltd.
Milton Keynes UK
UKOW04f2239041215

264060UK00001B/199/P